The Goldilocks God

ANGLICAN STUDIES

Series Editor
Sheryl A. Kujawa-Holbrook, Claremont School of Theology

This series responds to the growing need for high-quality and innovative research in Anglican Studies made available to the scholarly and ecclesial communities. Anglican Studies as expressed here is an interdisciplinary field, including Anglican history, theology, liturgy, preaching, postcolonial studies, ecclesiology, spirituality, literature, missiology, ethics/moral theology, ministry, pastoral care, ecumenism, and interreligious studies. Studies that engage global Anglicanism, as well as studies related to individual contexts are welcome. The series seeks monographs and edited volumes which explore contemporary issues and forge new directions in interdisciplinary research.

Titles in the series

The Goldilocks God: Searching for the via media, by Guy Collins
Sacramental Poetics in Richard Hooker and George Herbert: Exploring the Abundance of God, by Brian Douglas
Ministry in the Anglican Tradition from Henry VIII to 1900, by John L. Kater
A Eucharist-shaped Church: Prayer, Theology, and Mission, edited by Daniel J. Handschy, Donna R. Hawk-Reinhard, and Marshall E. Crossnoe

The Goldilocks God

Searching for the via media

Guy Collins

LEXINGTON BOOKS/FORTRESS ACADEMIC
Lanham • Boulder • New York • London

Published by Lexington Books/Fortress Academic
Lexington Books is an imprint of The Rowman & Littlefield Publishing Group, Inc.

4501 Forbes Boulevard, Suite 200, Lanham, Maryland 20706
www.rowman.com

86-90 Paul Street, London EC2A 4NE, United Kingdom

Copyright © 2022 by The Rowman & Littlefield Publishing Group, Inc.

All rights reserved. No part of this book may be reproduced in any form or by any electronic or mechanical means, including information storage and retrieval systems, without written permission from the publisher, except by a reviewer who may quote passages in a review.

British Library Cataloguing in Publication Information Available

Library of Congress Cataloging-in-Publication Data

ISBN 9781978713475 (cloth) | ISBN 9781978713499 (pbk.) | ISBN 9781978713482 (epub)

Contents

Acknowledgments	vii
Introduction	1
Chapter One: The Enigma of Elizabeth	11
Chapter Two: Kierkegaard's Courage	29
Chapter Three: The Science of the Soul	45
Chapter Four: "It can be no disgrace to confesse wee are ignorant."	61
Chapter Five: The Antiquity of Diversity	83
Chapter Six: The Promise of the God Who May Be	99
Chapter Seven: Forgers of Holiness	115
Chapter Eight: The Gift of Desire	137
Chapter Nine: Transfiguring Touch	157
Chapter Ten: Why Do We Fall?	175
Chapter Eleven: Treasure Hidden in the Field	195
Chapter Twelve: Love in the Goldilocks Zone	213
Bibliography	237
Index	247
About the Author	257

Acknowledgments

I remain grateful to Peterhouse, University of Cambridge, for incorporating me in an intellectual community rooted in commensality. This book is a small attempt to pay homage to the Petrean ideal of learning while eating. The recent death of Peterhouse's beloved head porter Gerald Meade occurred as this manuscript was being finalized. Someone who never forgot a face, even decades later, he embodied hospitality and friendship.

As an undergraduate at the University of St. Andrews, John Hudson, Gordon McPhate, and Robert Bartlett opened my eyes to much that continues to challenge and shape my understanding. I also owe another much delayed thank you to Joe Hawes and Chris Eyden for enshrining the radically inclusive hospitality of the *via media*. Gavin Hyman has helped me remain connected to the search for theological wisdom in unexpected places. The combined witness of these scholars, guides, and friends to the strange companions we call saints has been an important catalyst to this project.

I am grateful to the Lilly Foundation Clergy Renewal project for funding a sabbatical, which deepened my visceral experience of pilgrimage, inspiring new trajectories of inquiry. My gratitude also goes to the Edgerton House pilgrims who walked St. Cuthbert's Way, showing me the practical importance of way markers.

The intellectual liveliness of members of St. Thomas Church, Hanover, the undergraduates of Dartmouth College and participants in courses I have given through Osher@Dartmouth have contributed greatly to this text. My thanks to them for walking with me through fields that are often obscure, but rarely dull.

I remain indebted to the Anglican Studies series editor Sheryl Kujawa-Holbrook, for shepherding this book through the publishing process. My gratitude also goes to her colleagues Gayla Freeman and Neil Elliott at Rowman and Littlefield for their assistance.

The revision of the text gained much from the careful reading, scholarly corrections, and thoughtful observations of Reneé Bergland, Nicholas

Christakis, Gretchen Holbrook Gerzina, and Jeffrey John. To Neil Heavisides I owe many lifelong debts: most recently, as a reader suffused in the Anglican tradition who knows its resonances better than I ever will. Mistakes that remain are entirely my own.

It is a source of deep regret that Judith Esmay did not live to respond in her inimitable way to the thesis of this text. Judith revealed a Goldilocks-like God to so many, and for those who "knew her not" I hope this text may conserve something of her saintly exuberance.

Finally, I give hearty thanks for the supper-time interrogations of my daughters, Lyra and Beatrix. Together with the heroic willingness of my wife, Kristin, to bring clarity to the text, their quizzicality and zest continue to illuminate the way.

Hanover, NH
The feast
of St Wulfstan of Worcester 2022

Introduction

What if the story of Goldilocks were more than a nursery tale? What if it were the quintessential story about life, the universe, and everything? And what if it could illuminate both the philosophy of Aristotle and Heidegger while clarifying some of the most intractable problems of Christian theology? Like other quest narratives, *Goldilocks and the Three Bears* is the story of an adventurous spirit who bites off more than she can chew. Goldilocks disturbs the peace of the three bears. She breaks things. She gets into trouble. And yet her willingness to seek and try new things has turned her into an enduring symbol for good sense. Somehow a story about a truculent tearaway becomes the ultimate paradigm for discovering the conditions for things being "just right." Read in a certain light the Goldilocks story is also a parable of failure, echoing the thematics of the grail quests of the medieval period. Like Arthur's valiant, yet morally frail, knights, her courage, vulnerability, and perseverance, not to mention the hospitality of the bears, reward attention.

As a priest living and working in a college town, I experience a fair amount of the rich tapestry of human life. Life is not an unadulterated diet of writing papers, taking midterms, and partying. There are also the stories of students searching for meaning amongst the all-pervasive shallowness of a me-centric culture. In some ways things are worse in the Ivy League. Everyone is a "success" (on paper). Which makes admitting life's failures so much harder. Students are not simply looking for faith beyond fundamentalism. They are also looking for a way to forgive, and a way to love, as well patterns for living that are kind and honest.

Truth is an important core value at college. Yet, not all academic truths are created equal. In the truth-hierarchy, scientific truth trumps the truth of the humanities, and the truth in the football stadium trumps everything. The idea that religious truth might have any part to play in this situation is the kind of question faculty and students learn not to raise if they wish to be taken seriously.

Professors and students alike recount their fear of being found out as secretly religious in a setting that assumes all religion is fraud, superstition, or worse, proof of feeble-mindedness or self-deception. And yet surprisingly large numbers still risk it. This book is for similarly brave souls: intellectuals who are tired of concealing their religious yearnings, and believers who are weary of being instructed to conceal their intelligence. Churches can be as anti-intellectual as colleges are anti-religious. This book argues for a rejection of this mutual animosity and a recognition of intelligence as a gift of God.

College communities are not unique. They simply make the false divisions between intellect, heart, and spirit more jarring. Every human being is working everything out for the first time. Gentle souls, preparing for marriage, facing death, or bringing a new life into the world. Questioners, searching for meaning amid the maelstrom of human life. And those laid low by undesired changes and unwished for circumstances. The human experience is universal: life occurs, we pay attention.

The human life cycle from birth to death is not abstract. Life is a series of holy moments where people are yearning for meaning, forgiveness, and redemption. Faith is about discovering that even in the worst of times there are the best of times. Joy is not entirely absent in the face of suffering. For every person who has everything and finds it is not enough, there are those who have nothing and find that it is more than they need. A certain kind of religious belief can crush or constrict. By contrast, the wager of this book is that there are other approaches to faith that liberate, redeem, and enthuse. To be enthusiastic literally means to be filled with God (*en-theos*). The question animating this book is how do individuals in community discover, manifest, and replenish this enthusiasm? And how do they do it while holding on to more than a modicum of intellectual credibility? While there are religious traditions that respond to the life of the mind with hostility, denial, or fear, the route to the Goldilocks God is different.

The riches of human learning are great. Just as the theologian Friedrich Schleiermacher addressed the "cultured despisers" of religion, so this work attempts to weave a dialogue between theology and culture.[1] Rather than isolating faith from culture, the following chapters approach the "sacred" within the context of discourses more familiar as "secular" science, social science, history, literature, art, imagination, and myth. If this approach succeeds, the division between sacred and secular will be revealed as increasingly artificial (and unhelpful). This work also challenges the "theory" and "practice" opposition of much spiritual and theological writing. Rather than oppose one to the other, the following pages open a window onto resources within one community's weaving of the warp of "theology" or "spirituality" with the woof of "intellect" or "wisdom." The thread that joins these two lies firmly outside the academy, in the life of a community searching for the Spirit. Such an approach is perspectival and local, what might perhaps be described as parochial in the best sense of that word. It also hopes to make an implicit case for how a faith community may be the only place within which to uncover the way of Goldilocks.

In astrophysics the Goldilocks zone is a concept that describes the conditions needed for life. If a planet is too cold life will not develop. If a planet is too hot it will be destroyed. What is needed is something like Goldilocks's porridge (a planet hospitable to life) located somewhere in the thermodynamic middle: neither too far nor too near from the sun, neither too hot nor too cool. Paul Davies, one of the world's leading physicists and cosmologists, has further argued that the Goldilocks concept can be extended beyond individual planets to the universe itself. In Davies's reading, the very fabric of the universe is neither too hot nor too cold, but rather "just right for life."[2]

Something similar may be said of God. Spirituality and religion are like Goldilocks's porridge: they have many different thermal properties, which can just as easily mobilize forces that are life giving or life destroying. Religion has quite literally burnt people when the fires of fundamentalism are too hot and overenthusiastic. The great conflagrations of the Spanish Inquisition are a particularly virulent, and literal, example: *autos-da-fé* of public penance in which heretics were burnt at the stake for their wrongheadedness. From the treatment of Joan of Arc to the destruction of the Cathars in Southern France, the medieval church militant frequently forgot the commandment to love its enemies. Closer to the present, the mass suicides of a Heaven's Gates or an Adam's House cult show how every age has its own religious hotheads. These are the kinds of activities that give religion and spirituality a bad name, providing ready proof of the homicidal truth of religion. Violence between Roman Catholics and Protestants in Northern Ireland, the conflict in the Middle East, or the disputes in Kashmir between Pakistan and India are here held up not as the exception, but the rule.

Within contemporary America, a thriving conservative evangelical culture rejects gender equality and scientific teaching while promoting gun ownership and fostering hatred towards quite a long list of outsiders. Vaccine deniers and resisters are not all religious, but many are simply following the internal logic of their spiritual traditions. This explains why deep in the basement of the Baker Library at Dartmouth College there are murals depicting the clergy as crows feeding off the bones of humanity.[3] For ease of comprehension, and at the risk of radically adumbrating their full spectrum, we shall label these forms of militant religious experience, "toxic."

Far more common than fires of execution, collective suicides, or the geopolitical disputes that feed off and expose underlying religious divisions is an even greater threat to human thriving: religious chill. These are the unappealingly cold, if not downright icy conditions, that dampen down spiritual life before it can be kindled. While toxic Christianity runs too hot, it arouses equally hostile forces that blithely assume the elimination of religion will make the world a better place. That this has been tried most successfully by totalitarian leaders like Hitler, Stalin, and Mao is usually forgotten. States going out of their way to suppress religion have been quite accomplished at killing millions of their own citizens. Sociologically, such attempts never eliminated religious fervor. Instead, they displaced religious devotion from acclaiming the divine to adoring new, more secular, gods. If God and God's earthly representatives were the focus of the medieval and early modern periods, the party and the party's ministers became new objects of adoration, blind faith, and unquestioning devotion. Contemporary political movements sweeping the globe (like the January 6, 2021, assault on the United States Capitol) remind us that the ghosts of fascism, communism, and *uber*-nationalism have yet to be decisively laid to rest. They still haunt us. Especially in the democratic West.

The idea behind *The Goldilocks God* is that there is fertile middle ground between the hellish extremes of toxic Christianity and militant atheism. Or as they call it at seminary: the *via media*.[4] The argument that follows is simple. Classical Anglicanism emerged as a synthesis of Catholic and Reformed insights (with a healthy respect for the earliest centuries of ecumenical agreement before the separation from Orthodoxy). If the *via media* is to be sustained as a creative synthesis in the coming century it will need to keep fidelity to this matrix of Classical Anglicanism by repeating this synthesizing movement in relation to new sources of wisdom, secular and divine. For the middle ground to remain fertile, it needs intellectual and spiritual tilling to expose fresh furrows. The *via media* is not frozen in time: it is only ever found as a living way.

The repetition of this synthesis also requires a rediscovery of the *imago dei*, the image and likeness of God, as the defining feature of all human beings, of every culture, background, faith tradition, and way of life. The Jewish philosopher Emmanuel Levinas understood the face as the window onto the human soul, the primal site of encounter with the other.[5] It is through the faces of others that we experience the world. Our faces reveal us to the world, sometimes betraying more of ourselves than we realize. Pope Francis concludes his encyclical *On Fraternity and Social Friendship* with an invocation of the *imago dei* and the role of Holy Spirit in revealing God's beauty in the "different faces of the one humanity God so loves."[6] Scientists also celebrate how the face allows for a massive variety of human communication. From an evolutionary perspective, faces are sites of uniqueness that create identity and make human recognition possible.[7] Our knees or elbows are not quite so diverse or capable. Even something as "homogenous" as the terracotta army of China points to the need to keep the uniqueness of human identity. Where their faces are concealed by helmets, even the ears of the warriors were crafted as distinctively individual. Perhaps the visceral reason why so many resisted wearing masks in the pandemic has as much to do with what is lost when the face is obscured. Levinas viewed the face as the guarantee of ethics, the one place where we cannot but see the dignity and vitality of the other. Face to face encounters keep us honest. The face to face prevents the idolatry of abstraction. Hypocrisy, or being two-faced, is in this reading a denial of both the true image of the divine, and of ethical responsibility to the other.

In the story of the three bears, the sight of the little bear's face brings Goldilocks to her senses. In an act of pure Levinasian ethical encounter, first the sound of his voice, then the sight of his expression, wakes her from physical (and moral) slumber. Awakened, Goldilocks realizes where she is, and makes a swift exit. Goldilocks is an inherently conflicted personality. She does not dissimulate or mask her sense of moral failure, the destruction that she has wrought on the house. Nevertheless, she hints at a way for finding life in equipoise between equally unattractive alternatives. The instinct in the search for the Goldilocks God is similar: spirituality and religion make more sense when viewed through the experience of this practical and conflicted model of a girl who dared to make mistakes.

Her story is not the story of a genius or a saint. It is not the story of someone who has all the answers. It is instead the story of fearless experimentation. Goldilocks in this reading is better approached as an archetype or model for spiritual growth. And we shall encounter many examples of this Goldilocks archetype.

Goldilocks reveals there is no substitute for lived experience and exploration. One cannot theorize one's way to the most comfortable bed or porridge of the right temperature any more than one can speculate one's way to God. Yet we still try. It is tempting to compare humans in search of the divine to the Greek myth of Sisyphus, a king endlessly condemned to rolling a boulder up a hill, only for it to roll back down again. Anyone who has ever sought God has at times, if they are honest, felt like Sisyphus.

The story of Goldilocks is more hopeful. Instead of the pointless toil of Sisyphus there is clear narrative progression. Goldilocks gets somewhere. She practices empirical scientific method, and when it does not work, moves on. It is in the middle of everyday life that we find the deep wisdom of the Goldilocks imperative to seek the God who is neither too hot nor too cold. But this is not a wisdom limited to only a single religious tradition. The truths of the Goldilocks God are broader and deeper. Those searching for the middle way of the *via media* are better understood as theological magpies, merrily stealing whatever they need from the nests of others.

I frequently wonder whether there is a God, and have always harbored a certain distrust toward those who are unduly certain either that God exists or that God does not. How do they know? What makes them so very sure? Demagogues, cult leaders, and inquisitors share the certainty of being right. They know that their road is the only one worth traveling. For others of us, spirituality and religion have never been something to be certain about. Instead, it has always been fairly messy and unpredictable. The argument of this book is that in the field of everyday life (religious or otherwise) the perplexing and contradictory, the muddles and the confusions are sites of deep wisdom. Socrates understood that he did not know an awful lot about much. His wisdom was not about accumulating knowledge, so much as discovering some humility about what we cannot know. The same is true of those who start with the *imago dei*.

French philosopher and theologian Jean-Luc Marion agrees with Socrates and takes it a step further. It is precisely in our own incomprehensibility (and lack of understanding of ourselves) that we reflect the incomprehensibility of God. To put it another way. Socratic unknowing is not simply a human invention: it is theologically rooted in the very nature of what it is to know God.

The Search for Extra Terrestrial Intelligence Institute (SETI) has an open mind about the presence of alien intelligence in the universe. SETI thinks it would be "extraordinary if we were the only thinking beings in these realms." Equally, out of the 100 billion galaxies we can see SETI estimates ranging from as many as 10,000 alien life forms to as few as just one: us.[8] The experts at SETI are honest that they don't know. Yet they strongly suspect they will eventually find alien life. That seems to me to be a pretty accurate statement of my own approach to the quest for God.

The spiritual and/or religious search for God is a lot like the scientific quest for alien life. Like the scientists at SETI, those traveling the *via media* begin with the assumption that we do not have all the answers. We recognize that there are many other seekers after the true God, the God who is neither too hot nor too cold. Nevertheless, despite our doubts, we are convinced that if we keep searching we may end up finding what we are looking for.

Former Archbishop of Canterbury, Rowan Williams, explores St. Augustine's insight that the reason we search for God does not originate with us.[9] Maybe the religious quest is about discovering how God already seeks us out. What we think of as *our* quest may, in fact, be the way God self-reveals. Or, to use the language of Goldilocks, perhaps the Goldilocks story was a set up! Maybe the three bears deliberately allowed themselves to be taken advantage of so that she could make herself at home. And perhaps the narrative core lies in the hospitality and generosity of the three bears. It has always struck me as peculiar just how easily Goldilocks enjoyed breakfast and a nap before being discovered (with no discernible repercussions).

It is also important to say a word about the power of desire in the story of Goldilocks. For too long desire has been frowned upon as somehow un-Christian or selfish. Yet, thanks to scholars within the academy and feminists within the church, we are better placed to appreciate desire. Desire is not reducible to psychoanalytic categories or sexual experience. St. Augustine reminds us that in our desire for God, we are experiencing something of God's desire for us. Desire, as we shall see at key moments and in key doctrines, also describes movements at the heart of God. Part of the appropriateness of the story of Goldilocks lies in how this fable affirms the importance of desire, both human and potentially divine. In her study of the Trinity and the various ways it has been approached, the theologian, priest, and academic Sarah Coakley argues persuasively for a more sophisticated understanding of the complexity and prayerfulness of desire.[10] The desire of human yearning, and the desire of God, are where humans are inextricably entangled.

Goldilocks is a story of entanglement. We do not really know what the three bears thought of Goldilocks, just as we do not really know how God views humanity. This is an asymmetry that cannot be overcome. The quest to know God as a separate being on equal terms will never result in much satisfaction. Theologians have for centuries rejected the idea that God is "a" being. That theologians are much closer to atheists in rejecting such a being is under appreciated. God is beyond being. In the words of Levinas, *otherwise than being*. Jean-Luc Marion's *God Without Being* questions the entire history of being in Western metaphysics, preferring to envisage God as loving *without being*.[11] Both Levinas and Marion call into question thinkers who pursue a God's-eye-view of the universe (ending up instead with a human-sized ego for God). Whether it is the ethical demand of Levinas or the primacy of the loving gift of Marion, both force philosophy and theology to focus less on metaphysics. More significant is the practice of living and loving others (with God) in the world.

One night at supper my youngest daughter (who was six at the time), asked me what it is to be Episcopalian. Only she did not put it that way. She asked, "What is an Episcop," pause, "alien?" It was hilarious. She helped me realize that the spirituality of the religious tradition I grew up in is pretty alien compared to other communities. Her question also inspired me to explore what lies at its heart. Yet, the more I investigated the less I was convinced that it was anything to do with a particular belief, doctrine, or dogma. Instead, it seemed more about a particular way of being in the world, a certain set of embodied practices, than anything else. Less about believing. More about becoming. Which is when it hit me. In my quest to answer her question I was not discovering anything distinctively Episcopalian. I was instead uncovering a constellation of habits shared by Christians and others of all shapes and sizes for thousands of years. I am christening the constantly shifting relationships within this constellation a "spiritual thermodynamics." Just as the secular laws of thermodynamics provide a consistent window into what we can expect to occur in the physical world, so this spiritual thermodynamics offers a more ancient, and empirically verified, way of experiencing God. In exploring this one may be drawn to the historic *via media* of Anglican experience. And yet, to identify this spiritual thermodynamics entirely with the tradition is to miss the point. The spiritual thermodynamics experienced by those yearning for the Goldilocks God represents a sensibility rather than a body of knowledge. And this sensibility is found across many different traditions within Christianity.

The Goldilocks God is the kind of God discovered at the supper table and the workplace. Such a God is found in both joy and heartache; and is concerned above all with failures and sinners. The Goldilocks God is no sugar-coated God or loftily unreachable divinity. This is the real thing, neither too hot nor too cold. Thanks to Beatrix and her sister Lyra and their frank supper conversations I found myself being swept into the gravitational pull of the Goldilocks God. To say I found God would be misleading. I prefer to imagine that the Goldilocks God pulled me in.

Encounters with the holy always start with being decentered and pulled out of one's existing orbit. The challenge of spiritual growth is always about how this encounter changes the shape of our lives. The universe and solar system are still there, and the earth keeps turning. Yet something changes within the orientation of the human heart. What follows is the story of how this occurs. In the quest to find the Goldilocks God we will grapple with a litany of different challenges. But there is one recurring question that informs all the others: where (and what) are the signs that both illuminate and reveal the way that leads to the holy? Or, to give it a more Levinasian inflection, what does a seeker need to do to catch, and refract, something of the joy on the face of Goldilocks?

NOTES

1. Friedrich Schleiermacher, *On Religion: Speeches to Cultured Despisers*, ed. Richard Crouter (Cambridge: Cambridge University Press, 1998).
2. Paul Davies, *The Goldilocks Enigma* (New York: Mariner Books, 2008).

3. "Dartmouth Digital Orozco," Dartmouth College, accessed March 20, 2021, http://www.dartmouth.edu/digitalorozco/app/.

4. Many of the formative texts of the Anglican *via media* are found in the following: Geoffrey Rowell, Kenneth Stevenson, and Rowan Williams, *Love's Redeeming Work: The Anglican Quest for Holiness* (Oxford: Oxford University Press, 2001), Richard Schmidt, *Glorious Companions: Five Centuries of Anglican Spirituality* (Grand Rapids: Eeerdmans, 2002). For key assessments of the tradition: Charles Helfling and Cynthia Shattuck (eds.). *The Oxford Guide to the Book of Common Prayer: A Worldwide Survey* (Oxford: Oxford University Press, 2008), Mark Chapman, Sathianathan Clarke, and Martyn Percy (eds.). *The Oxford Handbook of Anglican Studies* (Oxford: Oxford University Press, 2015).

5. Emmanuel Levinas, *Totality and Infinity: An Essay on Exteriority*, trans. Alphonso Lingis (Pittsburgh: Duquesne University Press, 1969).

6. Pope Francis, *Fratelli Tutti: On Fraternity and Social Friendship* (Washington, DC: United States Conference of Bishops, 2020), 134.

7. Nicholas Christakis, *The Evolutionary Origins of a Good Society* (New York: Little Brown, 2019), 289ff.

8. "FAQ SETI Institute," SETI Institute, accessed March 31, 2017, http://www.seti.org/faq#seti2.

9. Rowan Williams, *On Augustine* (London: Bloomsbury Books, 2016).

10. Sarah Coakley, *God, Sexuality, and the Self* (Cambridge: Cambridge University Press, 2013).

11. Jean-Luc Marion, *God Without Being*, trans. Thomas A. Carlson (Chicago: University of Chicago Press, 1991).

Chapter One

The Enigma of Elizabeth

On September 7, 1533, a child was born to King Henry VIII. Convinced that his new wife Anne Boleyn would bear him a male heir, the king already had letters ready to go out across Europe heralding the birth of his prince. But the prince turned out to be female. In a hurry the proclamations were rewritten, and it is still possible to see where there was not quite enough space to fit the double "s" required to turn a prince into a princess. Two and a half years later, Elizabeth's mother was dead, beheaded by an irascible husband, caught in a web of political intrigue. Half a millennium on scholars are still revising their theories about why Anne had to go, and why Henry's passion turned so quickly into uxoricide.

Henry's disappointment in the gender of his new daughter did not prevent him from raising her in a manner befitting her royal status. In addition to her native tongue, Elizabeth became fluent in French, Italian, and Spanish, and was taught to read and write in Latin. Sixty years later she would translate Boethius's *On the Consolation of Philosophy*, "in less than a month for fun."[1] Tall, beautiful, intelligent, and accomplished alike in hunting and playing on the virginal (an early harpsichord), she grew up to become one of the most eligible women in Europe. While she never married, she gave birth to a uniquely pragmatic religious system, known by historians as the "Elizabethan settlement."

England in the mid sixteenth century was a time of crisis and seeming constant change. Religion and politics were deeply intertwined, and what was perfectly orthodox belief could turn into a death warrant—depending on who the monarch was. After Henry's death, his son Edward reigned for just six short years. He was succeeded by Mary, the daughter of Henry's first wife, Catherine of Aragon, the queen displaced by Henry's infatuation with Anne Boleyn. Like her step-brother, she also ruled for six turbulent years. Both Edward and Mary were problematic rulers. Under Edward, a mere ten years old on his accession, power went to various figures at court who pursued their own religious and political interests. Heretics (which meant

Roman Catholics) were targeted by sweeping changes that made the country much more Protestant. Under Mary, following her marriage to Philip, Roman Catholic King of Spain, power was perceived as passing to foreigners and the Pope. It was also under Mary that a passion for burning heretics (which meant Protestants) succeeded in stirring up further antagonism against Roman Catholicism. By the time the reigns of the boy king and bloody Mary were over, the only thing anyone could really agree on was that things had been much better under Henry.

When in 1559 messengers came to announce the death of Queen Mary and her accession to the throne, Princess Elizabeth was sitting under an oak tree in the grounds of Hatfield Palace. Her first act was to call together her new Council of State in the banqueting hall. Elizabeth consulted others, but she ruled as her father's daughter. Henry could be capricious, and his daughter inherited his ease of wielding authority. She was also her own person, and her reign was to be characterized by caution as she carefully steered clear of perils. Unlike Edward and Mary, she would not have her strings pulled by others. She did not encourage dissent. And unlike Henry, she was constant. She did not change religious or political policy to pursue her own marital interests. Quite the reverse, she used the ruse of those marital interests to pursue political and religious stability.

Against counsel to the contrary, Elizabeth avoided the danger of being ensnared in a marriage that would weaken her independence. More importantly to the health and security of her subjects, she avoided the pursuit of dogmatic certainty in religion. Elizabeth would have agreed with Voltaire's insight: "Doubt is an uncomfortable condition, but certainty is a ridiculous one." Elizabeth's reign suited neither Protestant reformers nor Catholic traditionalists. Instead, she pursued a middle way largely of her own making. While she had religious advisors, she abhorred religious extremists. She was no innovator. Robert Wright draws attention to how, in her own words, her church followed, "no novel and strange religions but that very religion which is ordained by Christ, sanctioned by the primitive and Catholic Church and approved by the consentient mind and voice of the most early Fathers."[2] In short, she was the very first person to pursue a deliberate religious and political strategy that was pure Goldilocks.

We will return to Elizabeth. Her story has important lessons for a present that is often divisive and partisan. She shows how it is possible to chart a steady course through major religious, political, and social challenges. Elizabeth did not simply give birth to a religious institution that, over time, would be renowned for moderation. She did something much more important. She recognized that maintaining community with others was more important than subscribing to a particular set of beliefs. In ideologically divided times, with figures on the right and the left mutually uncomprehending, seeing the world through an Elizabethan lens can help us rediscover our common humanity. Her reign was never secure, and she was always looking over her shoulder facing down some plot or other. But even before it was over, her rule was looked upon as a Golden Age. The poet Edmund Spenser even named her Gloriana. It was fitting tribute to the woman who essentially saved her country by intuiting that moderation is more important than forcing one's views on others.

Jumping forwards half a millennium we can see the implications of this perspective in the life of Verna Dozier. The daughter of an agnostic and a Baptist, she remembered being taken to hear Howard Thurman, spiritual advisor to Martin Luther King and other civil rights leaders. Dozier was spellbound. For the first time she realized it was possible to question received wisdom about spirituality. She started to realize that spirituality has very little to do with Sunday mornings. In her words, "what happens on Sunday morning is not half so important as what happens on Monday morning."[3] For over three decades Dozier taught in the District of Columbia public schools. She knew at first hand the challenges faced by people who looked liked her. As a black woman, she knew that the world privileged whiteness, maleness, and youth.

Dozier enlarged our sense of what our common humanity should look like. She recognized that to have faith requires us to challenge the cultural (and often ecclesiastical) constructs that privileged white over black and brown, male over female, and youth over age. Dozier understood that the work begun by Elizabeth was far from over. She also realized that the opposite of faith is not doubt but fear. She knew that love is justice in action. And, like Elizabeth, she taught that making a difference is much more important than interior belief.

Dozier knew that breaking down the barriers of racism, white privilege, and patriarchy was not an easy thing to do within the church. She also understood that such a work was not hers alone. She approached it from within the Goldilocks zone. She had the intellectual humility to know that she might not be right about everything. And yet she accurately predicted the three traps faced by people of faith. There is the trap of thinking that spirituality is all about saving souls. The trap of legislating morality. The trap of putting all one's energies into social service alone. Dozier understood that each trap was there for a reason—often a very convincing reason. She also knew that when believers reduced their faith to any one of those three activities that it ends up doing more harm than good.

Dozier saw things differently. She believed that faithfulness was about living into the dream of God. This is profoundly aspirational and puts the burden of living into the dream on the soul of every seeker. It is also quintessentially Goldilocks. Dozier recognized that faith should not be prescriptive. It should be transformative. In short, Dozier wanted to lift others up to discover the freedom of God's dream for themselves.

ARISTOTLE'S PRACTICAL WISDOM

More than two millennia before Dozier, the Greek thinker Aristotle was wrestling with a remarkably similar set of questions. Specifically, he wondered what humans need for happiness. While others theorized that repudiation of desire or the seeking of pleasure led to true happiness, Aristotle sought neither the way of denial nor the way of excess. Choosing a middle course, Aristotle suggested that the pursuit of human virtue is the surest road to happiness. Practice the virtuous life, and happiness will follow. The only problem with this deeply practical theory is that locating virtue is never particularly easy. Life is a series of choices between differing possibilities. Aristotle argued that seeking out the virtues was always a matter of identifying the center ground, between opposing extremes. In avoiding both the ferocity of the Protestantism of her brother Edward and the fervent Roman Catholicism of her step sister Mary, Elizabeth had echoed Aristotle's instinct for the middle ground.

Unlike his more theoretical and abstract teacher, Plato, Aristotle knew that finding happiness and seeking virtue were deeply practical concerns. Aristotle also understood that the path to happiness and the good life requires clarity about what to avoid as much as what to seek. Aristotle recognized that humanity often skews to its worst instincts. Humans are always faced by the extremes of excess (like overly hot porridge) and deficiency (the cold porridge). The key to the fulfilling life is finding the "mean" or the average between the two opposites. For Goldilocks the mean was the porridge that was just right, neither too hot nor too cold. For Elizabeth, it lay in a religious sensibility that was neither too radically self-centered and anti-traditionalist (Protestant) nor too hierarchical and anti-individualist (Roman Catholic). She did not abandon the interiority of belief that Protestants valued. And she did not reject the importance of the traditions that had been preserved by the Roman Catholic church. Instead, she sought to combine parts of each.

Aristotle had already laid the intellectual groundwork for finding the middle way. In explaining the virtue courage, Aristotle showed how courage is found when the extremes are rejected. Courage is Aristotle's middle point (his "mean" again) between foolhardiness (a state of excess) and cowardice (a state of deficiency).[4] Goldilocks's language of finding a temperature that is "just right" is an echo of the Aristotelian search for the mean or the middle way. But while Goldilocks makes no moral judgment about the excess or lack of heat, Aristotle is less forgiving. He saw that virtues, "are middle states, and that these virtues themselves and their opposing vices are states that find expression in choice."[5] Virtue is clearly found in the middle, while vices are the opposing states of either excess or deficiency. In another example, Aristotle describes justice as the phenomenon that is found in the "mean" position where things are, quite literally, "just right." It is in the nature of justice to be in equilibrium, while the opposing vices of gain (a situation of excess) and loss (what happens where there is deficiency) represent two opposing, yet equally problematic, formulations of injustice. Wisdom is another Aristotelian virtue situated firmly in the middle. To have an "excess" of wisdom, to be overly hot, is to be "cunning," and much to be deplored for Aristotle. Yet to lack wisdom, to be chilly in respect of wisdom, is to have something just as undesirable: "naivety."

Straying from the virtuous middle ground leads to what Aristotle did not hesitate to call vices. One of the marks of contemporary society is that we are very good at identifying vices in others, if less in ourselves. We are living at a time of unprecedented alienation, confusion, and division. Politically, we are segregated into increasingly blue or red states. Very few of us live in purple areas. We tend to live surrounded by those who are like us, and we barely know what to say to those who are of the opposing political tribe. Socially, we are just as divided between embracing "traditional" values or daring to "think for ourselves" as the subjects of sixteenth-century England. Economically, we are living at a time of intense and ever-widening financial disparity. Wage inequality is worse than it has been in over half a century. The richest grow ever richer, the poorest, reliant on the "gig economy," get ever poorer. Internationally, the promise of living in a global village is increasingly challenged by protectionism, nationalism, and fear of difference and immigration. The pandemic simply made these fault lines more obvious. While economies stagnate for the working poor, stock markets boom. And while the depths of economic and racial inequality are rendered visible in death rates, there remains no societal consensus that this is even a problem. Although Dozier was challenging white male privilege half a century ago, there is still a huge amount of racial reconciliation to be undertaken if genuine wholehearted equality is to become a reality.

Religiously, we are even more divided than sixteenth-century Europe. We are increasingly forced to choose between unquestioning fundamentalisms that delight in offending and attacking those who do not share our beliefs. "Conservative" Christian fundamentalists have so taken over the language of Christian belief that many other millions who follow Jesus are reluctant to even name themselves Christian. Meanwhile, the reflex atheism of "liberal" elites delights in repeating the professions of fundamentalism as proof of the moral bankruptcy of religion. Elizabeth lived with a similar set of polarities. She avoided in equal measure Puritan and Papist extremists. She feared the political danger and civil divisions that each posed. Both were existential threats to peace for the whole of her reign. Eschewing, and doing her best to repress them, she understood that a bipolar politics could not sustain civil society. Instead, she sought a middle way between the two. Under her the royal chapels were to be places that offended some reformers by singing hymns to the accompaniment of organ music; while offending traditionalists by rejecting Latin for the innovation of worship in vernacular English. She was not a good Catholic, but nor was she a good Calvinist.

Elizabeth's motivations were a form of both religious and political pragmatism. Dozier was much more explicit in connecting the project of freedom and equality to spirituality, and the dream of God. By contrast, the pre-Christian Aristotle offers *phronesis*: a form of deeply practical wisdom with which to pursue a virtuous life. The ideological mistrust and entrenched divisions of our own day provide the perfect backdrop for rediscovering these connected, yet different, approaches to wisdom. In reaching for the center, and avoiding extremes, the Aristotelian and the Elizabethan impulses may be combined to shape a "spiritual thermodynamics" that may equip us for realizing Dozier's dream of God. Such an approach is more interested in finding spiritual common ground than accentuating differences. Against divisive certainty, boastful pride, or smug self-righteousness, the route to the Goldilocks God is one that passes through ambiguity, inclusiveness, and ethical humility. To combine Aristotelian virtue ethics with Elizabethan religious pragmatism is to offer a new way of negotiating the ethical and religious challenges. At the same time, we need to be mindful of Dozier's insight that the pursuit of joy is a better indication of being on the right path than any quest for virtue for its own sake.[6]

This approach to spirituality rejoices in diversity and delights in the challenges of thinking differently. We are not alike. And if we are genuinely created in the image of God, then we have to assume that our intrinsic differences are part of what connect us to the divine. Without listening to, and learning from, black female voices like Dozier's, the quest for the Goldilocks zone is doomed to fail before it has even started. In the same way, as we approach the end of the first quarter of the first century of the third millennium students of Goldilocks will wish to listen to a rich panoply of other voices only just beginning to be heard. Gay and lesbian voices, transgender voices, bisexual voices, and the voices of those who are questioning gender as a fixed identity are some of the most important of these. If Dozier is correct, and we are invited to pursue the dream of God, in time, there will also be other distinctive voices for us to learn from. God's dream is always a diverse one. And to pursue the spiritual thermodynamics of Goldilocks is to be willing to learn from those who are different.

UNIVERSAL EQUALITY

One of the touchstones of the Goldilocks God is fundamental human equality. It is worth recalling that this revolutionary universal truth was first expounded by the apostle Paul. Subsequently it was taken up by the writers of the American constitution and every progressive since the Enlightenment. This was a radical idea in the first century, and it has been a dangerous idea whenever humans have dared to imagine it might be true. The fact that it continues to be such a difficult concept to abide by is proof of how ahead of its time the Pauline concept was. And yet, despite such difficulties, few today would openly suggest that the project of equality should be abandoned.

Paul knew at first hand just how dangerous and difficult the pursuit of truth could be. And yet, when it came to the universal love of God for all people, Paul was not to be deflected in pursuing it. For Paul universal equality was not a political or cultural concept. It was instead, a religious insight, grounded in his belief that in Christ there is no male or female, Jew or Greek, slave or free.[7] His belief was radical, because he was writing at a time when it was self-evidently *not* the case that men and women, slaves and free, Jews and Greek were all equals. In what was a deeply countercultural statement, Paul deconstructed the hierarchies of his day, claiming Christ as the supreme disrupter and leveler of social conventions. To be in Christ was to be part of a fellowship of equals, regardless of pre-existing social status.

Christianity itself has not been particularly swift at following this logic to its conclusion. However, given how long it took subsequent revisions and Supreme Court interpretations of the Constitution of the United States to establish freedom for all, regardless of gender or race, one cannot fault Paul overmuch. He was at least a good couple of millennia ahead of most. And yet, by whatever metric you are grading, humanity clearly has a long way to go. Were it not for Paul's striking egalitarianism, we would not be quite as far down the road as we currently are. And yet, as the increasing consciousness around race relations reminds us, our journey is still only just getting started.

Few have had an instinct for equality. Good Queen Bess was more promising than most of her contemporaries. After ascending the throne, Elizabeth declared that she did not seek to place "a window into men's souls." Instead, she issued *The Book of Common Prayer*, designed to structure a community of prayer, education, and social service in which all were equal. The Elizabethan church was not simply about worship. It was also a way of making sure that the poor were cared for, education delivered, and the fabric of human society strengthened. With one deft move she avoided much of the trauma of a European context that saw duchies, principalities, fiefdoms, city states, kingdoms, and electorates vying for one another's blood. Issues such as which language to speak in church (one's own, or Latin) were tearing the Continent apart.

Elizabeth wanted stability for a land that had experienced pendulum swings between Catholic and Protestant beliefs over the previous three decades. She was not by any stretch of the imagination perfect. There was still religious persecution as she sought to keep her throne and fend off foreign invasion (mainly Spanish, which meant by extension Roman Catholic). And to this day, those who walk in her footsteps have a profound sense of the failings, foibles, and feeble-mindedness of the institutional church that is her legacy. For her Archbishop John Whitgift the mission was clear: "we retain whatsoever we find to be good, refuse or reform that which is not evil." In practice it was a lot messier. Elizabeth frequently blocked the desires of her people (including her Archbishops). She sought not perfection, so much as institutional ambiguity, a certain *je ne sais quoi* that was probably maddening to her most trusted religious advisors. Nevertheless, by comparison with the Continent where persecution saw both Catholics and Protestants engaged in protracted bloody warfare, Elizabeth steered her English kingdom in an entirely different direction.

Over subsequent centuries the Elizabethan settlement eventually evolves into the *via media*, the hallmark of the global network known as Anglicanism. Elizabeth's intimation that there might be unity alongside doctrinal difference takes centuries before it becomes fashioned into Anglicanism (the endlessly confusing collective noun for that communion of churches, the Church of England, the Episcopal Church, and other international churches descended from the original Elizabethan settlement). It was in the Episcopal branch of Elizabeth's church that Dozier would spend her adult life in faithful service. While Elizabeth's father, Henry, wanted the freedom to do his own thing, remaining "Catholic without the Pope," he did not much care for the opinions or concerns of others. By contrast, Elizabeth created an ecclesiastical framework that was more interested in allowing people to pursue their own dream of God free from persecution, rather than worrying about what they might believe.

It has generated a cottage industry of analysis, and most investigators eventually come to recognize the truth of what H.R. McAdoo put so incisively: "Anglicanism is not a theological system and there is no writer whose work is an essential part of it either in respect of content or with regard to the form of its self-expression . . . the absence of an official theology in Anglicanism is something deliberate which belongs to its essential nature."[8] Such an absence constitutes the very core of the Anglican way of life.

Anglicans, and by extension, Episcopalians like Dozier, were shaped out of a royal desire to steer deliberately down the middle of the road. Over the centuries, this decision born of realpolitik evolved into an orienting religious and spiritual principle. Whether the faithful lean more to the Catholic, Protestant, or Orthodox (from which so much liturgy and theology is drawn), the tradition as a whole was designed to help people learn from one another, and stay connected despite very real (and potentially very deadly) differences.

In the twenty-first century many continue to expand upon the Elizabethan vision of inclusivity. There is still much to do working out the implications of the "radical hospitality" that is the breadth of God's love for absolutely all people. In the last century God's love for all humanity has been emphasized. Not just warring Catholics and Protestants, but everyone. The *via media* eschews the segregation of people into insiders and outsiders, sheep and goats, blue staters or red staters, or whatever divisive term happens to be trending on social media this week. Perhaps the strangest thing about seekers after the Goldilocks God is their diversity. In a global village that often seems to encourage homogenization and uniformity, there are as many millions of different ways of finding God as there are believers.

The Elizabethan settlement continues to provide a foundation for understanding the diversity of God's creation, and the variety of ways that people encounter God. *The Book of Common Prayer* of The Episcopal Church, for example, requires adherents to recognize the image of God as present in every human being. Like Dozier, it teaches against discriminating on the basis of sexual orientation, gender, national origin, or race. And like other followers of Christ, Episcopalians are required to look for, and serve, Christ in every other person. Belief in God as all-loving requires believers to extend that love to Buddhists, Jews, Muslims, Sikhs, atheists, and agnostics as well as members of other faiths and other Christian traditions. Perhaps even more boldly, we also believe God loves our mothers-in-law, siblings, bosses, immigrants, criminals, and political adversaries. In a culture that encourages, or at least facilitates, sectarian, socioeconomic, and political divisions, inclusivity is one of the most alien features of the Goldilocks God.

Sometimes it seems as if the world is afraid of being strange. In its rush to make everything transparent and clear there is little time for recognizing differences or places of friction. And yet, spirituality and religion are saturated with strangeness. Seeking God is not about having the answers. It is more about how one works through the questions. It is less about solving life's mysteries so much as making friends with the fact that life is mysterious. Some of the great fantasy writers of the last century grew up within churches of the Elizabethan settlement: J.K. Rowling, creator of Hogwarts, Madeleine L'Engle, the time wrinkler, and C.S. Lewis, imaginer of Narnia. These three alone are perhaps the most famous practitioners of Elizabeth's *via media* hiding in plain sight. It does not take a genius to recognize how their writing may have been inspired by the richly imaginative faith that they all shared.[9]

BLUNDERING AFTER GOD

To hold perspectives as diverse as Aristotle, Paul, Elizabeth, Dozier, and Madeleine L'Engle together at once is, if not impossible, then, at least paradoxical. I confess to being a considerable devotee of paradox. It reminds me how little I comprehend of the mystery of God. Paradox and mystery are natural partners. Paradox is an invitation to try and make sense out of that which does not always make that much sense. This tension, between knowing intellectually that we do *not* know God and the spiritual desire to know God, is an essential and insurmountable problem. It is both the reason *for* spiritual exploration and one of the most limiting factors. It is the ultimate spiritual paradox.

To search for the paradoxical God within the Goldilocks zone, it is necessary to embrace both the paradox and the mystery. God is both present and absent, and it is the difficult experiences of both that shapes the spiritual quest. The *via media* requires honesty about this if we are to find the conditions that are "just right." Many find themselves starting on the side of feeling God's absence more keenly. How could we do anything else this side of eternity? Yet, as Emily Dickinson suggests, "To the faithful, absence is condensed presence."[10] Even absence can point to presence. The purpose of theology and spiritual reflection is to help us discover for ourselves how it is not just in spite of, but *because* of, feelings of absence that we are driven ever onward into God's presence.

One of the challenges facing those pursuing spiritual integrity is recognizing how absence of God leads us into a dialectic with the presence of God. Theology even gives us ways of codifying this in the language it uses to describe God. There are positive statements about God (cataphatic) and there are denials about God (apophatic), or what is sometimes called negative theology. Orthodox theologians underline the importance of the apophatic as a reminder that our images and ideas of God are fragile, requiring us to be creative with them. As Christos Yannaras notes, "The apophatic attitude leads Christian theology to use the language of poetry and images for the interpretation of dogmas much more than the language of conventional logic and schematic concepts."[11] *Apophasis* goes hand in hand with *cataphasis*. Each has its great insights. Yet, each left to its own devices, threatens to make nonsense of God. At its best, the cataphatic helps us learn something of God using metaphors and images from the world in which we live (love, forgiveness, truth, art, poetry, etc.). Yet, at its worst, we forget we are speaking cataphatically, and we risk believing that God really is completely identified by any of these images. The danger of *cataphasis* is that we think that the words we use for God might accurately describe the divine.

The apophatic and the cataphatic always require one another. Vladimir Lossky, another Orthodox theologian, resolved his apophatic problem by speaking personally of God as Trinity, Father, Son, and Holy Spirit at the same time as speaking of the unknowability of God. Which is, of course, to start to speak positively, or cataphatically.[12] If the apophatic alone is "too cold," and the cataphatic alone is "too hot," what is needed is a combination of both that is "just right." This was also what Thomas Aquinas aimed for when he developed his idea of analogy. Aquinas recognized how words shape reality. We need words that can be used positively, cataphatically, to describe God. And yet, we also need to recognize that these words are not literal. His brilliant insight was to introduce the notion of analogical language, a form of language that avoids the pitfalls of language that is both excessively literal or excessively unknowable.

Speaking of God analogically allowed Aquinas to continue to talk about God. At the same time, he recognized that for all the talk of analogy he had not reduced God to some "thing" that humans comprehend. Aquinas knew he could not know God. Analogy was a way of keeping God-talk honest. It was also a way of naming the essential dialectic between the presence and absence of God. As Jean-Luc Marion has argued, Aquinas is not trying to present God as a metaphysical object about which we can successfully make positive statements. Rather, Aquinas's theory of analogy is just as much about reminding us that we can only speak analogically. In other words, our words do not circumscribe the divine. We do not know God. As Aquinas puts it: "With the exception of a revelation of grace we do not, in this life, know about God what He is and therefore that we are united to Him as unknown."[13] In contrast to later traditions that see Aquinas at the start of a tradition of naming God as metaphysically knowable, Marion reads Aquinas guaranteeing the unknowability of God (showing God as "beyond Being") in God's very self.

The elementary spiritual paradox is that words always struggle and fail to name God. And yet for some reason we keep trying. As D.Z. Phillips notes, "Language is not a screen which hides God from us. On the contrary, the idea of God *in* the language we have been explaining, is the idea of a hidden God."[14] It is not that language fails us, and we are somehow unprepared to talk about God. Rather, these struggles occur because it is in the nature of God *not* to be completely transparent to us: hiddenness is simply another way of talking about this divine oscillation between presence and absence.

Within the intellect and heart of each believer, there are times when God is so absent and so unknowable. At other times, we feel closer to God, more in touch with the divine presence. *Apophasis* and *cataphasis* are not simply abstract ways of thinking about God. They also encode the different ways in which people have experienced the interplay of the presence and absence of God.

It would be terrible if God were always utterly equally vividly present. This is why theologians suggest that God purposefully created distance between God's self and creation, so as not to overwhelm creation. The sixteenth-century rabbi and mystic Isaac Luria founded the concept of *zimzum* (withdrawal) within kabbalism for just this reason: "the withdrawal of the infinite divine *ein sof* from a certain 'place' in order to bring about an 'empty space' in which the process of creation could proceed."[15] Without God distancing God's self from creation we would be forced to worship God night and day. We would have no option but to recognize God. Such a situation would be horrific. Overwhelming presence would be just as bad, if not worse, than total absence. Despite the truth of that, the problem of the seeming absence of God has been the one that believers and would-be believers have struggled with the most.

Those seeking God on the *via media* are often marked by a love of rationality, pragmatism, and common sense (the cataphatic parts). Yet, those same seekers also recognize that God is a mystery beyond comprehending (the apophatic parts). God is paradoxical, and if either side of the paradox is forgotten, we have not God but an idol of our own making. To find God in the middle of everyday life, in the *via media*, is as much about recognizing that there are some aspects of God that can never be comprehended.

Rowan Williams is helpful here, prefacing his thoughts with the insight of the Australian cartoonist Michael Leunig: "The word 'God' cannot be grasped scientifically, rationally or even theologically without it exploding." Williams goes on to explore in great detail the nature of these explosions, or what he calls "the breakdown of speech when it turns to God and the breakdown of speech that is unable to turn to God."[16] Williams reminds us that the difficulty of language about God is not something to retreat from.

This also points to the spiritual benefits of doubt. What the modern world takes for granted as doubt emerged from the crucible of debates within Christian theology.[17] And as those debates spread out into other fields, faith can only be understood with respect to doubt.[18] Time and again, it is the questions that drive forward the search for God. The doubts that lead to questions are the very lifeblood of the spiritual quest for God. The search for the Goldilocks God is one that requires both intellect and heart to cooperate in asking questions that can take us into deep waters. Once again poets seem to grasp this best. Alfred Lord Tennyson puts it beautifully: "There lives more faith in honest doubt, / Believe me, than in half the creeds."[19]

Those looking for Christ experience how in times of gravity, human suffering, and deep need, there is always the counterpoint of grace. The desolations of serious illness, dying, and bereavement sound awful, and they often are. Yet, they can also be amongst the most joy-filled events of life. Feelings of spiritual absence can also lead deep into the presence of God. The flux of

God's absence and presence is revealed in a "hidden grammar" that is real but not always visible. This hidden grammar is the connective tissue that binds religious practice and ordinary life together. Just as physicists try to produce equations that can account for fundamental laws of the material universe, so a hidden set of rules root experiences of spirituality within the life of the divine.

Rules is probably putting it a bit strong. A better description would be "normative experiences." Birth. Death. Grief. Joy. Getting married. Having a baby. Losing a loved one. Divorcing. Going bankrupt. Graduating. These are the highs and lows of existence. The French mystic Simone Weil understood the necessity of being open to the spiritual experience of even the most awful of events.[20] The hidden grammar of faith reminds us that the identical experience can be graceful for one person and ruinous for another. A Goldilocks spirituality understands that we are always shuttling through absence and presence, intellect and heart, suffering and joy, as we search for the holy somewhere in the middle.

While we cannot understand everything about God, it may be possible to shed some light on what Wittgenstein would call the "language game" of those who have successfully, and nondogmatically, sought (and experienced) God. To search for the Goldilocks God is simply code for thinking about a version of God that is neither too hot (too scary, too judgmental, and too unforgiving) or too cold (too irrelevant, too remote, and too absent).

The Goldilocks God is revealed by paying attention to the linguistic notations and conventions that create the conditions for spiritual life. Nowhere will it be suggested that there is a "proper" or "correct" grammar for seeking God. The last thing the world needs is a spiritual equivalent of one of the many style guides prepared by those who know the "best" way for how language should be used. This book follows Dozier in that it is not prescriptive so much as descriptive.

Faith involves a fair amount of blundering through life looking for spiritual sustenance. Those seeking God along the *via media* tend to be less driven by orthodoxy, and more concerned with orthopraxis, or "right action." It is not what we say or even what we think that truly matters. Intentions are all very well and good, but Aristotle, Paul, Elizabeth, and Dozier all knew better than that. It is what we do and *how* we live that determines and shapes the true nature of our beliefs. Life is not lived in theory, but in action. As I learned in the parish where I was priested: belonging is more important than believing.[21]

One of the things that makes the Goldilocks God so very alien is how the peculiar deep grammar of the Elizabethan *via media* matters more than any particular doctrine, creed, or institutional teaching. This is the same point that Aslan makes (he calls it deep magic) in *Narnia*. Whether we call it magic or something else, everything was created and everything shares a common structure. It makes sense if you think about it long enough. If there is a God who created everything and everyone, then alongside and within our differences, we also have much in common. Differences are not what divide us in this model. They are, instead, the set of identifiers that let us discover what makes us capable of dreaming of God in a way that is utterly unique to us. Dozier knew that we all have to find our way to God in the way that makes sense for us as individuals. She also knew that we don't have to make the journey alone.

This will sound wishy-washy or dotty to those raised in stricter, or simply more theologically coherent, religious traditions where doctrine is studied more intently. Nevertheless, this is the "dottiness" of an entire ecclesiastical tradition premised on avoiding too much certainty.[22] It is profoundly dotty to think that there might be a church that welcomes both Protestants and Catholics, both Republican conservatives and Democratic liberals. Dottiness is the very opposite of a system that has everything neatly within its place. Dottiness is not consistent with perfection, so much as the slightly bewildered and perplexed. The dotty tend not to be focused on having their own way. They are too caught up in the miracle of living for that. The dotty are dotty because they are so busy radiating joy.

In Homer's *Iliad* we hear the story of Odysseus's journey back from the Trojan War. After years of exploits and heroic adventures, he eventually makes it back to his wife Penelope, and discovers her beset by suitors trying to win her hand. But Penelope is every bit as wily as her husband. Promising to marry a suitor when she finishes weaving a burial shroud for Odysseus's father Laertes, by day she knits. And by night she unpicks the stitches. She keeps this extraordinary act up for three years, before her ruse is uncovered by Melantho, a disloyal servant. Penelope deliberately deferred choosing a replacement for Odysseus, continuing to remain faithful to her marital vows even when she must have felt totally abandoned by him.

Penelope had no way of knowing that Odysseus will make it home, any more than Odysseus could know that he would survive the trials of the war and the return voyage to Ithaca. In her practice of weaving and unstitching she keeps alive the possibility that she will be reunited with Odysseus. Her stitching and unstitching is a fitting metaphor for the spiritual and religious life.

Seeking God is about learning how to perform acts of weaving and unstitching. In the dialectic between presence and absence it becomes possible to knit closer to the divine. Penelope's actions reveal how it is not the finished product that matters. What matters is not what is woven or even the template that is followed. What matters is how we learn, unlearn, and relearn how to make the space to begin again.

Queen Elizabeth practiced Penelope's artifice on a grand scale in both her state craft and her religious politics. More important than the final destination was a habit of weaving. She may have inherited this habit from her mother,

Anne Boleyn. It is also worth remembering in this context the venerable tradition of peace weavers practiced by the Anglo-Saxon and Viking women who created political and religious bonds at the earliest points in the emergence of England. Elizabeth should not be seen as practicing a strategy of religious and political practice that was entirely without parallel. Rather, she deserves to be contextualized within the ancient royal Christian practices of her predecessors.

The influence on Christianity by royal women has long and deep roots within the English church. One of the key historians and interpreters of the birth of Christianity within Anglo-Saxon England was the monk Bede. As the historian Sarah Foot has shown, Bede's *Ecclesiastical History* devotes a remarkably equal attention to the female saints, many royal, who shaped Anglo-Saxon Christianity.[23] Many of the monastic houses he points to as examples of best practice were minsters of women religious (notably, Barking, Ely, and Whitby). Across English and Continental history the influence of powerful women, at court or in religious life, remains quite remarkable. Jane Tibbets Schulenburg explores this in considerable detail in her magisterial work on female sanctity, noting the web of interconnections between the saints and the royal families of the European courts and monastic institutions.[24]

Going back to the introduction of Christianity to England by St. Augustine of Canterbury in 597, the influence of Christian queens is once again made visible. The classic story of the arrival of Augustine is recounted as a mission commissioned by Pope Gregory, determined to Christianize the pagan Anglo-Saxons. King Athelberht famously greets Augustine on the Kent shore and allows him to set up a pioneering mission. In time, Athelberht converts. Only, the history is actually more complex. Years before Augustine even visits England, Queen Bertha (daughter of the Christian Frankish King Charibert and Queen Ingoberg) is married to Athelberht on the strict understanding that she be allowed to practice her faith. As textual evidence from Pope Gregory to Bertha confirms, Bertha's role was critical in arranging hospitality to the mission of Augustine. Schulenburg explains: "in this letter Pope Gregory the Great clearly recognized the queen's influence and the decisive role which he expected her to play in the strategy of converting Ethelbert and his followers."[25] Schulenburg goes on to note that the letter from the Pope makes it crystal clear that it is the faithful Bertha who is singularly responsible for the conversion to Christianity of the people of Kent, comparing her favorably with Helena the empress mother of Constantine, another holy woman responsible for the rise and spread of Christianity. And, according to legend at least, another daughter of Britain. This particular letter, written four years after the arrival of Augustine, paints a picture of the Bishop of Rome leaning heavily on Queen Bertha to help bring a somewhat reluctant King into line.

Schulenburg even suggests that it may have been Bertha who first reached out to the Pope requesting Augustine's mission in the first place.[26]

This excursion into history reminds us that while royal women have not always had the power to maneuver as freely as their male consorts, they were adept at playing the hand they had. Without Bertha the success of Augustine's mission to Kent is difficult to imagine. Elizabeth's own actions have been interpreted as vacillation as she fended off suitors of her own. Yet, like Penelope (and one imagines, Bertha at the court of her lamentably pagan husband), she pursued a deliberate strategy of deferral, entertaining possible matches while ultimately succeeding in maintaining her independence, and the independence of her country, for 44 years. For someone whose Latin motto was "*semper eadem*," always the same, Elizabeth was far from inflexible. She adapted to circumstances, playing different factions off against each other. She knew how to weave. She also knew how to unpick. Machiavellian in never overreaching and almost always avoiding conflict, Elizabeth kept her principles well hidden. Steering a careful course between arrogant Protestantism and unapologetic Catholicism, Elizabeth pursued a different course.

Defamed as the daughter of the great whore of Babylon, Anne Boleyn, the woman responsible in traditional opinion for tempting Henry VIII from the true faith, Elizabeth could so easily have been a lightning conductor for radical Protestantism. Yet her true opinions, if such things can ever be known, seem to be present in a comment to a visiting French ambassador: "there was only one Jesus Christ and one faith, and all the rest that they disputed about but trifles."[27] Elizabeth intuited that it was not worth sweating the small stuff.

Outward action is more important than inner belief. In the words of one historian, "A rather lukewarm and *politique* Protestantism, Elizabeth's own religion has always been something of an enigma."[28] It is not simply that she anticipated Goldilocks, steering away from extremes, while maintaining flexibility. In refusing to be drawn into the labyrinthian doctrinal tunnels and rabbit holes that so fascinated her contemporaries (often with fatal consequences), Gloriana's enigmatic approach remains worthy of study and emulation. Unlike her brutal father, Elizabeth never had any children. Yet, in some shape or form, we are all recipients of Elizabeth's pragmatic instinct that religion need not be a force for division. Elizabeth gave birth to a more inclusive form of church; one that can even be what it was for Dozier, the dream of God. While spirituality always entails a fair amount of trial and error, when approached with a certain degree of imagination it may also reveal how everything might be just right.

NOTES

1. John Guy, *Tudor England* (Oxford: Oxford University Press, 1990), 251.

2. Quoted by J. Robert Wright, "Anglicanism: *Ecclesia Anglicana,* and Anglican: An Essay on Terminology," in *The Study of Anglicanism*, ed. Stephen Sykes, John Booty, and Jonathan Knight (London: SPCK, 1988), 481.

3. Verna Dozier, *The Calling of the Laity* (New York: Rowman & Littlefield, 1988), quoted in Schmidt, *Glorious Companions*, 292.

4. Aristotle, *The Eudemian Ethics*, trans. Anthony Kenny (Oxford: Oxford University Press, 2011), 19ff.

5. Aristotle, *Eudemian Ethics*, 37.

6. Verna Dozier, *The Rock that is Higher,* quoted in Schmidt, *Glorious Companions*, 308.

7. Galatians 3:28.

8. H.R. McAdoo, *The Spirit of Anglicanism: A Survey of Anglican Theological Method in the Seventeenth Century* (New York: Scribners, 1965), v.

9. J.K. Rowling is a member of the Scottish Episcopal Church, a sister church of The Episcopal Church and the Church of England. The Scottish Episcopal Church was also responsible for consecrating the very first Episcopal bishop, Samuel Seabury, in Aberdeen in 1784. Madeleine L'Engle was an active American Episcopalian. C.S. Lewis was a member of the Church of England, the church brought over by colonists from England, and from which The Episcopal Church emerged following the Revolution. To this day the English monarch remains the "Supreme Governor" of the Church of England.

10. Letter to her cousin, Susan Gilbert Dickinson, in about 1878. I am grateful to Renée Bergland for introducing me to this reference.

11. Christos Yannaras, *Elements of Faith: An Introduction to Orthodox Theology*, trans. Keith Schram (Edinburgh: T&T Clark, 1991), 17.

12. See Rowan Williams, "Lossky, the *via negativa* and the foundations of theology," in *Wrestling with Angels*, ed. Mike Higton (Grand Rapids: Eerdmans, 2007), 1–24.

13. Aquinas, *Summa Theologiae* Ia, q.12, a.13, ad 1 quoted in Marion, *God Without*, 231.

14. D.Z. Phillips, *Faith After Foundationalism* (London: Routledge, 1988), 289.

15. Dan Joseph, *Kabbalah: A Very Short Introduction* (Oxford: Oxford University Press, 2007), 74.

16. Rowan Williams, *The Edge of Words* (London: Bloomsbury, 2014).

17. Dominic Erdozan, *The Soul of Doubt: The Religious Roots of Unbelief from Luther to Marx* (Oxford: Oxford University Press, 2016).

18. The importance of doubt within faith is the focus of my book *Faithful Doubt: The Wisdom of Uncertainty* (Eugene, OR: Cascade, 2014).

19. Alfred Lord Tennyson, "In Memoriam," xcvi lines 11–2 in *Selected Poems,* ed. Christopher Ricks (London: Penguin, 2008), 167.

20. Simone Weil, *Gravity and Grace* (London: Routledge, 1952).

21. My gratitude to Joe Hawes for first teaching me how fundamental this concept is for travelers on the *via media.*

22. Urban Holmes, *What is Anglicanism?* (Harrisburg, PA: Morehouse, 1982).

23. Sarah Foot, *Veiled Women I: The Disappearance of Nuns from Anglo-Saxon England* (Burlington, VT: Ashgate, 2000), 22.

24. Jane Tibbetts Schulenburg, *Forgetful of their Sex: Female Sanctity and Society, CA, 500–1100* (Chicago: Chicago University Press, 1998).

25. Schulenburg, *Forgetful*, 191.

26. Schulenburg, *Forgetful*, 194.

27. Richard Rex, *The Tudors* (Stroud: Amberley, 2011), 156.

28. Rex, *Tudors*, 154.

Chapter Two

Kierkegaard's Courage

There are inevitable frictions between the followers of Christ and the followers of worldly wisdom. Many of the most creative theological insights have emerged out of these tensions. Part of what made Paul, Gloriana, and Dozier so successful was their recognition that the mystery of God exceeds the human ability to contain or comprehend the divine. Responses, faithful or otherwise, to the person of Christ have also been animated by the challenge of making sense of this strange figure who is presented by tradition as both human and divine. The paradox of Christ drives theology and faith forwards. On the one hand Christ is the closest expression of intimacy and unity with God, and on the other, the identity of Christ seems something of a mystery. Every age seems to find a different Christ. In the earliest quest for the historical Jesus, Albert Schweitzer noted that looking back to discover the real Jesus was like peering down a deep dark well and finding the reflection of one's own face. Schweitzer turned from biblical criticism to helping the needy, devoting his life to finding the faces of others in need, rather than gazing at his own reflection. In a certain modality of intellectual analysis, Schweitzer might be reprimanded for having failed to persist in his historical search. But from another perspective, Schweitzer may be credited with finding Christ where the New Testament had been pointing all the time.

Schweitzer reminds us that any true engagement with the question of Christ will require life-changing action. His experience also suggests that those looking to understand Christ might not want to rush too quickly to make sense of Christ. We, too, risk finding our own faces peering back at us from the deep well of history. Part of this risk is structural, and has nothing much to do with our own capacities. Christ also seems to have been internally divided. Although Jesus was close to God, scripture is careful to record Christ's forsakenness and alienation from God when hanging on the cross. Jürgen Moltmann's classic exploration of the cross of Christ continues to discourage attempts to impose too much sense on this experience of alienation.[1] The cross is destructive of theological attempts to rationalize, at the same time the cross is the ultimate site of Christian theology, the ground zero for all theology. The cross warns subsequent interpreters not to rush to conceptualize this terrible rupture within the nature of God. It stands as a sign to proceed with caution, lest we form the God-human in our own image, rather than the other way around. Even when he rose again, whatever and however one interprets that, at first Christ is not recognized by those who knew him. Despite the patriarchy of the age, he appears first to women whose legal testimony as witnesses was invalid. It is almost as if the gospel writers were not content with recording resurrection. They also wanted to challenge the standard by which the society of the day measured truth. And yet, despite the strange counter cultural actions of this crucified human-God, he re-energizes his beleaguered disciples into a hopeful community to share the good news of love and forgiveness.

EMBRACING ONE'S INNER RESIDENT ALIEN

In a searing critique of the Christian church, Stanley Hauerwas and William H. Willimon explored what they thought was wrong with the church in North America. They wrote from acknowledged positions of knowledge and power.[2] Their central thesis was that the church they served and loved had become an extension of broader American culture. It had lost its distinctiveness, what scripture names, "saltiness." Hauerwas and Willimon argued persuasively, and uncomfortably, that the church had reneged on its calling to be a radical community of love and forgiveness. Instead, they argued, the church had become overly preoccupied, indeed, utterly bound up with, meeting the political and cultural needs of the American state. Most churches had become little more than institutional wings of American political life, red state churches and blue state churches. Christians had forgotten that their values were not meant to be entirely aligned with the country's need for civics.

Long ago, Søren Kierkegaard leveled similar criticisms at the Danish Church of the nineteenth century. The authors wryly observed, borrowing a metaphor from immunology: "As in Kierkegaard's Denmark, North America is a place where people have absorbed just enough Christianity to inoculate them against the contagion by the real thing."[3] Hauerwas and Willimon sought to rouse the church from slumber and help it become what it was meant to be. The basic problem was that the church had lost the sense of service and prophetic calling of Jesus the resident alien. Instead of proclaiming the Crucified God, the church had become another partisan prop in the establishment culture wars.

Although they first rang the alarm bell the year the Berlin Wall fell, they could as easily be writing today in response to the ongoing partisan fusion of politics and Christianity. Willimon and Hauerwas were also aware that this was not a novel problem. The central historical and symbolic event behind their critique went back to the Constantinian shift that first privileged the church within the state. With the conversion of the Emperor Constantine to Christianity in 325 the church moved from being a sect that was hunted down, marginalized, and underground to an establishment force. Jesus stopped being the one who was executed by the Romans for being disruptive and challenging conventions. Instead, he became the conquering Christ who laid down rules, validating late Roman society, ensuring imperial harmony and homogeneity.

Two centuries before Constantine, in the letter of Clement, the churches in Rome and Corinth were described as sojourning (the Greek is *paroikousa*). As Giorgio Agamben explains, to sojourn is the kind of thing a resident alien might do. Sojourning is a way of living lightly that contrasts with the way those who live within an establishment, Constantinian or otherwise:

> It designates the manner in which foreigners and those in exile dwell. It is opposed to the Greek verb *katoikein*, which designates how a citizen of a city, state, kingdom or empire dwells.[4]

Before Constantine, the church knew itself to be an alien body in respect of wider culture. It sojourned, rather than ruled. Thanks to Constantine's conversion, Christianity became the legal institutional religion of the Empire, uniquely privileged. Believers went from being foreign sojourners in exile to permanent dwellers. *Resident Aliens* started from the assumption that while the conditions of that establishment waned and morphed over the centuries, believers had not always noticed.

In one particularly haunting analogy, Willimon and Hauerwas compare the church to an out of touch grandee:

> Like an aging dowager, living in a decaying mansion on the edge of town, bankrupt and penniless, house decaying around her but acting as if her family still controlled the city, our theologians and church leaders continued to think and act as if we were in charge, as if the old arrangements were still valid.[5]

Written more than a quarter of a century ago, these words still ring true across large parts of the Christian church. Having diagnosed the problem, Hauerwas and Willimon argued that the church should renounce its privilege and recognize its true identity as a colony that is in the world, but not of the world. It was time to become, like Jesus, a resident alien once again.

Unsurprisingly, not everyone rushed to agree with our two theologians. Many argued that the church is not even meant to be a colony. Colonies smack of separatism or retreat from the world. They are generally not the healthiest of places. The theologians had clearly touched a nerve and many respondents disagreed with their analysis. And yet, America may not officially be an imperial Christian power, but it has inherited a uniquely inflated view of the divine status of its power. Americans on both sides of the political spectrum continue to endorse a vision of a country that is not only uniquely chosen but superior to other countries. All countries are patriotic, but not all countries are quite so earnest and voluble about their myths.

Willimon and Hauerwas were on to something important. The cultural appropriation of Christianity within America has not always been positive, to put it ever so mildly. Something is wrong when large sections of the population assume Christianity is synonymous with hate, division, exclusion, and intolerance. It is no wonder few want to confess being Christian at college or in public life.

Followers of Jesus would be better served spending less time seeking political influence by throwing rocket fuel onto the culture wars. To recognize Jesus as a spiritual immigrant is also to notice that following him requires something similar. Drawing on the Aristotelian-Elizabethan perspective of the Goldilocks God, maybe there is a third option not yet envisaged by our two theologians or the politicized nationalism they critique. An option that seeks to break down the opposition between those who are "in" the true church and those who find themselves "outside" of it. There is not that much different between a colony that is always opposed to the culture around it and an established church that is always trying to shape the culture around it. They are two sides of the same ecclesiastical pathology. Each longs to be the sole true church. And neither sounds much like the search for a synthesis between being in the world and being called to travel lightly into God's kingdom.

The unique gift of the way of Goldilocks, and something that may sound alien to the ears of many faithful believers, is that the ordinary wider world *does* matter. Not the world of culture wars and politically weaponized religion, but the world of ordinary human experience.

Where *Resident Aliens* sought to save the church by stopping it from being subsumed by the dominant American culture, the Goldilocks intuition is different. To be open to the spiritual thermodynamics of Goldilocks is to admit that there is always a complex interplay between culture and faith. And in the topography of culture making, there are many alternatives to the Constantinian or toxic versions of Christianity. Anglicans have historically forged cultures of faith that entwine faithful habits in the midst of the world. Given the horrendous reputation that toxic Christianity has, the temptation to avoid the public sphere and retreat to private, inward facing, ecclesial institutions is enormous. Yet, this is not really the way of those searching the *via media*. What is required instead is the courage to enter more fully into the world while remaining obedient to God's radically inclusive love.

THE COURAGE TO LOVE

The Anglican ethos arises from a sensibility to build and transform culture, and is inherently resistant to separatism. At the same time, it recognizes how the church is always in need of reformation. The church should not be confused with the kingdom. To understand this better, we will look more deeply at the thought of one of the most famous resident aliens, Søren Kierkegaard. Lutheran by birth, Kierkegaard was intensely spiritual. He was also blistering in his critique of the institutional church of his day. Equipped with biting sarcasm and a tendency to scoff at the self-important, he made few friends in the religious hierarchy. A loner who was mocked for his appearance, an intellectual pariah, and a failed romantic, Kierkegaard never chose the comfortable or easy route. Yet, it is to Kierkegaard we need turn if we are to better comprehend the nature of spiritual courage.

Kierkegaard famously noted that to dare is to risk losing one's footing. To not dare, he continued, is to lose oneself. Kierkegaard understood that courage is the fundamental ingredient of human thriving. Without courage we fail to be the people we are meant to be. Kierkegaard's realization that it takes courage to become an individual has been taken up by atheists as well as the religious. His existential focus remains as powerfully attractive to those outside the church as baptized insiders. Kierkegaard understood that it is not what we believe that matters. What matters is whether we have the courage to act upon those beliefs.

Courage does not appear out of nowhere. It arrives when we recognize that we are facing many dangers. As Kierkegaard puts it, "This is the way a person always gains courage; when he fears a greater danger, he always has the courage to face a lesser one; when he is exceedingly afraid of one danger, it is as if the others did not exist at all."[6] Kierkegaardian also makes a nautical contrast between a sloop and a warship. Kierkegaard's readers would have been familiar with a sloop as a single-masted sailboat, just as they would have been familiar with the enormous warships with which the European powers fought their wars.

To demilitarize the original analogy, in essence Kierkegaard is distinguishing between travel by bicycle and helicopter. One travels lightly, and is best suited to routes that have been thought through. The other requires serious provisioning, but is then equipped to go anywhere. For Kierkegaard this represents the difference between the merely sagacious and those who are willing to do everything. The sloop (or the bike rider), knows everything about its journey down to the very last detail, and yet it never leaves sight of the coast (or the road). By contrast, the courage required for faith is more serious. The seeker needs to be willing to risk exploring the unknown. Only in the unknown, what Kierkegaard calls the deep, do we learn who we are, and who we might become. As Kierkegaard concludes, "the great warship does not learn its destination until it is out on the deep."[7] Kierkegaard was not making a point about warfare. He was making a point about being willing to surrender control about where we are headed. Purity of heart consists in being able to focus on the deep. And only by setting out for the deep can the faithful become both themselves and connected to God. For Kierkegaard, fear, by contrast, occludes the human ability to see the good and venture out into the deeps.

TALK LESS, SMILE MORE

Kierkegaard was reacting against the internal impulse within Christianity to stay in the shallows. Over the centuries, many of the most toxic and virulent forms of Christianity have sought to minimize the unknown, partly by laying claim to knowing everything. Richard Hooker saw this kind of Christianity in the late sixteenth century, and abhorred it. Perhaps uniquely for his age, Hooker maintained a healthy skepticism about the pretensions of religion to actually know God:

> Dangerous it were for the feeble brain of man to wade far into the doings of the Most High; whom although to know be life, and joy to make mention of his name; yet our soundest knowledge is to know that we know him not as indeed he is, neither can know him; and our safest eloquence concerning his is our silence . . . He is above, and we upon earth; therefore it behoveth our words to be wary and few.[8]

These are words that should be part of the ordination service. Hooker is essentially saying the same thing as Aaron Burr and Alexander Hamilton in the musical *Hamilton*: talk less, smile more.

Hooker's wariness about speaking is simply the start of what turns out to be a not inconsiderable volubility about the implications of the holy and holy living in the world. A good Elizabethan Christian, Hooker had no qualms about allowing the holy to permeate every aspect of life. Yet, unlike so many of the doctrinally dogmatic views of his contemporaries, Hooker continues to provide hints at how we might seek God within our own age. Hooker was Elizabethan to his core, inclusive and pragmatic. He was not a zealot or a demagogue who believed that he was uniquely correct. Quite the reverse. He had intellectual and spiritual humility. In Rowan Williams's elegant turn of phrase, Hooker was one of the inventors of the distinctively Anglican mood of "contemplative pragmatism."[9]

Combining prayerfulness and pragmatism has been a distinctive characteristic of those traveling the *via media*. It is in this spirit that Hooker provides the parable of the three-legged stool. Despite, or perhaps, because, it sounds so rickety and unsubstantial, the metaphor of the humble stool has stood the test of time. The three lenses of scripture, tradition, and reason create a fragile stability that can easily be lost, and will always collapse if one element is missing. Urban Holmes notes the similarities between Hooker's model and the theological approach of pre-Reformation theologians Thomas Aquinas and Augustine.[10] Yet, while these Catholic thinkers were working within a church that affirmed tradition and reason, Hooker develops the stool at a time when the reformed church was questioning the efficacy of both these non-scriptural sources. For Hooker, turning to scripture alone (as so many reformers argued) could not produce all the theological and spiritual answers that believers sought. From the earliest moments of the Reformation, there were significant disagreements between Protestants about how to read scripture. Everyone claimed its authority, none could agree on how to interpret it. The stool offered a corrective, one capable of creating a synthesis out of a dialogue between tradition, reason, and scripture.

The Reformation chronology is instructive. Hooker did not fundamentally disagree with the theological idea "by scripture alone" (*sola scriptura*) of Martin Luther and sixteenth-century Protestantism. However, he did recognize that an interpretive framework is still required. At the same time, Hooker did not entirely reject the traditional Catholic idea of authority residing in ecclesiastical councils or other traditions (like bishops). In delineating two additional sources alongside scripture (tradition and reason), Hooker creates an imaginative way of ensuring that theology remains inclusive. Not simply inclusive of people, but also inclusive of the varieties of spiritual, ecclesial, and sacramental experience.

Hooker had essentially articulated a theoretical framework for discovering the optimal conditions for experiencing the Goldilocks God. And the way Hooker does this is unique, creating a synthesis that draws upon the rivers of both Reformed and Catholic thinking (as well as parts of Christian tradition that belong to a more Orthodox delta). The way he allows it all to flow together was quite unusual for the time. As Williams explains, Hooker's thought can be deeply paradoxical: "Tradition, the discourse of the non-elite or less literate, is defended on the basis of the same Reformed theological method that campaigned for the open Bible and Christian literacy."[11] Here the creative "poles" of tradition and scripture are not separated and held over and against each other, but brought together to inform one another. The *via media* laid out by Hooker is not one of compromise between three distinct sources. It is instead one of imaginative synthesis: an ongoing dialogue between different theological imperatives.

Hooker's theological intuition is at the root of a lot of subsequent ecclesiastical oddness for churches rooted in the Elizabethan settlement. The community of faith is not restricted to simply following scripture or inherited tradition. The community was also asked to synthesize these by attending to reason (and by extension, a whole host of concepts and ideas that are not strictly part of either scripture or tradition). So much of what seekers value in spirituality is neither obviously scriptural nor obviously traditional. And yet, thanks to reason, there are some remarkable notions that have ended up strengthening the community's understanding of both scripture and tradition.

This can all be quite maddening when first encountered. For those wanting to be told what to think or believe, Hooker is little help. On the other hand, his insights liberate the would-be faithful to use their God-given gifts of reason, intelligence, and understanding. By embracing reason alongside scripture and tradition, seekers discover a way of decoding different and contradictory opinions. Hooker had the common sense (of a contemplative pragmatist) to realize that not everything in scripture was self-explanatory. Many things need interpretation. To make an appeal to authority is never to settle a question once and for all. And, unlike some more contemporary theologians, philosophers, and scientists, Hooker knew that reason is not singular. It cannot be revered on its own. It needs to be set within a creative synthesis alongside tradition and scripture.

DUAL CITIZENS

Hooker's rickety stool, and Elizabeth's vigilance against doctrinaire belief, were measures designed to prevent any single perspective swamping the full range of beliefs present within the community of faith. This Anglican sensibility might be thought of as providing a vaccine against idolatry. Hooker and Elizabeth were never particularly interested in creating a church of the like-minded. What they were interested in was a church that was as broad-based as possible. Before the language of diversity existed, they were creating ecclesial space for a spectrum of interior belief through uniformity of external action. They were not interested in creating a colony or cult in which everyone saw the world through the same set of lenses. Rather, they were focused on the pragmatic question of how to shape a human society, a society of the faithful, in which people worked together to overcome the trials and tribulations of existence.

To rephrase a little, if the Goldilocks God is not the toxic God, neither is it the Disney God. As Ann Loades explores in her review of Anglican spirituality, the tradition is stronger for this. Her survey of its major figures, influences, and tributaries offers a wonderful resource for those at any stage of exploration. Loades also draws attention to the unique way in which the tradition helps us, "to reflect on some of our nightmares."[12]

The Goldilocks God is not for those who want everything to be sanitized, safe, and without jagged edges. The Goldilocks God is instead the God for real human beings, the kind who can be honest that they are divided amongst themselves and alienated within themselves. It is not just that we do not always know how to find our way to God. Sometimes á la Socrates and Kierkegaard we don't even know who we are.

The writer Theodor Kallifatides was raised in Greece before emigrating to Sweden, where he went on to spend the vast majority of his adult life. In his memoir, he recounts how he eventually found his way back to his only true homeland: the Greek of his mother tongue. Despite being feted for his literary writings in Swedish, something about the Greek language itself remained his real home. Like so many immigrants who return years later to visit their homeland, he recounts how he was often perceived and treated as a foreigner. And yet, this did not stop him feeling that the Greek language remained his abiding home.[13]

People of faith live similarly bifurcated lives. We may feel like resident aliens, like the path breakers Aristotle, Jesus, Paul, and Elizabeth. But for most of us a better metaphor is dual citizens. Citizens of two cultures, the broader culture as well as the culture of faith, hope, and love. Like Kallifatides, believers know that for all their intimate knowledge of the two cultures (the world and faith), there is only one true homeland. This is true even if, like Kallifatides, we spend more time in our adopted lands, and less time in the place from which we came (and to which we all shall return).

The story of the philosopher of religion Anthony Flew presents another interesting example of what it means to become a dual citizen. Flew spent his entire life writing academic critiques of religious belief. He thought up some of the most sophisticated and powerful philosophical arguments to reject belief in God. He was adamant about the nonexistence of a heavenly home. Then on reaching his ninth decade he famously switched positions.[14] He became an ardent advocate for God. Flew's preeminence as a philosopher may make him unique, but his path back to God is well-trodden. His reversal was not born of a winning intellectual argument (after all, he had spent his life refuting such arguments). He knew all the arguments. And no argument changed his mind. His reversal was rather about giving in (in the positive sense of embracing a gift) to where his heart yearned to reside.

THE HEART OF COURAGE

Finding that homeland when one has been fleeing it all one's life takes enormous courage. Spirituality is less about arguments for or against God, and more about finding Kierkegaardian courage across the whole spectrum of life. Bravery is the thread that connects so-called everyday life to the heart of the spiritual life. Kierkegaard might go further. Until one has discovered the courage required for being an individual, it is not possible to relate to the divine. And as Kierkegaard argues in *The Sickness Unto Death*, the forging of individuality parallels the forging of the relationship to the divine.[15] These are interrelated tasks, and in the next chapter we will see a similar dynamic of self-creation in the thought of St. Augustine, the North African theologian and bishop. The human self for both Kierkegaard and Augustine is constituted in the act of relating to the divine. Spirituality in this reading is not something additional to ordinary human experience, it is simply what happens when we recover what Paul Tillich called the courage to be (who we are meant to be).[16]

So exactly how do we do this? Kierkegaard offers important clues. He was also a man of his age, and metaphors of sloops and battleships are not as persuasive today as they once were. A more contemporary guide to understanding courage is Brené Brown. Brown is an exceptionally high achieving shame researcher who by her own account spent a considerable amount of time resisting the topic of alienation. Even when her research took her deeper into the topic of shame, she resisted connecting it with her personal experience. It remained an intellectual abstraction, an area in which she had theoretical expertise. It was not a topic that touched her own life until circumstances forced her to acknowledge it.

Brown writes movingly about her experience of having a breakdown.[17] She tells the story of how her therapist helped her realize that what she was experiencing as a breakdown may, rather, be a "spiritual awakening." The experience of breakdown, an instance of alienation taken to breaking point, is not something anyone rushes to embrace. But for Brown, the breakdown led her to a deeper understanding of self and a positive re-evaluation of life. She saw what she was missing. And at the heart of this was the phenomenon of courage.

Brown used to think that her research, to use her words, "hijacked" her life. After her breakdown ("spiritual awakening") she instead came to see how her research had rescued her. The more Brown recognized what was holding her back, or what was alienating her, the more she realized that there was an alternative way to live. She even coined a new word for this new way of living: wholeheartedness.

Brown turned her personal experience of failure into a source of renewal. She also came to realize how the quest for perfection will always lead to failure. This realization echoes the choreography of other biblical figures, medieval saints, and ordinary folk. One of the most tormented figures in a history of spiritual leaders who struggled with interior demons was the Augustinian monk and initiator of the Reformation, Martin Luther. Luther viscerally felt *anfechtungen*, which is probably best translated as assault or temptation. After grappling with them for so long, he eventually learned not to flee these feelings, but to use them to move beyond his own powerlessness and rest in the mighty fortress of God.

In allowing herself to be vulnerable, and comfortable with failure, Brown undercut the power of fear and shame. Alienation from the familiar, from loved ones, and even from one's very self, is one of the prime drivers of the quest for God. For some, this is quite literal. Many of those setting out on a pilgrimage, the ultimate physical manifestation of the spiritual quest, do so after things have gone wrong in their lives. Such decisions require enormous amounts of courage. In general, few set out looking for God when everything is going just fine. When things are tough spiritual questions suddenly appear more relevant and genuine.

If we rely entirely on ourselves the path often leads to failure. Yet, in practicing something along the lines of Brown's wholeheartedness or Kierkegaard's courage, we encounter a more promising way of working through alienation and failure. Brown understands that pretending away failure and alienation simply gives them too much power. The alternative is to befriend failure, and use the challenges that come our way to be open to the mystery of life.

In Brown's words, to thrive we first need to find the courage to fail. Courage is, quite literally, at the center of wholeheartedness. Etymologically, formed from the Latin word for heart (*cor*), theology has much to say about the courage of the heart. Alienation strikes at the heart, which in turn opens one up to God. St. Augustine put it succinctly when he wrote "our hearts are restless" (*cor nos inquietum est*).[18] He then went on to say that the only thing that can counter that restlessness was the prospect of resting in God. Alienation is simply another way of describing the essential restlessness of the human heart.

Theologically, the fundamental alienation has always been imagined as that between finite beings and God. One way of approaching Christianity is as a story about how God goes out of the way to become vulnerable. God did not have to become a resident alien, but God chose to. Taking the defenseless form of a human child, the birth narrative of Jesus describes a God who surrenders power, taking on the vulnerability of human flesh. One of the most classically Anglican doctrines is that of *kenosis*, or the divine self-emptying of incarnation. God divests God's self of power in the defenseless infant, born of Mary in a humble stable. Jesus's journey to the cross embraces his vulnerable humanity, connecting with the resident aliens of his own day: fishermen, women, the sick, itinerants from other tribes, occupying forces, the possessed, and tax collectors. Jesus appears to have spent most of his time with those on the margins. Incarnation was God's way of being wholehearted. In the figure of Jesus, God risks everything, becoming vulnerable to all the failure, hurts, and disappointments of ordinary human life.

Like Luther and Jesus before him, Søren Kierkegaard experienced something similar, describing it as *angst*. Less barriers to the divine so much as portals, Luther's *anfechtungen* and Kierkegaard's *angst* were German and Danish experiences of alienation. In the two hundred years separating us from Kierkegaard, experiences of alienation amongst those seeking the divine have continued to proliferate. From literary genius Fyodor Dostoevsky, to philosophers Miguel de Unamuno and Gabriel Marcel, the religious feeling of alienation catalyzed entire generations. These, and many other, "anxious angels" represent one of the most significant forces in the theology of the first half of the twentieth century.[19] They also represent a remarkably broad religious and geographical constituency. Alienation is universal. It does not discriminate on the basis of religious belief or geography. It is a sign of its ubiquity that responses to alienation flourish in spiritual works by Catholics, Orthodox, and Protestants, as well in the secular writings of atheists and feminists. And while alienation may lead straight to courage, it can just as easily lead to despair. What is remarkable about existentialism is how it began with religious awareness of alienation, and then spread out throughout human society.

HOW TO GROW A HEART

It is possible to try to protect or anaesthetize the heart from being hurt, but theologians, shame researchers, and existentialists know that this is not a viable long-term strategy. Nowhere is this clearer than in Dr Seuss's story of *The Grinch*, the eponymous stealer of Christmas presents. Having stolen all the gifts of the Whos in Whoville, the Grinch is puzzled when the Whos do not give up. Despite having lost everything, on Christmas morning they gather and sing welcome to Christmas Day. The Grinch cannot understand it. When it finally dawns on him that Christmas resides not in the parcels he has filched, but in the joy of the season, he experiences internal self-alienation. He reneges on his dastardly larceny, returning the gifts to the townsfolk.

Theodor Geisel tells us how us the Grinch's heart grew three sizes that day. What was loss for the Grinch—returning the stolen presents—actually turned out to be gain. Hearts grow where we have the courage to have a close encounter with alienation and vulnerability.

Geisel's life was also a story of the growth of the human heart through alienation. A child of German-speaking immigrants growing up in Springfield, Massachusetts, Geisel would have been keenly aware of feeling like an outsider. As a fourteen-year-old he encountered the former President of the United States, Theodore Roosevelt, when he came to Springfield to fix medals on children who had helped sell war bonds. As Roosevelt went down the line pinning medals on the children he praised each of them. Yet by the time he came to award Geisel his medal, the President had run out of ribbons.

With no medal to give, Roosevelt instead declaimed, "What's this little boy doing here?" and the scoutmaster bustled Geisel off the stage. Geisel had expected to be acknowledged as a "Somebody," but was instead made into a "Nobody." One biographer wonders whether this incident also provided emotional and intellectual fuel for the idea of the Whos of Dr Seuss.[20] Little Geisel's painful exposure on the stage would later become fuel for brilliant storytelling.

Nor was that everything Geisel had to draw on. As a Dartmouth undergraduate, Geisel got up to all sorts of antics. Relieving himself from a fraternity roof top was probably one of the more risqué of recorded incidents. But it was his capacity to poke fun at authority through his literary endeavors that seems to have landed him in the most trouble with College authorities. During Prohibition Geisel was caught drinking gin in his student rooms, for which the Dean banned him from all extracurricular pursuits. In order to edit the satirical publication *Jack-O-Lantern* Geisel began to use the pseudonym Seuss to keep writing under the radar. With the passage of time his high jinks and creativity are now viewed with great fondness.[21] What was perceived as alienating at the time, and what no doubt caused palpitations for the Dean, is now part of his enduring appeal.

If Geisel had not been so subverted by Roosevelt, and so challenging to Dartmouth, it is doubtful that there would have been a Dr Seuss. Geisel's story, while one of extraordinary accomplishment, is instructive for its human ordinariness. It highlights how adversity, the particular form of alienation that comes from the exterior, is not always a limiting force. Such reversals, from loss to gain, are a familiar dynamic in the spiritual quest.

LUTHER THE DOUBLE AGENT

God's response to human alienation is often framed by spiritual writers, theologians, mystics, and believers as having something to do with love. But lest we confuse this with its human counterpart, it is helpful to recognize a qualitative difference: something Martin Luther explicitly named as "alien." Luther knew from his visceral experiences of *anfechtungen*, that the assaults and temptations that drew him away from God could only be overcome by something not of his own making: something utterly alien. The irony is clear. Luther thought that only an alien faith or grace given to humans by God might overcome human alienation from the divine. He knew that he could not restore himself to harmony with God by his own intervention. The depth of alienation was too deep for that.

Luther puts it succinctly, "There is a double life, my life and an alien life . . . "[22] For Luther the double life is the tension between one's ordinary human life (of being a sinner, alienated from God), and one's life of righteous faith (receiving the "alien life" provided by God). By naming this "alien life" Luther underscores how righteousness is a foreign gift that comes from God. It is nothing that we can lay claim to. We have no possession over it. To translate this back into the language from earlier: God gives out dual citizenship. Or as Brown might gloss it, unless you are vulnerable enough to have the courage to fail you cannot hope to experience an altogether different love from outside lifting you up.

Luther's personal experiences of alienation and failure were the genesis for a radical new insight into the nature of God's love. His courage lay in recognizing that he did not possess the resources he needed to make everything right. He needed outside help. Luther further recognized that we each share this double life of being both saint (a recipient of the alien life of God) and sinner (aware of the depth of our alienation from God). The glory of this insight is that overcoming alienation is never a final or one-off event. Alienation is always part of the ongoing human experience. Faith is the experience of living with alien life, or dual citizenship, given by God. For Luther, to be Christian is always a matter of being a double agent. We are always conflicted, always simultaneously sinners and saints. Always needing the courage to fail before we can experience being forgiven.

Luther was right. At least, to a point. Seekers of the Goldilocks God cannot but be double agents with conflicted loyalties. We are loyal to our own identity, but we are also loyal to the alien divinity that sets us free from alienation. We know what it is like for things to be too hot or too cold. But we would much prefer it if things could be just right.

Perhaps the greatest problem with Luther's approach is that he makes grace more powerful than anything else. (We shall return to this question again in the final two chapters.) For Luther, we are all so very truly, madly, deeply alienated that only God's grace can rescue us. By contrast, my intuition is to treat with healthy skepticism spiritual accounts that make things appear so black or white. The grace of God may very well be the only thing that can overcome alienation. Yet, at the same time, lovers of Goldilocks are wary about suggesting that human nature is so terribly fallen that we have no hope of connecting to God.

It seems self-evident that humans are not so very close to God that they cannot help falling in love with God. That is the "too hot" position of religious fundamentalism that threatens to blur the gap between the individual self and the divine. Yet if this is untrue, isn't the opposite also false? Can it also be true that humans are so alienated and far from God that we are utterly lost and permanently out in the cold? Might not the truth be a little more nuanced?

We have seen how alienation can be a route to the divine, and how the spiritually adventurous learn to embrace it and grow with it. Perhaps alienation is also a reminder that we are a little closer to the divine than we suspect. Maybe Luther was right about being a double agent, but wrong about putting the burden for all the action on God. Maybe alienation is not the experience of how God rescues us all on God's own. Maybe alienation is instead a sign of how God always meets us half-way? At the same time, alienation, and the courage it calls forth, are not the only ways seekers experience God. As the next chapter explores, God is also encountered in wonder and wisdom.

NOTES

1. Jürgen Moltmann, *The Crucified God*, trans. R.A. Wilson and John Bowden (London: SCM Press, 1974).

2. Stanley Hauerwas and William H. Willimon, *Resident Aliens: Life in the Christian Colony* (Nashville: Abingdon Press, 2014). Hauerwas was a theologian at Duke University Divinity School, Willimon a bishop in the United Methodist church. A Methodist at the time of writing, Hauerwas has since become an Anglican.

3. Hauerwas and Willimon, *Resident Aliens*, 4. The authors note their indebtedness to theologian E. Stanley Jones for originating the metaphor of Christianity as an inoculation against the "real" Christianity.

4. Giorgio Agamben, *The Church and the Kingdom*, trans. Leland De La Durantaye. Photographs by Alice Attie (London: Seagull Books, 2012), 1.

5. Hauerwas and Willimon, *Resident Aliens*, 29.

6. Søren Kierkegaard, *The Sickness Unto Death*, trans. Howard V. Hong and Edna H. Hong (Princeton: Princeton University Press, 1980), 8–9.

7. Søren Kierkegaard, "Purity of Heart," *Upbuilding Discourses in Various Spirits*, trans. Howard V. Hong and Edna H. Hong (Princeton, 1993), 84.

8. Richard Hooker, *Lawes of Ecclesiastical Politie*, ed. John Keble (Oxford: Oxford University Press, 1841), vol. 1, I.ii.2, 201.

9. Rowan Williams, *Anglican Identities* (Cambridge MA: Cowley Publications, 2003), 24ff.

10. Holmes, *Anglicanism?*, 11.

11. Williams, *Anglican Identities,* 38.

12. Ann Loades, "Anglican Spirituality," *Oxford Handbook of Anglican Studies,* eds. Chapman, Clarke, and Percy, 149–164.

13. Theodor Kallifatides, *Another Life: On Memory, Language, Love, and the Passage of Time* (New York: Other Press, 2017).

14. Anthony Flew and Roy Abraham Varghese, *There is a God: How the World's Most Notorious Atheist Changed His Mind* (New York: HarperOne, 2008).

15. Kierkegaard, *Sickness*.

16. Paul Tillich, *The Courage to Be* (New Haven: Yale University Press, 2000).

17. Bréne Brown, *Daring Greatly: How the Courage to Be Vulnerable Transforms the Way We Live, Love, Parent, and Lead* (New York: Avery, 2015).

18. Augustine, *Confessions*, trans. R.S. Pine-Coffin (London: Penguin, 1961).

19. George Pattison, *Anxious Angels: A Retrospective View of Religious Existentialism* (London: Macmillan Press, 1999).

20. Donald E. Pease, *Theodor SEUSS Geisel: The Man Who Became Dr Seuss* (Oxford University Press, 2010), 15ff.

21. The Dartmouth Medical School now bears his name.

22. Martin Luther, *WA* 40, 1.287 quoted in Daphne Hampson, *Christian Contradictions: The Structures of Lutheran and Catholic Thought* (Cambridge: Cambridge University Press, 2001), 26.

Chapter Three

The Science of the Soul

A thousand years ago, a Benedictine abbess from the Rhineland found fame for her healing abilities. Hildegard of Bingen was popular among contemporaries for her medical knowledge. She wrote books on the medicinal properties of plants and elements, and the sick sought out her healing hands. Hildegard was a student, both of nature, and a classical tradition of science that traced itself back to Galen. Dividing the world into four elements (fire, earth, air, and water), Galen's scientific approach sought to understand the physical world and human bodies in terms of the balance between these essential humors. Monasteries and secular schools were important centers of scientific education throughout the medieval period. Only after scholars mastered the trivium (grammar, rhetoric, and logic) would they go on to the quadrivium of (arithmetic, geometry, music, and astronomy).

Some of the great mathematical and astronomical innovations came from those who were saturated in prayer as much as classical learning. Many of the most well-known medieval physicians were also prominent figures of great religious houses. In one vignette, Abbot Baldwin of Bury St Edmund curses Herfast, an interfering Bishop of Norwich, who promptly falls off his horse and is injured. When Herfast is brought back to the abbey, Baldwin tends to him using his skill as the leading court physician (and the bishop recovers).[1] The science of the heavens was another area in which the religious led the way. Historian of science Seb Falk investigates how the cloistered were responsible for the cutting edge of astronomical and mathematical exploration: inventors of astrolabes, clocks, and complex computational tables. Between liturgical needs (finding the time to pray the monastic hours, dating Easter and holy days) and agricultural needs (when to plant and when to harvest), monasteries had both spiritual and practical reasons for predicting both daily and astronomical time.[2]

Born just as Abbot Baldwin died, Hildegard's understanding of natural science was the best her age could offer. And yet, today, Hildegard is less likely to be remembered for her knowledge of nature's healing properties and more for her devotional writings. Before the advent of the split between science and religion, Hildegard's life was one of harmony between the scientific and the religious. Nor was she alone in this. As we shall see, students of the soul like Hildegard also delighted in exploring areas that we now tend to think of as exclusively lying within the domain of science.

For an eleventh-century woman (or, indeed, any eleventh-century figure), Hildegard's passion for learning was simply astonishing. She did not choose one path of knowledge to the exclusion of another. Rather, she saw the whole of life, spiritual and physical, as profoundly interconnected. Contemporaries sought her out not simply for her medical or spiritual insight, but for her wise counsel on a host of matters. In the collection of letters that survive we are given a glimpse of those who turned to her: from the leading royalty of her day to fellow monastics, priests, archbishops, even Popes. Today she would be described as a celebrity or an influencer.[3]

Hildegard had curiosity about all things, spiritual, metaphysical, and physical. She was both scientist of the soul and natural scientist. Every area of study revealed the wisdom of God to her, and all were worthy of her full attention. Perhaps her most enduring legacy is a series of visions that she received and later shared in beautiful manuscript form. Aged forty-two, she recalls how "a fiery light of exceeding brilliance came and permeated my whole brain, and inflamed my whole heart and my whole breast."[4] And how right she was. Her profound meditations on the nature of God and creation were extraordinary. Illustrated with gloriously elaborate images, her account of these visions is nothing short of astonishing. To read these today is to marvel at the enormity of her imagination and the skill of those who illustrated her visions. It is to experience wonder at first hand.

In these visions, known as Scivias, or know yourself, Hildegard reveals a deep love for God and the community of faith, as well as a passion to share the depth of her insight. One of the most remarkable features of this text is how Hildegard depicts Wisdom. Personifying it as female, Hildegard reserves to Wisdom the most important place: "Among all of the other virtues, she is his greatest, and is joined with him in a sweet embrace, in the jubilation of burning love."[5] The passion of this metaphor is clear. Wisdom is not a matter of cold rational analysis. Wisdom was instead the way that the burning ardor of God was expressed and encountered in creation.

This approach to wisdom, the science of the soul, is one more marked by wonder than the analytic. This is not to say it is not intellectually coherent. For Hildegard, Wisdom was the first of God's creations, and the animating principle by which all creatures (in heaven and earth) are ordered. What is remarkable, however, is how deeply passionate her approach to knowledge is. This is not your dry and dusty bookish wisdom. This is both personal and emotive. In short, it was a way of channeling wonder: an experiential approach to learning that saw all knowledge within the creation as profoundly connected to its divine Creator.

In the mid-nineteenth century the German theologian Friedrich Schleiermacher described spirituality as a "sense and taste for the infinite."[6] There is a powerful symmetry here between the feeling that Schleiermacher emphasized and the passion with which Hildegard explored the divine. Both understood that awe and wonder are perhaps the most fundamental realities behind any spiritual quest.

Like Hildegard, I cannot help but wonder at what is, what has been, and what might be to come. I know I am far from alone. To live is to ponder and to be perplexed. It is also to possess an almost uncanny ability to turn some of the most ordinary features of existence into occasions for reverie. The mystic and the natural scientist see the same flower. Yet, both experience different forms of wonderment as they imagine how the flower came to be, what sustains it, and what it means to perceive it as beautiful.

Spirituality has no monopoly on wonder. The simple act of being human gives us all more than enough to wonder about. The brute fact of life itself calls for the question whether there is any meaning to life, and why there is something rather than nothing. Atypically astonishing highs, like tragic lows, receive so much attention that we easily neglect the greater mass of unexceptional wonders saturating existence. The beat of a pulse, the cresting of a wave, or a setting sun are all more than enough to wonder at. We have no need of a Large Hadron Collider smashing subatomic particles into one another to know that the universe is awe-inspiring. Like Hildegard, the poet William Wordsworth, and so many others, something as humble as a flower or a river is a reminder of the awe-inspiring reality of creation.

WONDER-FILLED QUESTIONS

The inclination to marvel is an inextricable part of what it means to be human. Aristotle, the Goldilocks theorist of practical virtue, was one of the very first to articulate this. In the *Metaphysics* he discussed both how the experience of wonder first led people to philosophize, and how wonder continues to invite wrestling with big questions.[7] Generations of subsequent philosophers, atheists, agnostics, and believers have shared a sense of wonder just as surely as they share a cardiovascular system. To be drawn to explore the Goldilocks God is to admit the reality of Aristotle's and Hildegard's experience of wonder. It is wonder that forces us to explore. And it is wonder that opens our hearts to the science of the soul.

Individuals differ in believing that the cosmos was begun by the Big Bang, a Creating Deity, or some other explanation. Maybe, to channel the spirit of science fiction writer Douglas Adams, the whole thing is an experiment created by super intelligent mice.[8] Whether one believes that the universe had no starting point or that it just happened entirely randomly this does not stop us asking the question of why there is something rather than nothing.

The twentieth-century German philosopher Martin Heidegger thought that this fundamental question (of why there was something rather than nothing) was the central philosophical question. Why *is* there a world, a universe, a galaxy in the first place? Why is there an is-ness rather than nothing?[9] Heidegger never found an answer. Yet that never stopped him engaging with the question. One suspects that these two facts are interrelated. Part of the reason this is such an enduring question has to do with the impossibility of answering it from a strictly philosophical or scientific viewpoint. Philosophy and science cannot answer the really big questions. They take us only so far, not the whole way.

This is not to claim that spirituality can do better. It cannot. The spiritual quest for God does not offer clearer or better answers than science or philosophy. What it can offer is a more generative and productive range of questioning. It reframes and amplifies the questions. Sometimes the rush to provide answers can be dangerously deceptive. While toxic Christianity boasts of answers, the spirituality of Goldilocks is more agnostic. As a wise character in one of Ursula Le Guin's classic science fiction parables puts it: "To learn which questions are unanswerable, and *not to answer them*: this skill is most needful in times of stress and darkness."[10] Of course, in times of stress and darkness we are more likely to note the absence of this skill. The rush to provide simplistic answers that are inherently unsatisfying is a feature of both inauthentic spirituality and totalitarian ideology. Le Guin would recognize our current cultural situation of "fake news" and corroded trust in science, politics, and journalism as entirely predictable. In public life we have largely ceased wondering, rushing instead to answer the unanswerable bluntly and without ambiguity. Wonder, by contrast, thrives on ambiguity, creativity, and imagination.

Theologians and their philosopher counterparts follow the path of Le Guin, rejoicing in the complexity and ambiguity of knowledge. For philosophers, the field of epistemology, the study of knowledge, continues to be a tremendous growth area. From another direction, scientists continue to explore the limits of what can be known about the natural world, biological life, and the mysteries of human consciousness. Yet, when faced with why there is a natural world or human consciousness to begin with, neither philosophers nor scientists can offer anything like comprehensive answers.

No one really knows why there was a Big Bang rather than a Quiet Whimper, a Slow Silence or Nothing Whatsoever. These theories have not answered the question of why we are here any more than Galen's four element theory could satisfactorily explain the origin of matter. Even the physicists who understand the Big Bang best cannot offer a reason *for* the Big Bang. In fact, the very question would seem to be counterfactual. The Big Bang created not just space but also time, so to think about what was before the Big Bang is beyond the bounds of normal scientific enquiry. St. Augustine of Hippo realized this some time ago. In his *Confessions* he recognizes how time and creation occur concurrently. For Augustine, there is no time before creation. Rather, time is created alongside creation. Jean-Luc Marion glosses Augustine: "God anticipates and is in advance of the world in a way not given temporally precisely because God gives time as he creates the world—in an advance without world or time."[11] Here Augustine is following the logic of Genesis, where we read how God creates night and day, framing the division and measuring of time as part of God's creative work. Humans cannot look beyond to a moment before time. In the same way, there are no good explanations for why human consciousness is the way it is. We can explain a little of the how, but not so much the why.

The theory of evolution is our best theory yet for understanding how planetary life emerged. Yet, the mystery of human consciousness remains a puzzle. Humans are exploring and learning all the time. And as scientists will readily affirm, the more that is discovered the more questions we unearth. More knowledge does not simply increase the sum of all knowledge. Increased understanding instead leads to a multiplying of the realms about which we know very little.

In 1698 when Thomas Savery first discovered steam power to pump water out of mines, that was not the end of wondering about the laws that govern the physical operations of the universe. It was simply one critical point in a process that would change and develop over the succeeding 150 years as steam power evolved to move not only pumps, but trains and boats. With fresh discoveries new questions and possibilities are raised.

The first person to posit an atomic theory was Aristotle's predecessor, the Greek philosopher Democritus. However, it would take another 2,500 years before scientists were able to definitively confirm the reality behind Democritus's theory of atoms. We now know that atoms are not even the smallest constituent parts of the universe, with numerous smaller particles identified in the form of various types of quarks, leptons, and bosons. Scientific curiosity has been going on since the dawn of human history, and it shows no signs of slowing down. Quite the reverse. As human curiosity increases, and discovers new fields to explore, our list of unanswered questions grows longer.

One of the many fascinating insights from contemporary physics is that even something as apparently "fixed" as the laws of the universe may not be as universal as we once thought. Physicist Paul Davies makes a strong case for the local nature of the laws that physicists observe from within our universe. There was immense chance and contingency in the conditions prevailing at the start of the universe. Not everything occurring at the very start of the Big Bang needed to happen the way it did. And if things had been different, some of the most basic "laws" of science might be otherwise:

> What we have hitherto taken to be universal laws of physics, such as the laws of electromagnetism, would be more akin to local by-laws or state laws, rather than national or federal laws. And of this potpourri of cosmic regions, very few indeed, would be suitable for life.[12]

The more we learn about physics and the laws of the universe, the clearer it becomes how very astonishing it is that there is anything like life in the first place. It is not simply that the conditions of possibility for generating life are vastly improbable. The more we discover, the more it becomes necessary to revise our conception of physics.

Outside science or philosophy there are even more ways that wonder is maximized. Art thrives on wonder, and in enormously diverse ways. The ballerina's capacity to move audiences by her gracefulness and the emotional honesty of movement introduces an arena for wondering that has little to do with reason. In the same way, an impressionist painting should not be judged as somehow faulty when compared to a photograph of the same scene. Both ballerina and artist introduce new marvels to wonder at. When faced with such beauty or complexity we tend not to wonder whether there is a scientific answer for why the ballerina is so graceful. We admire the discipline required, just as we admire the amazing musculature and grace of gliding ballerinas. Appreciation of such performances is more than respect for the physics of their physique.

AN EMOTIONAL UNMOVED MOVER?

Functionally, art has a tendency to move the listener or observer. In being moved we are forced to confront deep questions. One may wonder why the artist used a particular color or pattern. However, the deeper questions will always be, what does it mean? As small children so honestly and persistently wonder, but why? More importantly, what does it mean for us, or for me? Wondering about outer form invariably leads to wondering about inner meaning. Modern art does not move in the same way as classical or medieval art, but there is no denying that all have impressive motor power. Even some of the most shocking modern art works (one thinks of Marcel Duchamp's urinal

"Fountain," Damien Hirst's formaldehyde sharks, and Tracey Emin's unmade bed) have the capacity to jolt viewers into new ways of living in the world.

The capacity to be moved is part of wonder. Wonder emerges from being moved at the presence of something worthy of one's attention. Like alienation, wonder ushers in a dynamic that moves individuals out of themselves. One could even call alienation and wonder the Copernican movements of the soul. They are external forces that uproot humans from the naïve belief that we are the center of our universe. While this displacement is painful, it also introduces larger reality. Just as life on earth depends on orbiting the sun, so the difference between surviving and thriving is all a matter of what provides constancy, connection, and fundamental relationship. As the enormous energy of the sun guarantees life on earth, so spirituality is about sensing and tasting something vast that will sustain the soul.

In the medieval world of scholastic theology several powerful arguments for the existence of God were presented by Thomas Aquinas. Most of these would have been inconceivable without the influence of Aristotle. Aquinas took the best philosophy available to him and constructed his theology in dialogue with it. It is also important to note the deep influence of Islam in opening up European access to many of Aristotle's texts. One of those Aristotelian-influenced arguments advanced by Aquinas was to posit God as the unmoved mover, or first cause. Aquinas wondered whether God could be conceived as the initial point in the cosmos that set the rest of the cosmos in motion.[13] The argument was one of five different arguments Aquinas made that have been summarized as "cosmological arguments," arguments based on the very existence of the cosmos.

In the case of the unmoved mover, Aquinas explored whether God could be the source of all subsequent motion in the universe. It is important to note that this theory of the unmoved mover does not fit as well with the notion of a creating deity as it does with scientific suggestions that the universe began in a Big Bang. Aquinas's unmoved mover is arguably more in tune with subsequent scientific cosmologies than classic Christian reflection about God. While there is much that is intuitively appealing about this argument, it does not explain the need for a God rather than any other natural phenomenon that could kick start the universe. Nevertheless, this notion that God might be a "mover" is worth examining.

As a thought experiment, what if God really is the mover, but just not in the way conceived by Aquinas and Aristotle? What if the movement of God is not simply restricted to a mechanical kind of causal motion (like the Big Bang) so much as a more human type of movement? What if the fundamental law of spiritual growth is not motion, but emotion? Remember Hildegard and how for her Wisdom was the greatest of virtues, joined in sweet embrace with God? Being emotionally moved and connected is one of the most powerful experiences. In an age where Christianity often struggles to gain intellectual credence, emotionally it continues to make enormous sense.[14] We do not know if there is a God. Yet we all know the need to be loved and to love back in return. And we need to be reminded of this.

With this in mind, what if Aquinas's unmoved Mover could be reframed as an Emotive Mover? Less of a God who kicks things off and then hides away, and more a God who is fundamentally emotionally connected to humankind, and the whole of creation? This also has the advantage of returning us to the affectivity and intimacy of Hildegard's Wisdom rather than the haughty objectivity of much that passes for contemporary thought. Maybe this could also shed light on how alienation (plummeting emotional depths) is structurally connected with wonder and its soaring emotional highs? After all, it is in highs and lows that we are quickest and most ready to name the presence of the divine.

Although it was a while ago, I remember the intensity of emotion of being present at the birth of my children. It was a viscerally overpowering experience, literally decentering. It was also one filled with awe and wonder. There are also other times, like being in conversation with an old friend, when one finds oneself being deeply moved, but in an entirely different kind of way. Emotions are complicated, but they undoubtedly enrich and shape life in ways that the intellect alone cannot.

Perhaps the emotional experience of being moved draws us closer to understanding what it means to be swept up by the divine. It is not something that can always be predicted or rationally explained. I have tended to be woken from intellectual slumber by ephemeral things, fleeting moments of ordinary life that have the power to move my thoughts to greater questions.

In the feeling of being moved, we transition from being at the center of our world to placing our focus elsewhere. It may only happen for a brief moment, but in being moved we lose ourselves as we become centered more in the object of our wonder. This dynamic of being lost in wonder when faced with the other, whether a person or a spiritual reality is a universal and recurring experience. Being open to the pull of the other is one of the most powerful spiritual experiences.

Wonder is not abstract or intellectual. Wonder is emotional and subjective. At the same time, wonder reorients us to the objectively true. Wonder pulls us in, decenters us, and pushes us out of ourselves. Like Hildegard, Verna Dozier was full of wonder. She rejoiced in the diversity of the human family and wanted others to rejoice along with her.

The experience of being moved in awe-filled response to something other than oneself is among the greatest possible of all joys. However, we are not always moved towards joy. To be moved is to experience a deeply emotional connection, but these soul movements are not always positive. As philosopher and literary scholar Richard Kearney has written, "The shortest route from wonder to wonder is loss."[15] Loss draws us up short, grabs our attention, and destabilizes us.

As the animation *Inside Out* so hilariously and thoughtfully revealed, emotions may be important, but they are not always transparent to the subjects who are feeling them. Part of what it means to be an emotional being is to not always be in control of one's feelings. Sometimes it is not clear which particular emotion is actually in the driver's seat. Sometimes we are clueless about what we are feeling. And while we may wish that joy was always in charge, too often it is a different, less pleasant, emotion.

This unknowability can be a tremendous burden. It can also be liberating. If it is not possible to completely grasp who one is or what one is feeling, it is hardly unreasonable to have humility when faced with other questions. Following both Socrates and St. Augustine, John Caputo is adamant about this: "we do not know who we are."[16] If we are mysteries to ourselves for at least some of the time, why should deeper questions make any more sense? True mysteries are not inherently solvable.

There is considerable agreement here between science and religion. The science of the Big Bang theory does little to solve the mystery of the beginning of the cosmos. And yet, an even more helpful insight from the scientific world is hidden in the name of a cosmological theory, M-theory. A mathematically complex attempt to bring together string theory that vastly exceeds my ability to explain it, the "M" in M-theory is left deliberately open by its founding mathematical physicist, Ed Witten of Princeton. The M in M-theory could stand for "membrane, mystery or magic." Or as Paul Davies glosses, it might even stand for miracle.[17] One of the so-called Grand Unified Theories of Everything (GUTS), M-theory would explain how absolutely everything is interconnected (if one could understand it). Yet even this brilliant theorem cannot answer the recurring question, "but why?"

THE WONDER OF MYSTERY

Unfortunately, not everyone looking for the divine is as honest as M-theorists. One of the tragic mistakes of much recent spirituality has been to approach the mystery of God like an airport paperback mystery where everything fits neatly together in the final chapter. Unfortunately, God cannot be so simplified. The divine, if it exists, must by very definition be the ultimate mystery. If one cannot always understand one's own emotions, and if we cannot answer the question why there is something rather than nothing, it seems very odd to make clearer claims about the nature of God.

Being aware of, and open to living with, mystery is a key part of the grammar of the Goldilocks God. Subsequent chapters will return to some valiant and thoughtful attempts to chart the contours of this mystery. Spiritually, God is exponentially more mysterious than our inability to understand ourselves or the origins of the cosmos. God is also far more capable of moving us, and inducing wonder and awe. The monastic philosopher St. Anselm of Canterbury realized that the very thought of God was enough to make one realize that God was inherently beyond the capacity of humankind to imagine anything greater. While praying to God in his *Proslogion*, Anselm reflected in quite some detail how God is best described as "that than which nothing greater can be imagined." Since the idea of God will always be an idea greater than anything else we could ever imagine, Anselm assumed that God's existence followed from this.[18]

Anselm's great achievement lay in showing how nothing greater than God can be imagined. Nevertheless, he never pretended to having decisively solved the mystery of God's actual existence. What he had in fact done, was describe his own experience of the paradoxical reality of God. It will always be true that God in God's very self can never truly be conceived of by a human. Anselm was really saying what God is not, rather than describing how God is. Ultimately, both the "idea" of God and the "actual existence" of God have to be, by their very nature, mysteries.

The failure of Anselm to provide convincing proof of God's existence is a good thing. For one thing, it was never something he set out to do. He simply set out to wonder aloud a bit more deeply about the nature of the God whom he believed in as he prayed to that same God. Anselm was the first to recognize that a God who can be proven would then not qualify as being a God who exceeds our understanding (something he explicitly requires God to be). It is in the nature of the divine mystery that it cannot be solved. And Anselm knew that.

When we appreciate the importance of mystery we can begin to see how some of the most cherished arguments between believers and nonbelievers are irrelevant and misleading. No believer should be able to claim that their knowledge of God is proof of God's existence, just as no nonbeliever should be able to claim that their knowledge of the workings of scientific method are proof of God's nonexistence. If God were a vase on a table in the next room, the two would have something to prove or disprove. For better or worse, God is not an object. This is a truth believers and atheists alike trip up on. The God of the scriptures, the God of Moses and Abraham, Mary and Jesus, like the God of other traditions, is a God of mystery.

As hymn writer John Wesley put it so beautifully, to respond to God is to be lost in "wonder, love, and praise." God is not the subject of scientific or philosophical study. The God that emerges from such studies is really nothing very special, and certainly bears little resemblance to the divine mystery that animates the hearts and minds of countless believers. Just as no one can reason themselves into a profound sense of love or anger, so no one should be able to reason themselves into a profound sense of belief.

In pondering life's deepest mysteries we encounter signs of God's presence. No church should lay claim to having the answers to life's mysteries. Instead, as Rowan Williams suggests, the church is the institution that hands down the questions from generation to generation. Wondering is simply a necessary step towards asking more of those questions. An individual's answers can never be permanent or all encompassing. Instead they develop as we change and as we learn more about how others have wrestled with the same questions. There are few activities more suited to the way of Goldilocks than being inherently hospitable to questions forged out of wonder.

The French philosopher, scientist, and mathematician, René Descartes, spent a lifetime trying to figure everything out. Like most of the other thinkers we have encountered, Descartes saw no inherent contradiction between religious and scientific quests. Equally importantly, Descartes believed "wonderment is the first of passion of all," a sudden surprise to the soul that moves the mind toward understanding and away from ignorance.[19] Descartes also believed that it was *because* of God that it was possible to wonder at the world; and that one's wonderings would eventually take one back to God.

Descartes is perhaps most famous for doubting everything and then realizing that the one doing the doubting, the *I that doubts* (the *cogito* in Latin) cannot itself be doubted. Before he says "I think therefore I am" Descartes really means "I doubt therefore I am." Yet, despite his affection for reason, his life was not completely dedicated to the pursuit of rationality. Just like Anselm, Descartes was not first and foremost a neutral observer of rationality. Both thinkers spent their lives in a passionate search for God. They shared the road with Goldilocks. They used the intellectual tools available to them, of philosophy, grammar, rhetoric, and logic to explore the mystery of God.

If wonder is the first of all passions, it is also the passion that sustains and directs people to reach out and connect with others. It is impossible to hold on to or exhaust wonder or passion. Like unquenchable fires, wonder elicits a passion that is uncontainable. Aristotle, Hildegard, Anselm, Aquinas, and Descartes are remembered today for their scholarly achievement. However, it was their ardent commitment to fanning the flames of wonder that underpinned the actions of their lives.

Fifty years old and with more than a hundred works to his name, on the day of his death, Thomas Aquinas noted, "Everything that I have written seems like straw to me compared to those things that I have seen and have been revealed to me." Wonder lay at the heart of Aquinas's experience of God. And despite being the most gifted and arguably most important theologian of the

Middle Ages, nothing he wrote could come near to expressing the fullness of the wonder he had experienced.

Aquinas's deathbed confession is a classic example of Goldilocks spirituality. And it is helpful to be reminded of the humility of his own life, in contrast with later scholasticism. The great innovators of theology have often had much less grandiose ideas about their legacy than their most enthusiastic disciples of subsequent centuries. It is out of wonder that first tentative steps are taken to explore the mystery of God. Yet even a lifetime clarifying and articulating that mystery is as nothing compared with the fullness of the mystery.

The poet Dante Alighieri's *Divine Comedy* is a pilgrim journey through hell and purgatory and ultimately into the celestial spheres of heaven. For Dante, paradise is mapped onto the cosmology of Ptolemy, which conceived of the stars and planets as a series of moving spheres radiating out from earth at the center. Well-versed in both Aristotle and Aquinas, Dante's picture of heaven is one that combined the cutting-edge physics and metaphysics of his day in which to situate the heavenly spheres. As he journeys from the earth into the rotating spheres above that hold the stars and the planets, Dante draws ever closer to the unmoved mover of Aquinas's argument, namely God. When questioned by St Peter, Dante is asked to give an account of his faith and replies, in language that is completely in harmony with Aquinas:

> I believe in one true God,
> sole and eternal who, Himself not moved,
> moves all the spheres by love and with desire.[20]

He goes on to underline how his belief comes both from "proofs / that physics gives, and metaphysics, too . . . " as well as prophets, psalms, and gospels. Like Aquinas the theologian he so admired, Dante ultimately recognized that the pursuit of faith, hope, and love required physics and metaphysics, even if it could never be entirely circumscribed by them.

HEROISM BORN OF WONDER

Paul Gallico's classic *The Snow Goose* centers on Philip, a solitary hunchback with a deformed arm.[21] Philip lives in southern England, on the Essex marshes, in an abandoned lighthouse with only the birds for company. In addition to the wounds to his body he also carries mental hurt. Anxious to flee the pity and sympathy of his fellow humans, he tends instead to the birds in his remote sanctuary. Gallico paints the scene sparingly. For while Philip has fled human society, he is no stranger to wonder.

Delighting in the natural world, Philip is brought into a deeper communion with creation. His reputation for caring for the birds draws Fritha, a young girl, to seek him out to tend to a wounded bird. This snow goose eventually heals and flies away. But it returns, drawing Fritha and Philip closer together. In the summer of 1940 everything changes, as Philip sails his small sailboat to the shores of Dunkirk to help evacuate the stranded British army.

Gallico carefully avoids reading too closely into Philip's motivations. Instead, he allows the story to be taken up by the witness reports of the soldiers Philip rescued. It is their wondrous accounts of his heroic intervention, accompanied only by the snow goose, that give the story its climax. Philip dies a hero, saving countless troops who otherwise would not have made it from the shallows to the troop ships in deep water. Yet his heroism is not the totality of the story. Fritha and the snow goose also share responsibility for saving the lives of the soldiers.

It is Fritha's wonder-filled love of the snow goose that transforms Philip's isolation into a deeper communion with his fellow human beings. While the crippled hero assumes the personal risk and danger of saving the soldiers, it is Fritha and his guardian angel, the snow goose, who save Philip. Wonder at the world around them, embodied in their shared care for the snow goose, forged the love that bound Fritha and Philip together. This is a deeply Christian wonder at the mystery of life that is expressed in caring for the vulnerable, first the snow goose and later the stranded soldiers.

Wonder in the face of mystery cannot simply result in awe. It also awakens the isolated into a community of sacrificial love. Together, Fritha and Philip reveal how wondrous love effects a movement from alienation to mutuality. It is neither intellect nor knowledge that saves the Dunkirk troops. Rather, it is through Fritha and Philip's wounded love that they become agents of healing. Wonder is not simply a subjective emotional experience. It also awakens and transforms those touched by it to serve the world around them.

Aristotle would have interpreted the story of Fritha and Philip as one revealing "greatness of soul." Although neither meet the criteria of traditional martial heroes, both reveal *megalopsucia*, literally a greatness of the soul. Against the vices of vanity and smallness of soul, *megalopsucia* occurs when we have a certain confidence in living a virtuous life:

> He who is truly great-souled, therefore, must be good, and what is great in each virtue would seem to belong to the great-souled man.[22]

By cultivating wonder we discover this possibility of living the virtuous life, or what Aristotle calls being good. This is the ultimate purpose of wonder. This desire to be good and live virtuously is also a central motivation for those looking for the Goldilocks God. We may start on this journey because something brings us up short or because something goes wrong. At some point, we wonder how we may make the world a better place.

It is helpful to conclude with Hildegard. Although she was clearly an enormously creative individual, the message of her life is not that only a few can be heroic. Hildegard taught that every human being has something of God within them. And when we open ourselves to wisdom, we encounter the divine: "She is with everyone and in everyone, and so beautiful is her secret that no person can know the sweetness with which she sustains people."[23] In being open to wonder or in seeking wisdom, then, we are not alone. Wisdom and wonder are how we find our way back to God. By personifying Wisdom, Hildegard shows how the humanity (and divinity) of wisdom is essential, not an afterthought. It is only by affirming our humanity that we can follow her in becoming scientists of the soul.

Hildegard's search for God is one that accentuates and embraces the feminine aspects of the divine. Not simply in the sweetness of wisdom, but also in the sweetness of Mary, the bearer of Jesus. In one of her most beautiful poems, Hildegard underlines the miracle of Mary's arduous work:

> O how great a miracle it is
> That into the humble female body
> A king has entered
> God has done this
> Because humility surpasses all.[24]

This humble *scientia* of Hildegard is an embodied knowing, a wisdom that recognizes the essentially cooperative nature of Mary with the divine. Hildegard's Eucharistic devotion affirms both the divinity of Christ and the essential work of Mary. This science of the soul is both refreshingly familiar and unembarrassed with embodiment. Hildegard embraces the mystery of God working together with Mary. There is no concern about a division between the divine and the human or spirit and matter here. Rather, her science of the soul dedicates itself in praise to the quintessential Christian mystery of God's Word made flesh.

NOTES

1. Jocelyn of Brakelond, *Chronicle of the Abbey of Bury St Edmunds*, ed. Diana Greenway and Jane Sayers (Oxford: Oxford University Press, 1989), 54.

2. Seb Falk, *The Light Ages: The Surprising Story of Medieval Science* (New York: W.W. Norton, 2020).

3. For an excellent introduction see Joseph L. Baird, *The Personal Correspondence of Hildegard of Bingen* (Oxford: Oxford University Press, 2006).

4. Hildegard von Bingen, *Scivias*, trans. Mother Columba Hart and Jane Bishop (New York: Paulist Press, 1990), 59.

5. Bingen, *Scivias*.

6. Schleiermacher, *On Religion*, 23.

7. Aristotle, *The Metaphysics*, trans. Hugh Lawson-Tancred (London: Penguin, 1998).

8. Douglas Adams, *The Hitchhikers Guide to the Galaxy* (London: Pan Books, 1979).

9. Martin Heidegger, *An Introduction to Metaphysics*, trans. Gregory Fried and Richard Polt (New Haven: Yale University Press, 2014), 2.

10. Ursula K. Le Guin, *The Left Hand of Darkness* (New York: Ace, 1987).

11. Jean-Luc Marion, *In the Self's Place: The Approach of Saint Augustine*, trans Jeffrey L. Kosky (Stanford: Stanford University Press, 2012), 198.

12. Davies, *Goldilocks Enigma*, 167.

13. Aquinas, Summa Theologica (I,q.2,a.3).

14. For an excellent example of the power of emotional arguments see Francis Spufford, *Unapologetic: Why, Despite Everything, Christianity Can Still Make Surprising Emotional Sense* (New York: HarperOne, 2014).

15. Richard Kearney, *Anatheism: Returning to God After God* (New York: Columbia University Press, 2011), 13.

16. John Caputo, *On Religion* (London: Routledge, 2001), 18.

17. Davies, *Goldilocks Enigma*, 113–14.

18. Anselm, *The Prayers and Meditations of Saint Anselm*, eds. Richard Southern and Benedicta Ward (London: Penguin, 1973), 238ff.

19. René Descartes, *The Passions of the Soul and Other Late Philosophical Writings*, trans. Michael Moriarty (Oxford: Oxford University Press, 2016), article 53, 220.

20. Dante Alighieri, *The Divine Comedy*, trans. Robin Kirkpatrick (London: Penguin, 2012), *Paradise*, 130–33, 436.

21. Paul Galico, *The Snow Goose* (New York: Alfred A. Knopf, 1946).

22. Aristotle, *Aristotle's Nicomachean Ethics: A New Translation*, trans. Robert C. Bartlett and Susan D. Collins (Chicago: University of Chicago Press, 2011), 76–77.

23. Bingen, *Scivias*, 364.

24. Quoted in Miri Rubin, *Corpus Christi: The Eucharist in Late Medieval Culture* (Cambridge: Cambridge University Press, 1991), 142.

Chapter Four

"It can be no disgrace to confesse wee are ignorant."

Goldilocks's encounter in the home of the three bears is profoundly physical. It is also a story that evokes classic themes of spirituality: hospitality, nourishment, and community. As Hildegard's visions and poetry reveal, the intersection between the physical and the spiritual is the classic nexus of the holy. Sacraments reveal the holy within the ordinary. Bread and wine showing the presence of God. Water signing the new birth and entrance into a new community. The exchange of rings marking the promise and hope of a lifelong relationship. The anointing of the sick and the dying. Sacramental actions manifest parts of human experience that are inextricably connected to the divine. Like the moves of a dance, sacraments are the way individuals and communities learn, and keep alive, this connection. This chapter investigates some of the spiritual thermodynamics found in the sacrament of Holy Communion or Eucharist.

In the Greek conception of the afterlife, the river Lethe formed the barrier between the living and the dead of the underworld. To progress to the underworld, it was necessary to drink of *"lethe,"* which, literally translated, means oblivion, forgetfulness, or concealment. To forsake life, and be ready for existence in the realm of the dead, the Greeks believed humans had to forget everything. Acts of remembering distinguish being fully alive from being in the realm of those who have forgotten all, the land of the dead.

Ever aware of the dangers and fallibility of human memory, the faithful have presented God as a reliable source of memory. St. Augustine illustrated the trinity using a triad based on this very idea. Augustine explored how the relationship of three persons of the Trinity (Father, Son, and Holy Spirit) could be conceived of as memory, intelligence, and will. Identifying the Father with memory, Augustine accords memory precedence, while underlining how intelligence and love spring from it. Memory in this triadic structure is identified as the source from which the entire triad springs.

Jean-Luc Marion's reading of Augustine is careful to note that this psychological metaphor does not place Augustine as somehow privileging or anticipating the Cartesian tradition of the thinking subject. Rather, the priority that Augustine gives to memory should, instead, be seen as revealing the essential paradox of selfhood: *memoria* is before thinking, making thinking possible. Part of what *memoria* does is point beyond the self's thinking to that which is outside of it. As Marion puts it: "*Memoria*, therefore, displays an essential ambivalence: it renders absence present but also keeps absence absent."[1] The paradox is that what cannot be remembered is never part of memory. And yet, memory is always pointing to that which is not remembered, or what Marion calls "the secret of the self," the recognition that our memory constitutes us before we can even think about who we are.

In the medieval period, the shrine where pilgrims came to pray before a saint was often described as a "*memoria*," the place of memory. Saints were often described as "of blessed memory," and they provided a connection from the believer to God. Sanctity itself can be seen as the natural trajectory of those who were willing to invest time and energy keeping the memories alive of other holy men and holy women. Uncertainty driven by the frailty of human memory drives the development of specific practices of Christian remembering. Across different generations and different cultures Christian practices of memory creation, preservation, and transmittal remain consistent.

LETTING OTHERS REMEMBER

Henning Mankell's coffee drinking detective, Kurt Wallander, is one of the great literary characters of Scandinavian crime fiction. Turned into television drama, in one episode Wallander (played by Kenneth Brannagh) misplaces his police service weapon. Not given to acts of recklessness he is shocked to the core and suspended from the police while an investigation takes place. Viewers know why. Wallander is experiencing the first signs of dementia. Like his father before him, he is losing track of where he is. He is starting not to be able to remember everything.

We are shown Wallander walking along a beach having an imaginary, but utterly real, conversation with his own father (who has been dead several years). In the tragedy of discovering his dementia, he has received one special gift. He is finally starting to understand something more of his father. And his father is present to him. In an imaginary dialogue of great pathos, he asks the memory of his father "but who will do the remembering?" His father replies, "Let others remember for you." As he speaks the camera cuts to Wallander's granddaughter skipping through the waves. It is a deeply evocative and poignant moment. It is also a scene pregnant with meaning and what can only be described as hope. Thanks to how the director frames the scene, viewers see how the memory of his father is as real to Wallander as the child jumping waves. Something similar occurs in Eucharist. The drama of Eucharist is not simply a retroactive memorial pointing backward, it also shows the future.

In its earliest centuries the church found itself underground both metaphorically and literally. Services took place in catacombs or other hidden places out of sight of prying eyes. Before becoming the official Imperial religion under Constantine, Christians needed to keep their faith hidden for fear of persecution. Followers of Christ were less resident aliens and more straightforward outlaws. Pagan observers viewed the focus of their underground worship, the feast of Eucharist, as a cannibalistic act. Romans knew that Christians ate the body of Christ. They also knew Christ was a person. It made perfect sense to accuse Christians of practicing cannibalism.

In the Roman world it was perfectly ordinary, indeed, a basic requirement of being civilized, to make sacrifices to the gods. Roman pluralism approached gods the way capitalism approaches goods. One of the great strengths of the Roman way of life was how new gods could easily be incorporated into the pantheon of gods. Typically, this was the Roman response to any new culture or deity. Yet, while they were used to sacrificing to the gods, there was no precedent for the outrageous Christian belief that they ate their God.

While Eucharistic teaching took centuries to develop and crystalize the presence of God in the sacrament, by the late medieval period the paradox of God's presence had become deeply embedded in culture. Miri Rubin in her magisterial analysis of the Eucharist in medieval culture shows both how Eucharistic theology develops, and how the Eucharist penetrates every aspect of medieval life. In her wide-ranging study, she concludes with an examination of the development of the feast of Corpus Christi. A symbol for this Eucharistic flowering can be seen in the vision of Juliana, a devout Cistercian in the religious house of Mont Cornillon in Liège. Devoted to Eucharist, she has a vision of a moon with a "little break in part of its sphere." The dream recurs, and twenty years later it is interpreted by the writer of the *Vita Julianae* (the Life of Julian):

> Then Christ revealed to her that the Church was the moon, and that the missing part of the moon stood for the absence of one feast in the Church, which he would want his faithful to celebrate on earth.[2]

Eventually, Juliana's feast of Corpus Christi is introduced locally, and in time, with a little help from the Pope, as a feast that slowly gains universal appeal. Over time, the feast saturates the medieval social and political landscape, as much as the religious landscape, as processions, feasts, mystery plays, and confraternities take up the feast with enthusiasm. In what follows, it is my hope to resituate Eucharist within this medieval tradition as a public sacrament that challenges the division between the sacred and the secular. The practices of Eucharist that emerge are less those of ceremony designed solely for celebration within a church. Rather, it becomes possible to recognize Eucharist as a sacramental reality continually spilling out into the wider culture, evoking responses that are both sacred and secular.

The middle ages take up the challenge of God's presence in Eucharist with verve. While Romans were puzzled, the medievals exult in the strange contradiction of the body of Christ. Rubin quotes a poem from c. 1450 that illustrates some of these contradictions encountered wherever the sacrament was shared:

> It seems white and is red;
> It is quike and semes dede;
> It is fleshe and semes bred;
> It is on and semes too;
> It is God's body and no mo.[3]

The poem addresses the apparent contradictions of bread and wine appearing to be other than the body and blood that they truly are. The fourth line also addresses the doctrine of concomitance, the notion that Christ's body and blood only appear as separate in the two forms of bread and wine. Yet they are truly one, a unity of Christ's physical and spiritual body. The poem clarifies why the Romans had been perplexed. Where Romans sacrificed, Christians consumed.

Through the shared Eucharistic meal the church in all its different iterations, sects, denominations and nondenominational forms, encounters Christ in bread and wine. According to Christian tradition it is the closest encounter with the divine that is possible this side of eternity. In the famous assessment of the Catholic theologian Henri de Lubac the Eucharist makes the Church. For all his criticisms of Catholic tradition, Martin Luther never sought to replace the Eucharist. Instead, he deleted what he thought were medieval accretions while stressing the preaching of a sermon. In Eucharist, the community of faith continually rediscovers what it means to experience the presence of the divine as a living memory: both a memory of the past and a re-membering, a putting together again, of living presence.

The Greek *eucharist* literally means "Thanksgiving." Whenever Eucharist is celebrated the community gives thanks to God for the life, death, and resurrection of Christ. Each Eucharist points toward God through the mystery of consecrated bread and wine. In experiencing the re-membering of Eucharist, the faithful find themselves woven into God's own *memoria*. Another Greek word signals why Christians persist in the Eucharistic meal: *anamnesis*, "remembering." Presiding over the Last Supper, Jesus takes bread and tells the disciples that the bread is his body, and that they should take and eat it in remembrance of him. The *anamnesis* shows how Eucharist is a remembering and enacting of Christ's invitation to share bread and wine in his memory.

In sharing a common spiritual meal of bread and wine, participants are strengthened by the memory and ongoing presence of Christ's life, death, and resurrection. They are joined in a deeper communion with Christ and with all those who throughout time have celebrated that meal with him. So in addition to being a sacrament of remembering, Eucharist is also a sacrament of recognition. It allows participants to recognize Christ as the one whose body is broken, who suffers and dies for sinners, and who rises again to be recognized in the breaking of the bread.

The scriptural story of the road to Emmaus offers a template for this archetypal experience of Christian recognition. After the death of Jesus, the disciples are traveling when they meet a stranger who expounds to them the scriptures. They are impressed, and their hearts and minds are lifted up by his teaching. However, it is only when the stranger breaks bread with them that they recognize him for who he truly is: the risen Christ. Breaking bread together reveals the stranger to be their friend, risen and alive. Critically, it is this breaking of bread that enables them to understand what the stranger had been teaching them. Richard Kearney observes how in the Resurrection encounters,

> Christ, when risen, does not appear as sovereign king but as a foreigner, again and again—as a gardener, a fisherman, a beggar man, a cook, a wanderer at the inn. Emmaus is not a house; it is not a cathedral; it is not a temple. It is a station along the way.[4]

The encounter at Emmaus points to a Eucharistic hospitality centered on strangers and located in the midst of ordinary life.

Jean-Luc Marion pays close attention to the "Eucharistic site of Theology." For Marion, the celebration of Eucharist continues to provide the classic matrix for making sense of the scriptures. This is what Marion calls the Eucharistic hermeneutic: only in the hearing and responding to the Word in the Eucharist do we understand and make sense of what that Word means.[5] He goes on to affirm that all theology is (Eucharistically) celebrated first, before it can be written.[6] In this sequence, theology flows from the prayers and devotion of Eucharist. Eucharist is not simply a liturgical action among others. It is the primary site where God is made present. The Eucharist does not only make the church: it also constitutes theology. It is with a similar logic that Marion reads Augustine's *Confessions*. Only by praising (confessing) God, are we able to approach God. And in this act of praise and confession, we receive the gift of finding out who we are: "The entire undertaking of the *Confessiones* tends to establish precisely God as the closest, more interior to me than my own interiority . . ."[7] Only as we join in praise do we recognize God's proximity to us.

Eucharist makes God's presence closer than we can imagine through both the confession of praise and sacramental reception. Participants experience Christ not simply in bread and wine, but also in the community. Eucharist forms Christ, making Christ's body visible once again. It is through participation in Eucharist that individuals come to recognize their roles as members of the body of Christ. Even when we start to forget who we are, the encounter with Christ in bread and wine remains possible. And in the repeated act of communicating, consuming the consecrated elements, our bodies are literally made one with the Christic body. This does not require a belief in high medieval scholastic theories of divine presence. All it requires is an embodied participation in the communal act of remaking the body of Christ.

The mystery of Eucharist is a sacramental encounter in which God strengthens humans, both physically and spiritually. Eucharist is God's way of making human beings profoundly welcome. God makes God's self available, in bread and wine, through the devotion of the community. If that seems shocking or alien, then maybe we are closer to understanding the pagan shock about Christ's presence in Eucharist. God's welcome is not immaterial or spiritual. It is instead a spiritual welcome that *depends* on the materiality and physicality of bread and wine to manifest that which is essentially beyond comprehension.

In the Eucharistic prayer of consecration there is a movement that underlines this sense that something occurs. Borrowed once again from the Greek, the *epiclesis* (literally, "invocation") is the part where the priest asks the Holy Spirit to overshadow the elements of bread and wine, in order that God may transform them into the body and blood. Whether one understands this transformation literally, symbolically, or any number of ways in between, the *epiclesis* signifies how Eucharist is a living action.

Like the rest of the Eucharist, the *epiclesis* unfolds as a Trinitarian act, in which the prayers of the faithful enter into dialogue with the threefold God, Father, Son, and Holy Spirit. In Eucharist seekers grow closer not simply to God in Christ through the power of the Spirit, but also to the wider body of the community of saints, living and departed. As de Lubac puts it: "Just as the Church is entirely concentrated in the Eucharist, it may also be said to be entirely concentrated in a saint."[8] The repeatability of Eucharist points to its role as a sacrament of strengthening and renewal. Eucharist is how God meets spiritual hunger. It also works the other way. Eucharist admonishes, empowers, and sends out the faithful to feed others.

In Anglo-Saxon, there is an explicit linguistic connection between the word for Lord and the sharing of bread. The word for Lord, *hlafdor*, quite literally, includes the word for loaf, the *hlaf.* To be a Lord (or a Lady, *hlafdige*) was to be someone who provided bread. In the same way, Eucharist is never simply about receiving bread. Once the connection between God and God's gift of bread is discovered, we are expected to contribute something to building up the wider community. Anglo-Saxon, again, makes this clear. It is not simply the Lord who was defined by bread. To be a follower is to be a *hlafeata*, a person marked by the exchange of the loaf. Just as the loaf constitutes the connection between Anglo-Saxon lords and ladies and their followers, so bread sustains the connection between Christians and Christ.[9] Maybe it is time to retire the word "Christian." Perhaps it would be better to be described as "breaders" or people of the bread.

Sharing this bread forms Christians. And while communion wafers may seem prosaic to those who have known them their entire lives, this has not always been true. Rubin underlines the extraordinary nature of Eucharistic bread during the medieval period: "Wheat was usually grown as a cash crop which was sent to the market while those who produced it ate darker bread. Imaginative literature often mused upon and expressed a wish for regular consumption of white bread in a utopian world. The eucharist, the small wafer made of the finest wheaten dough, was transported into that realm of fantasy."[10] For medievals, Eucharist did not simply signify the extraordinary presence of God. The bread itself was a marvel.

Not simply in its physicality: everything about the Eucharist invited both wonder and wisdom. In order to comprehend the nature of the real presence of Christ theologians developed increasingly complex methods for analyzing the way how words denote and signify reality. Rubin offers one of the most lucid and thoughtful summaries of this complicated history within Eucharistic theology for those keen to travel the byways of its philosophical underpinnings.[11] As we shall see in the next chapter, the medieval mind was richly imaginative. Even something relatively simple quickly became complicated. In the grammatical analysis known as *distinctiones* of the Middle Ages, the single word for "bread" (*panis*) in just one manuscript (British Library MS Harley 5751) has been shown to have seven different meanings:

> first, in the sense of material bread (*panis corporalis*), as in the words, "our daily bread"; second, as in spiritual bread, as "man shall eat the bread of angels"; third, as an equivalent to teaching (*doctrina*), "He gave them the bread of life"; fourth, in the sense of repentance (*penitencia*), as "in my bread of tears day and night"; fifth, in reference to the body of Christ, "the bread which I will give you is My flesh," sixth, referring to Christ himself, "I am the living bread which came down from heaven," and finally *panis* is the equivalent to a word, as in

the Gospel, "Not on bread alone does man live but on every word that proceeds from the mouth of God."[12]

The Chaucer scholar Peter Travis explains how these grammar school distinctions, "are inextricably mixed up with issues that are of a logical, rhetorical, metaphysical, and even theological cast." As theories of Eucharist develop across the medieval period, these various lenses became inexorably applied to the simple invitation to receive the body of Christ in the sacramental bread. The bread is never simply consumed, it also invites struggle and debate, as believers and non-believers wrestle with what it signifies.

At the same time, let us not confuse such breads with the "blessed bread," that is bread not consecrated, that was made available during the medieval celebration to everyone at the end of the service. For hundreds of years access to Eucharist was restricted to special times in the year for laity. Not everyone was allowed access to the body and blood of Christ. But the church recognized that the laity still needed bread that was spiritually charged. One can well understand why, by the time the Reformation occurs, these debates have become intricate. Bread is never simply bread. And the Eucharistic bread is never simply bread that feeds those hungry for God. It is also the site of entry into a tremendous range of grammatical, rhetorical, logical, metaphysical, and theological debates and inquiries. All the while, it continues to nourish those receiving and adoring it.

THE ELIZABETHAN EUCHARISTIC REFORMATION

People of the bread have enjoyed disagreeing with one another about Eucharist for quite some time. One of the insights of the *via media* is that so many of these internal ecclesiastical arguments are inherently unsatisfying. As we saw in chapter 1, thanks to Good Queen Bess, a new way of defining church was chanced upon. With Continental Europe tearing itself apart on the basis of religious affiliation to either Roman Catholicism or Protestant confessionalism, Elizabeth experimented with an ecclesiastical model that did not require all of its members to believe the same thing.

One of Elizabeth's first acts was to side-line the existing traditionalist bench of bishops that had been put in place by Mary. However, instead of simply replacing them with radical Protestants, she proceeded more gently. Declining simply to swing the religious pendulum back from Mary to where it had been under Edward, Elizabeth instead authorized a third version of *The Book of Common Prayer*. A decade earlier, Archbishop Thomas Cranmer had retained much of the original Roman Catholic canon of the mass, translating the prayers into English and simplifying, rather than dramatically changing doctrine. Cranmer's 1549 changes were so mild that one of the most traditionalist bishops, Bishop Stephen Gardiner, declared the book compatible with his conscience.

Cranmer was at heart a simplifier, editor, and translator. Freeing the liturgy from accretions and complexity, Cranmer sought to grant the people access to the holy in their common tongue. Signs of Cranmer's original theological moderation are clearest at the point where clergy were to give the consecrated bread and wine to the people. Cranmer's English translation changed the words from Latin to English, but did not significantly shift the Latin focus from the sacrifice of the mass and the presence of Christ in the sacrament. The rubric, the instruction that told people what to do at this point, and the words of the priest that it precedes, make this clear:

> And when he delivereth the Sacramente of the body of Christe, he shall say to every one these woordes.
>
> The body of our Lorde Jesus Christe whiche was geven for thee, preserve thy bodye and soule unto everlasting lyfe.[13]

This makes it sound as if the body of Christ was being given to the faithful. While this made perfect doctrinal sense to Catholics like Gardiner, the belief in the real presence of Christ in the mass was at the heart of a whole constellation of Protestant criticisms leveled against the church. The medieval church had created an entire economy, financial as well as spiritual, around the sacrifice of the mass, making the sacrificial presence of Christ in the mass an irresistible target for reformers.

Allowing Gardiner to keep his conscience created problems for those reformers. Following a Protestant backlash against Cranmer's cautious revision, a second new prayer book was produced under Edward VI three years later in 1552. Retaining most of Cranmer's original translation, unlike its more conciliatory predecessor, the new book made critical changes to the words to be used at the giving of the bread and wine:

> And when he delyvereth the bread, he shall saye.
>
> Take and eat this, in remembrance that Christe died for thee, and fede on him in thy heart by faith, with thankes geuving.[14]

With a stamp of printer's ink the body of Christ was gone, ordinary bread replacing divine flesh. In its place, an interpretation made it crystal clear how the Eucharistic bread and wine should be understood. Out with the sacrament of the body of Christ, in with language of remembrance. No longer were the faithful to feed on Christ's body in the bread. Now they were to feed on Christ in their hearts with thanksgiving.

This dematerializing of Christ's presence in bread and wine would have elated radical Protestants as much as it angered traditional Catholics. When in 1559 Elizabeth asks parliament to authorize a new *Book of Common Prayer* she had two compelling precedents available to her to choose from. Wishing to retain the language of the people for the new prayer book, the choice was between a book that had angered everyone (the 1549 prayer book) and a book that angered Catholics more (1552). Elizabeth largely avoided the false polarity.

Instead, she created a third option, attempting to draw the country together in a book that would side-step the differences. Together with her religious advisers she, quite literally, combined elements of the two previous prayer books, forging a position between totally rejecting traditional Latin sacramentality and identifying wholesale with experimental Continental reformers. At a distance of more than four hundred years it is hard to grasp how radical this was, and how very perilous Elizabeth's choice was. Both as a woman and as a heretic (for a good many Protestant and Catholics) she was in uncharted territory. In 1559 no one would predict that Elizabeth's way, her Elizabethan Settlement, would set the course for succeeding generations. In "The Ordre for the Administracion of the Lordes Supper, or Holy Communion" even the way the Eucharist is named is inclusive: hospitable to both Protestant and Catholic interpretations.

If one judges success by the long stretch of peace she ushered in, Elizabeth's wager was successful. Her Golden Age was also more than simply peaceful. It was also a time of remarkable intellectual, musical, artistic, and commercial flourishing. Elizabeth brought a degree of stability to an England that had swung between Catholic and Protestant beliefs over the previous three decades. While she was far from perfect, and continues to earn her share of detractors, Elizabeth ushered in a less divisive approach to doctrine than Mary or Edward. Drawing positive comparison between Elizabeth's *real politique* approach and that of Machiavelli, the historian of strategy John Lewis Gaddis notes:

> God's church, under Elizabeth, would be staunchly English: whether "Catholic" or "Protestant" mattered less than loyalty. This was, in one sense, toleration, for the new queen cared little what her subjects believed. She would watch like a hawk, though, what they did.[15]

There was still religious persecution as she sought to keep her throne and fend off foreign invasion from the Catholic forces of Philip II of Spain. Elizabeth developed under her spymaster Walsingham a surveillance state out of the fear of invasion and internal betrayal. She also directed her bishops to clamp down on overly Protestant activity, guiding the country and church along a course that revealed the resiliency of her pragmatism. While she gave Roman Catholic agents provocateur no quarter, especially as the threat of war or regicide grew, she also cracked down on Puritan and Protestant pieties that threatened the harmony of the common weal.

In better moments, Anglicans and Episcopalians continue to steer down the middle of this path first charted by Elizabeth. It is as if we have imbibed the story of Goldilocks from an early age. While some of us lean more to the Catholic, the Protestant, or the Orthodox, the tradition itself is more robust. It was designed to help its members learn from one another and stay connected to each other despite their differences. It continues to be a tradition that positively encourages plural interpretations of what precisely is being remembered in Eucharist.

Thanks to the political and religious stability of Queen Elizabeth's settlement, the sixteenth century church of England avoided defining the nature of the divine presence in bread and wine. Keeping both the traditional 1549 catholic language of Christ's presence in bread and wine *and* the 1552 language about remembrance was a stroke of genius. While Eucharist reveals the mystery of Christ's presence, Elizabeth's approach left it to individuals to decide exactly how.

Ever since, the churches descended from Elizabeth have spent less time reflecting on the bread and wine and more on the receiver of the bread and wine. Richard Hooker was again one of the first to make this explicit. Thomas Cranmer's own Eucharistic beliefs were particularly well concealed, and extremely hard to surmise. He abandoned transubstantiation by 1548, but his later position seems to have asserted the spiritual presence of Christ. Cranmer's theology was marked both by an admiration for Lutheranism and by a desire not to offend the anti-Lutheran King Henry VIII. In some ways Cranmer was the perfect exemplar of the search for the *via media*. He trod carefully around the views of others, especially those more powerful than him. And he did not seek to impose his own views on the church as a whole. Diarmaid McCulloch notes how Cranmer comes closer to the Eucharistic position of Zwingli's successor in Zurich Heinrich Bullinger.[16] For Bullinger, Eucharist is a sign pointing to a happening in parallel, that occurs simultaneously in the present through God's work alongside that of the sign. In Cranmer's own words:

> And although Christ be no corporally in the bread and wine, yet Christ used not so many words, in the mystery of his holy supper, without effectual signification. For he is effectually present, and effectually worketh not in the bread

and wine, but in the godly receivers of them, to whom he giveth his own flesh spiritually to feed upon, and his own blood to quench their great inward thirst.[17]

This quote is important in that for all that it comes from the great architect of the resonant poetry of *The Book of Common Prayer* the prayer book itself is never this explicit.

Richard Hooker suggests later that Christians continue to concern themselves less with questions about the transformation of the bread or the wine, and more with the transformation of the believer who receives the sacrament. In contrast to Catholic, Lutheran, or Zwinglian orthodoxies that opined on how Christ was present in the sacrament, Hooker was honest enough, and brave enough, to admit that, "it can be no disgrace to confesse wee are ignorant."[18] Such Eucharistic agnosticism was incredibly radical for his day. Boldly *not* taking a position was not an obvious move for a theologian. Yet it was precisely by avoiding pontificating on the matter that Hooker evaded the entire question of how Christ was present or not present in the Eucharist. It was a move straight out of the Elizabethan Goldilocks playbook.

COMMUNION BEFORE BAPTISM

Seekers of the Goldilocks God continue to have no settled or unanimous view about *how* Christ is present. What they do recognize is how the mystery of Christ's presence requires a human response. They combine the seriousness of Catholic teaching that God is present in the Eucharist with the Protestant insight that central drama of Eucharist is not the transmogrification of bread and wine, so much as the transformation of lives. Eucharistic elements of bread and wine are not the focus of what is changed. They are catalysts for wider transformations that occur within the hearts, minds, and souls of those who are being re-membered in the presence of the divine.

The most profound lessons are learned not through logic or rationality, but by osmosis and experience. And so much of what we learn and remember is first learned by our bodies. As children so wonderfully reveal, we learn by soaking up everything around us. Eucharist is an act of remembering that shows seekers how to soak up and develop basic Christian habits. Many of those habits are learned first by the motions of our bodies, following the dance of the liturgy, and only later do the motions settle into our hearts, minds, and souls. The communicating of Eucharist is profoundly physical. Standing, sitting, kneeling, crossing, singing, bowing, exchanging signs of peace, smiling, even crying, and, of course, receiving bread and wine: these are the acts that form the faithful into the body of Christ as much, if not more so, than the dialogue of the liturgy.

The church resisted excluding people from Eucharist based on intellectual capacity or their ability to understand the faith. Over the last half century, the church has also recovered the primacy of baptism as the sacrament that defines the Eucharistic community. Many grew up receiving Holy Communion for the very first time at Confirmation. Some churches offer First Communion as a deliberate waypoint in the child's life journey, but many offer Communion immediately after baptism. We know that no one is worthy of be included in baptismal fellowship or Eucharistic fellowship based on their own merits. Baptism before Communion remains the dominant tradition within world Christianity. It is also a tradition that has come under increasing scrutiny within the Episcopal church where many communities offer communion before baptism.

This question is partly about grace. Nevertheless, the encounter with Eucharist remains one of the primary ways in which people experience the grace of God in ordinary life. Without experiencing Eucharist, where else can one encounter the ongoing Trinitarian drama that is the story of Christ's life, death and resurrection? What is also at stake is the question of who we believe God desires to communicate with. If we think God only has care for a religious elite or a chosen few then it makes perfect sense to retain communion for the baptized. If it is believed that God only reaches out for deeper intimacy with a subset of humanity, then it makes sense to see Eucharist as nourishment for saints alone. Of course, such a theological understanding would be quite narrow. By contrast, if the purpose of Christianity is to cooperate with God's ardent love for the whole of humanity, then barriers (ecclesiastical or otherwise) to full communication need to be examined and challenged.

The pastoral and theological intuition of many traveling the *via media* is that communion is not simply for the faithful. It is also for the broken, the unsure, and the not-quites. Here the situation of Goldilocks is relevant. Is the provision of hospitality (by the three bears) to someone outside the family (Goldilocks) an unmerited disaster? Or does it point to something more profound? Does the Goldilocks story encourage a Eucharistic reading? And if it does, is it a warning *against* hospitality, or simply a reminder of the inherent tensions within the practice of hospitality? Hospitality is always to take a risk. And in recognizing God in the Host, experientially and theologically, Eucharist appears as a topsy turvy banquet open to strangers, aliens, and enemies: a feast for sinners, beginners, and cynics alike. Eucharist is the food for the baptized and saints. It is also food for half-believers: the type of people who may believe something, and may even believe it rather deeply, but have never had the opportunity or inclination to sign on to the whole package. Half-believers have a desire to believe. They also often have a strong sense of the divine. They are simply unready to take on everything unquestioned, and prefer not to be duped. Sometimes, one suspects, this is as much because of their humility as anything. They do not want to pretend that they have the insight of an Augustine of Hippo or a Hildegard of Bingen. And so they settle for a more modest approach.

Offering the Eucharist to unbaptized seekers may be seen as a response to the spiritual yearnings of half-believers, agnostics, and all those who might happen to darken the door of a church in a vulnerable moment. What theological argument might refuse such brave people participation in God's most sacred meal? The medievals were, once again, somewhat ahead of us. In the twelfth century Peter Comestor posed the question of what is given in the Eucharist, before answering himself: "It is given both to the good and to the bad, and it is received both by the good and the bad. But the good receive it unto their salvation, and the evil to their damnation."[19] We may not agree with Comestor's theology of the afterlife, but it is hard to disagree with the proposition that Eucharist has always been given to the good and the bad.

It is also rather difficult to identify the good solely with the baptized and the bad solely with the unbaptized. As Rubin's study of the great variety of Eucharistic practice and belief in the Middle Ages shows, the Eucharist was always available for those who sinned. There were even increasingly elaborate ways in which the church ensured that sinners were made ready to receive. In many cases, sinners were restricted from communicating. But these restrictions also served to model the kind of preparation required for the faithful to be able to receive (at a time when communicating was often infrequent). Surely, the theological question is what would God's reason be for preferring the sinning baptized to the sinning unbaptized? And if that question sounds somewhat anachronistic and strange, we may be closer to understanding the nature of Eucharistic grace.

It has been rightly objected that this is to mischaracterize the purpose of Eucharist. Eucharist, according to traditional teaching, is communion with the body of Christ, and only those who are part of the body of Christ can receive the body of Christ. It is common to hear the suggestion that only those who are immersed in the grammar of Christianity can make sense of the experience of sharing in the body of Christ. Others who receive the body without being part of Christ's body are profaning that body.

All this seems eminently true. It also seems hard to argue with the belief that *everyone* in all times and in all places cannot help but profane the body of Christ whenever they receive communion. That seems to be the point of the Lord's Supper, a meal at which Jesus pointed out who would betray him in the very act of giving him bread. We are all in the position of Hooker. We have to confess that we are not simply ignorant, but also unworthy. This point has been made well by Hannah Bowman. Bowman argues for a theology of the cross signifying how Christ's cross destroys the barrier between the sacred and the profane. Bowman, like the Romans, recognizes the Eucharistic scandal: the proclamation of an outrageous gospel that always points to the cross. In her excellent review of various rethinkings of communion she concludes with a story from her lay Eucharistic ministry to Los Angeles County jails. Sliding communion under a filthy jail door to a prisoner in solitary confinement was for this believer in the real presence of Christ in the sacrament, "perhaps the holiest moment of my life."[20] It is almost impossible not to read Bowman's sacramental act through the lens of the Eucharistic devotion of millions of the faithful over countless centuries.

Nobody is worthy of the presence of Christ. In the face of God, all are sinners. The point of baptism is to acknowledge that despite that reality, the grace of God nonetheless redeems and reconciles. Bowman's sacramental experience of sharing communion in prison recalls Rubin's conclusion about medieval Eucharistic practices: "From the very nature of its sacramental status, it belonged in every area of life, mediating between the sacred and the profane, supernatural and natural."[21] Eucharistic theology needs to continue to make this mediation between the sacred and the profane. One of the ways this occurs is by allowing the full mystery of its grace to be experienced by apparent outsiders and in places not obviously sacred. In many ways the Eucharistic practice of the church needs to be prodded to become, once again, a practice intersecting with and saturating the wider culture. To frame the question this way is to challenge the church to recover something of the diversity of medieval Eucharistic devotion outside the walls of the sanctuary, not to further confine it to that sanctuary.

To be faithful is to be redeemed and reconciled again and again. If that is true for believers, it must surely also be true for the half-believers, the agnostics, and those for whom the whole thing is deeply puzzling. This is why Christians have tended to push for Eucharist to be repeated more often rather than less often. The remembering is continual. As Rubin explains when discussing the beguines of the twelfth and thirteenth centuries, it is also deeply carnal. For the English theologian Robert Grosseteste, beguines like Juliana of Cornillon were, "the most perfect and the holiest in religion, because they live of their own labour and do not burden the world with their needs."[22] They also revealed a Eucharist devotion that is something understood by bodies better than minds:

> The *Vita* of Cistercian or beguine female saints reveal strong strands of eucharistic devotion in these circles, a fascination with the tangible, physical contact with the suffering Christ, through his offering of himself in so vulnerable a form in the world. Christ in the eucharist could be watched, adored, smelt, touched, and taken into one's body, and for some of these experiences little mediation was necessary.[23]

Rubin underlines the sense in which Eucharist opened up proximity to the divine. While the church has always sought to control and regulate Eucharistic experience, the beguines point to a more transgressive and radically inclusive experience of Eucharist. If we contextualize current discussions in the history of those more fluid times, we may have a better understanding of how the sacrament works, and who it works for. For the medieval women who were not allowed to participate fully in the institutional structures of the church, Eucharist provided an intimate and impassioned point of access to the holy. In the same way, God may still hope to use the physicality of Eucharist to reach out to those who are as yet outside the body of Christ.

The beguines were baptized. And yet, it is precisely because of their extraordinary devotion that it seems even more important to interrogate the order of baptism and communion. It may be that the church is being asked to surrender more control over Eucharistic access. Since the time of the beguines the church has moved away from yearly communion and to requiring individual confession before communicating the sacrament. Anticipating the logic of potentiality that drives Christian experience (which we shall explore in subsequent chapters), maybe Eucharistic practice needs to be more carefully crafted around potentiality. Maybe it should be less about who we *are* and more about who we desire to become.

The beguines lived at a time when the church was simultaneously culturally dominant as well as anxiously trying to ensure uniform access and uniform Eucharistic practice. This is no longer the context of most living within the West. Those yet-to-be baptized also have need of experiencing the marvelous drama of reconciliation, forgiveness, and the call to become one in Christ. Infant baptism is often argued for (or in some communities, rejected) on the basis of the nature of the grace of God. If God's grace is capable of including in Christian community a soul not yet, or no longer, in command of reason, it seems narrowing to suggest that God's grace cannot touch other souls as yet unbaptized. The church established early on how the unworthiness of the priest celebrating was not a barrier to Eucharistic grace. The people needed to be assured that the sacrament was valid, and truly conveyed God's grace. If an unworthy priest cannot impair the sacramental experience, then maybe an unworthy and unbaptized communicant may also not be a bar to its efficacy.

Retaining communion until after baptism risks restricting the operations of God's grace and turning Eucharist into a mechanical transaction. Theologically, it is not clear what prevents God's grace being present in Eucharist before baptism. Jesus did not call his disciples to first be baptized before following him. First, he called them to follow. And while the Last Supper was one of the last events of Jesus's ministry, it was a meal he freely shared with Judas, knowingly pointing him out as the very person who was going to betray him. Christ died for sinners, which suggests Christ might want to continue to share his Eucharistic body with sinners of all types.

The Episcopal Church, like the Church of England and other churches in the Anglican Communion, teaches that all baptized Christians are welcome to communicate in the Eucharist. For many (and in many dioceses, most) Episcopal congregations, all are welcome, whatever their baptismal status, to participate in Eucharist. There are important arguments for ecumenical unity behind retaining the requirement for baptism to precede communion. Moreover, Communion before baptism is not always accompanied by teaching about the centrality of baptism and Eucharist. Some of the most ardent supporters of "open communion" may be motivated less by theologies of hospitality or the proclamation of the cross, and more by a general reluctance to engage with or talk about theology and spiritual formation. Some proponents of "open communion" may even reflect uncertainty that anything significant occurs in the Eucharist. These approaches are unlikely to lead to a flourishing of new Eucharistic practices in the way that Juliana of Cornillon and countless of her contemporaries increased Eucharistic devotion and participation. If the church is to affirm the practice of Communion before baptism, it needs a theological approach rooted in both the scandal of the cross and Juliana's devotional commitment to the re-membered presence of Christ in the sacrament. For this to occur, we need to listen to voices like Bowman that return us to the theological question of where Christ is encountered, and for whom Christ suffered on the cross.

The pandemic has also provided a fresh lens through which to approach these questions. As churches closed their physical doors it became necessary to open new doors. At St. Thomas, Hanover, the video conferencing platform Zoom was chosen, allowing worship to remain as a live dialogue between priest and people. As part of this "remote" and geographically dispersed worship, Eucharist continued to be celebrated. In the medieval church, squints were carved into the church to allow people to see from the public part of the nave of the church the celebration of the mass as it was happening in private chapels. In a similar way, videoconferencing makes it possible for anyone with a device to squint in on the Eucharistic celebration. As Eamon Duffy has shown, squinting for the medieval church was not simply passive or alienating. It was a way of participating in the mystery of the sacring, the devotional moment that was of such importance in medieval times: the moment in the Eucharistic prayer when the priest elevated the consecrated Host. Viewing the Host was "the high point of lay experience of the Mass," and in large churches the timing of simultaneous celebrations of the Mass was arranged, "so that their sacrings were staggered, none preceding that at the main Mass at the high altar."[24] In contrast to classic Protestant critiques of such practices, Duffy is at pains to note how these windows onto the holiest moments in the mass were driven not by a clerical hierarchy but by the desires of the laity: "This was Eucharistic worship in which lay people called the shots."[25]

During the pandemic some found viewing the celebration to be a difficult and undesired experience. Yet for a great many others, like those in the Middle Ages before them, squinting at the Eucharistic celebration became a form of genuine Eucharistic participation. It was all that was available, and eagerly received. During the pandemic, the prayer of spiritual communion was one in which worshippers prayed their yearning that Christ might "come spiritually into my heart." Quoting the story of the woman who is healed by touching the hem of Jesus's garment, but not his body, the prayer invokes this same desire for healing that even though they cannot sacramentally receive, they might yet "be healed by like faith in You."

The pandemic made it impossible for even the most devout to receive the bread and wine. And yet the turn to the prayer of spiritual communion did not eliminate participation. Eucharistic grace was still experienced. Given a choice, the people of the bread would much prefer to receive bread and wine. Yet, whenever this is not possible, the pandemic has shown that hearing and seeing the sacramental actions can also provide spiritual sustenance. By refraining from live-streaming the consumption of Eucharistic elements, pastoral care was shown for those squinting, unable to consume. When communities are no longer forced to rely on electronic forms of squint, as they gather around altars again, they will be even more eager to share in the Eucharistic feast. Abstinence has not taught us to survive without communion. The yearning for physical communion is real. Abstinence has simply revealed how the liturgy of the Eucharist is more than mere mastication.

The church is not to be confused with the kingdom. And yet, the mission of the church is to announce and proclaim God's kingdom, the rule of love, in the here and now. The inbreaking of that kingdom is meant to reveal a new order, subverting human distinctions between insiders and outsiders, the weak and the powerful, the sinners and the saints, even that between the redeemed and the damned. If Eucharist is proleptic of the heavenly kingdom, Eucharist will mirror not simply a theology of the cross, but also a theology of hope. If that theology of hope does not include an eventual eschatological restoring of all people into fellowship with one another and with God, then it would make sense to restrict Eucharist to the baptized. If one's afterlife is a relatively select gathering, then Eucharist will reflect that. Alternatively, following the trajectory of thought of Origen and Irenaeus, one can envisage a model of God's kingdom that ultimately does not leave a single soul behind. The practice of Communion before baptism then becomes a foreshadowing of how Eucharist both anticipates and creates a similarly radical, and decidedly unworldly, universalism. Universalism is foreign to toxic Christianity. By contrast, for many of those on the *via media* it is difficult to imagine God's love unless seen through a prism of its essential boundlessness. Communion before baptism in such a model would invite people into community of love without borders, a sign of a kingdom not yet arrived.

THE MYSTERY OF EUCHARIST

Eucharist does not simply point toward God's restoring and gathering together of all people: it also enacts reconciliation. And as Hooker understood, it does this while remaining a mystery. The English word sacrament translates the Greek word *mysterion*. Every sacrament is meant to be a mystery. In the mysterious sacrament of the communal meal of bread and wine, seekers and faithful alike are re-membered by God and literally made into God's body in community with others.

Elizabeth's carelessness about her subjects' innermost beliefs and Hooker's Eucharistic agnosticism both accentuate the mystery. They point to how individual cognition about the Eucharist does not matter. It is not what we think, but what we do, and what we desire, that shapes participation in Eucharist. There is an interesting correlation here between this classic Anglican agnosticism and what Marion calls the "fecundity" of the Eucharist, and how it creates theological understanding.[26] Both point to how theology can never grasp Eucharist. Instead, Eucharist is the fertile site for encountering the possibilities of the Spirit drawing the faithful into deeper communion.

In more traditional language, this is the central Eucharistic mystery of how the Eucharist enacts life emerging out of death, both in the story of Christ, and in the lives of the participants. One of the clearest expressions of this simultaneously life-giving yet essentially unknowable fertility comes from the French philosopher and theologian Paul Ricoeur. Nearing his own death, Ricoeur wrote a final testament, *Vivant jusqu'à la mort*. In it Ricoeur describes "the grace of a certain kind of dying."[27] Ricoeur went on to draw attention to the agnosticism with which Jesus himself approached the Last Supper:

> The Last Supper conjoins the moment of dying unto oneself and serving the other in the sharing of food and wine which joins the dying person to the multitude of survivors reunited in community. This is why it is remarkable that Jesus never theorized about this or never said who he was. Maybe he didn't *know*, for he *lived* the Eucharistic gesture, bridged the gap between the imminence of death and the community beyond.[28]

Ricoeur's reflection is in keeping with Elizabeth's settlement and Hooker's prevaricating sensibility. He presents Jesus's final sharing of bread and wine as the site of deep theological agnosticism. Yet he also reveals how this agnosticism is not disempowering or disabling. Instead, Jesus's refusals (to say who he was or even what he meant by the Last Supper) create possibilities for the life-giving community. Ricoeur reminds us that the ultimate meaning of Eucharist is in drawing life out of death, granting life to the dying, and joining the living with those who have gone before them.

In Eucharist God literally puts us back together, by sharing in the broken body of Christ. Indeed, our individual experiences of dying to self, losing, failing, and falling, connect us to the life-giving plenitude of the sacrament. Through bread and wine, fragments of our lives become known to the God who was willing to be broken for all humankind. God does not hold our brokenness against us. God makes God's self known to the broken. To those who know failure and frailty, this gives hope that all may, somehow, be alright.

Eucharist also propels forward. In this reading Eucharist is also the key to how we may approach the scriptures with hope for a meaningful encounter. Rowan Williams notes that when Christians join a celebration of Eucharist they are not simply passive recipients of hospitality:

> they allow themselves to be interrogated by the story of Christ's self-sacrifice, to be questioned as to whether their present lives are recognizably linked with Christ's and to be reconnected by the renewing gift of the Holy Spirit.[29]

For Williams, faithfully communicating the sacrament is not simply about sharing in a past memory or becoming part of a community who will remember us and hold us up. Eucharist is also a question of accountability. It is the way that seekers and followers are turned into helpers, healers, and bringers of life to others.

Eucharist is fundamentally the living mystery of God's love transcending and defeating death itself. It is also the story of how God tries to make humans at home with God and with one another. Dwelling within the mystery is what makes all the difference, whatever one may or may not believe in one's heart, mind, or soul. Participation is a matter of life and death. Once again, belonging to God matters more than believing in God.

Williams is also correct: Eucharist is also one of the primary sites where we are "interrogated," "questioned," and "reconnected" with Christ's story. These are the ways we are prodded *not* to forget, ways that hold us from crossing the Lethe into an underworld of forgetting. Without such challenges, the faithful risk becoming overly comfortable. Contrary to popular imagining, Christianity is not about finding peace of mind. Rather, it is about bringing peace to others by challenging the misconceptions, illusions, and false certainties that flourish in those whose minds are firmly closed.

Remembering is more than a recitation of things learned from others. Remembering is an active process of moving from deathly forgetfulness to life-giving participation in the world. The same dynamic is found in the Greek word for truth. Truth is an unconcealing, what one might call a revealing in the act of remembering. Literally, the word truth (*aletheia*) is a movement away from forgetting, a compound of "*a*" and "*lethe*." To know truth is to reject the oblivion of the underworld Lethe. It is to be enfolded in the memory of the saints, those who remembered first, as well as the God from whom all memory arises. Eucharistic remembering shatters the assumption that we are fundamentally disconnected from the divine or from one another. Instead, it is a divine strategy for giving people from every race, language, and way of life a foretaste of how all are equally remembered and equally beloved. And, when they are no longer able to remember for themselves, the Eucharistic fellowship remembers for them, from generation to generation.

NOTES

1. Marion, *Self's Place*, 74.
2. Quoted by Rubin, *Corpus Christi*, 170.
3. "The sacrament of the altar," BL Royal 17 A 16, fol. 27 quoted by Rubin, *Corpus Christi*, 146.
4. Richard Kearney in Richard Kearney and Jens Zimmerman (eds.), *Reimagining the Sacred: Richard Kearney Debates God with James Wood, Catherine Keller, Charles Taylor, Julia Kristeva, Gianni Vattimo, Simon Critchley, Jean-Luc Marion, John Caputo, David Tracy, Jens Zimmerman and Merold Westphal* (New York: Columbia University Press, 2015), 258.
5. Marion, *God Without*, 149ff.
6. Marion, *God Without*, 157.
7. Marion, *Self's Place*, 50.
8. Henri de Lubac, *The Church: Paradox and Mystery* (New York: Alba House, 1969), 5.
9. Pauline Stafford, *Queen Emma and Queen Edith: Queenship and Women's Power in Eleventh-Century England* (Oxford: Blackwell, 1997), 56–57.
10. Rubin, *Corpus Christi*, 147.
11. Rubin, *Corpus Christi*, 12–35.
12. John N. Miner, *The Grammar Schools of Medieval England: A.F. Leach in Historiographical Perspective* (Montreal: McGill-Queen's University Press, 1990), quoted in Peter W. Travis, *Disseminal Chaucer* (Notre Dame, IN: University of Notre Dame Press, 2009), 66.
13. *The Book of Common Prayer*, 1549.
14. *The Book of Common Prayer*, 1552.
15. John Lewis Gaddis, *On Grand Strategy* (New York: Penguin, 2018), 133.
16. Diarmaid MacCulloch, *Thomas Cranmer: A Life* (New Haven: Yale University Press, 1996), 614.
17. MacCulloch, *Cranmer*, 615.

18. *The Folger Library Edition of the Works of Richard Hooker*, Vol. II, ed. W. Speed Hill, "Of the Laws of Ecclesiastical Polity" (Cambridge, MA: Belknap Press, 1977), V.67.12., 342.

19. Rubin, *Corpus Christi*, 66.

20. Hannah Bowman, "Communion without Baptism and the Paradox of the Cross," *Anglican Theological Review* Vol. 102.3 (Summer 2020): 391.

21. Rubin, *Corpus Christi*, 335.

22. Rubin, *Corpus Christi*, 171.

23. Rubin, *Corpus Christi*, 168.

24. Eamon Duffy, *The Stripping of the Altars: Traditional Religion in England 1400–1580* (New Haven: Yale University Press, 2005), 96–97.

25. Duffy, *Stripping Altars*, 114.

26. Marion, *God Without*, 157.

27. Paul Ricoeur, *Vivant jusqu'à la mort* (Paris: Seuil, 2007), 45, quoted in Kearney, *Anatheism*, 77.

28. Ricoeur, *Vivant*, 91, quoted in Kearney, *Anatheism*, 78.

29. Williams, *Edge*, 85.

Chapter Five

The Antiquity of Diversity

In Salman Rushdie's *Haroun and the Sea of Stories* a little boy goes on a fantastic adventure.[1] Haroun's father, Rashid, is a storyteller, and the plot revolves around his ability to entrance listeners with vivid and moving stories. Only the stories dry up; or as we discover, the tap that provides Rashid access to the sea of stories has been disconnected. It falls to Haroun to try and reconnect the tap, and he is inevitably pulled ever deeper into the strange world of those who maintain and manage the sea of stories.

Rushdie makes it clear that there is a magic in stories that is not wholly amenable to the inquiries of rational analysis. Haroun is introduced to a magical world of elves who regulate and maintain the story supply. The hero of Rushdie's story, however, is not the storytelling father. It is Haroun, the one who listens. Part of the paradox of Rushdie's book is that it is the attentiveness of Haroun to his father's storytelling that is ultimately redemptive.

This chapter explores a second classic spiritual habit of those seeking the *via media*: listening to, and responding to the scriptures. We have already seen how the Eucharist locates the believer's approach to the scriptures, generating a fertile hermeneutic. Some religious traditions view the text of scripture as conveying a single, perfect, pristine message that has been given by God. This message is clear, unified, and should not be questioned, far less doubted or debated. Scripture in this view has but one author and one meaning. As a convenient shorthand, I will term this approach, "literalist." One scholar has called the notion that scripture has only one meaning a "fantastic idea." He did not mean that literally.[2] This chapter investigates alternative ways of interacting with scripture that shed light on a more fertile hermeneutic: one that approaches scripture through the more imaginative lens of Haroun and Rashid and their journey to discover the source of the stories.

These alternative approaches are not solely the products of a Eucharistic hermeneutic. They also stem from what has long been known about the confusing and often contradictory messages within scripture. The complexities of scripture invite us to affirm its variety, richness, and pluralism. They also highlight the inherent difficulty of finding a singular overarching meaning to the texts. Scripture in this sense has much in common with postmodern ways of reading that listen to excluded and hidden voices. And yet, this approach is not a recent invention. As shall be seen, alternatives to literalism are amongst the oldest ways of reading. While these ancient ways of reading have been largely forgotten by proponents of toxic Christianity, these imaginative practices are inescapable for those traveling the *via media*.

For centuries, it was understood that scripture required a diversity of interpretations. As a convenient shorthand, we will describe this broad family of wildly diverse approaches to scriptural interpretation by the habit they promote: wrestling. Unlike literalists who seek to lock down meaning, wrestlers like Haroun and Rashid seek to open it up. One of the defining misconceptions shared by both toxic Christianity and militant atheism is the primacy given to literal readings. Thankfully, the testimony of Eucharistic experience, the tradition of the church, and the academic approach to scripture point in a different direction.

DAVID AND GOLIATH

One of the best illustrations of the need for wrestling rather than literalism is found within the scriptural story of the defeat of Goliath at the hand of David. This well-known story is told in the first book of Samuel, and deserves quoting in full.

> When the Philistine [the champion Goliath] drew nearer to meet David, David ran quickly towards the battle line to meet the Philistine. David put his hand in his bag, took out a stone, slung it, and struck the Philistine on his forehead; the stone sank into his forehead, and he fell face down on the ground.
>
> So David prevailed over the Philistine with a sling and a stone, striking down the Philistine and killing him; there was no sword in David's hand. Then David ran and stood over the Philistine; he grasped his sword, drew it out of its sheath, and killed him; then he cut off his head with it.[3]

It is a simple story of the defeat of the giant Goliath at the hands of the young shepherd boy David. And yet, in these four lines of text there are more questions than answers. How did Goliath die? According to these verses he was killed by the stone from David's sling striking the Philistine facedown and killing him. And yet, as the last line of the passage shows, *after* Goliath has already been named as killed by the stone and no sword, *then* David grasps his (presumably Goliath's) sword "drew it out of its sheath, and killed him." So how was he killed? By a sword or by a stone? Was he killed twice?

The biblical scholar David Gunn champions literary approaches to the Hebrew Bible. In his investigation of the story of David and Goliath, Gunn confronts this clear contradiction about the death of Goliath.[4] Yet, as Gunn discovers, once one starts to wrestle with the story the questions do not go away. They multiply. The more Gunn delves into the story, the more questions he generates. By the end of his exploration, he has more questions than answers. The David and Goliath story is not simply a problem of a modern English translation failing to be clear. The David and Goliath story is, rather, a microcosm of the problem of making sense of scriptures that have never been uniform or consistent. Attempts to resolve whether the stone or the sword killed Goliath only open up further questions. Nor is this simply a question of finding an earlier "more authentic" text. The more Gunn explores the history of the biblical texts, the more he discovers something very strange. As he puts it pithily, "The further into antiquity one seeks, the more diversity one finds."[5]

Scholars know that the harder one looks at biblical texts the more questions emerge. The further one goes back in time the more variety there is within the different texts that underlie modern translations. Add to that the fact that the creation of the canon, the authorized text of the bible, was a historical event that occurred very late in the Jewish experience, and not particularly early in the Christian experience (for obvious reasons). What we think of as the bible today is a construction of communities of faith in the early centuries of the Common Era. As part of this construction, no single pure and uncontested text of the scriptures has ever existed. In the sixteenth century when Protestants turned their focus to scripture they adopted most of the existing Roman Catholic canon of scripture, but most of them also cut out the Apocryphal books. If Christians cannot even agree on which books belong in the bible, how much less possible is it that we might be able to agree on whether Goliath was killed by a stone or a sword?

A literal approach to the David and Goliath story will always end up confounded and confused. The wrestling approach intuitively understands that the bible does not simply deliver truth neatly packaged. The bible frequently speaks in a plural voice, and about much more than whether a stone or a sword felled Goliath. Truth is instead something that "happens" in wrestling with the text. This is a little like the unconcealing of *aletheia* encountered in the last chapter. The truth of David and Goliath is not a simple historical question involving death by a stone or a sword. Rather, the plural truths of David and Goliath are to be found in wrestling with the text to discover meaning. Ironically, literalists and contemporary historical critical approaches often find themselves chasing the same chimera: one authentic, single, final, and authoritative text. By contrast, those who are willing to wrestle with the text can lay aside the need to find the "one" meaning of the text as they recognize how scripture has always spoken in a variety of ways. The challenge of wrestling with the scriptures is the challenge of being open both to the voices of historical criticism *and* to the possibility that the texts are still speaking. Their truths are not dependent on a singular historical reality. It is more complex, or in Marion's language, more fertile.

WRESTLING WITH ANGELS

The importance of wrestling is found throughout the bible. The book of Genesis tells the story of Jacob physically wrestling with an angel. Hosea 12.4–6 interprets the story as Jacob prevailing in his fight with an angel. But the Genesis text describes the one Jacob wrestles with as a "man." Only later does Genesis suggest that Jacob was wrestling with God. As even a conservative biblical commentator and theologian notes, "The struggle and its inconclusive outcome are highly ambiguous."[6] On the one hand the story recalls the struggle of Esau and Jacob in Rebekah's womb. On the other, it seems to be presenting the wrestling as another image of Israel turning away from God. And yet the way the conflict ends, with Jacob receiving a new name, has tended to focus this wrestling as a route toward the divine, rather than something to be avoided. By the end of the story we are told that this man/angel was actually God, and that Jacob has done the unlikeliest of things to occur in scripture, seen God "face to face." The story cannot help but generate a profusion of readings. Through the lens of this classic and ambiguous story of conflict we may yet deepen our understanding of what it means to wrestle with scripture.

Every encounter with scripture can turn into an unexpected workout. It would be misleading to imagine that wrestling is always a positive experience. In this case the wrestling leads to a blessing, and Jacob is renamed by God as "Israel" the one who has struggled with God and prevailed. However, as both earlier and later episodes in the story of patriarchs and Israel's narrative show, everything does not always work out quite so well.

Theologically, scriptural stories are sites of poetic encounter, presenting possibilities for drawing closer to the divine. In a way, each reader is like Jacob. The story suggests a need to become personally involved in the struggle to make sense of the divine. In his struggle, Jacob has his hip pulled out of its socket. In the same way, any encounter with the stories of God will effect change. What is particularly startling about this story is how Jacob's persistence wins. The encounter between Jacob and the man/angel/God only ends after Jacob agrees to let go. And the condition for letting go is Jacob's desire for a blessing. In responding to this request for a blessing, Jacob is told by the man/angel, "You shall no longer be called Jacob, but Israel, for you have striven with God and with humans, and have prevailed."[7]

Jacob's striving is one of the closest encounters with the divine recorded in the scriptures. It reveals a God found in visceral encounter. It also provides a model of the to and fro of argument and debate. God does not shy away from this engagement. Instead, God allows the struggle with Jacob to rage all night, finally giving Jacob new insight and new perspective. The story of Jacob is not the story of disinterested learning, carefully evaluating pros and cons. Instead, it is an experience more akin to that of a fighter in the ring, vulnerable and willing to put everything on the line. At the same time, it is a story resistant to understanding. Why is it that Jacob is able to see God "face to face" when scripture in so many other places suggests this is impossible for humans? And who really was the person Jacob wrestled with? If it was a man or an angel, in what sense was it also a "face to face" encounter with God? What are we to make of these paradoxes? And what are we to make of the paradox of this presentation of Jacob/Israel as seemingly disobedient toward God, and yet also seeking blessing? The story seems to create something of a feedback loop: it generates meaning not as we locate answers to these questions, but, rather, as we wrestle with them—just like Jacob.

Other forms of wrestling are found in the New Testament. The first disciples heard the stories of Jesus at first hand, and through interacting with those stories they learned who he was and the nature of his ministry. Jesus mostly spoke in parables, stories that are uniquely resistant to singular interpretations. Parables are extremely paradoxical forms of stories. They are not linear; they defy literalism and they throw down the gauntlet to listeners. They encourage diversity of interpretation, promoting polyvalence and multiplicity rather than uniformity or singularity.[8] This was a deliberate strategy of Jesus. Time and again, Jesus forced his listeners to forge meaning for themselves. He rarely explained. Instead, he reversed the expectations of what a teacher's role was. He did not limit complexity and he did not spell things out. He required his listeners to work to draw meaning out of his stories like water from a well.

While we are not hearing the stories first-hand, we interpret in the same position as those disciples. Some of the most arid debates arise from questions concerning how one should interpret scripture. Should a certain passage be read literally, metaphorically, or symbolically? Or are there other forms of interpretation? Part of the gift of viewing the scriptures as forms of wrestling is that many of these questions fade into the background. At the same time, if we are to give scripture what it deserves we need to be aware of how others have wrestled with the text. We need to be willing to learn from their grappling, and the practices of interpretation of previous generations and different ecclesial communities. The Episcopalian or Anglican rarely approaches scripture through a confessional prism. We are instead given the extraordinary liberty of learning from all those who have faithfully wrestled with the text.

This requires readers to be particularly attentive to the interpretational practices of the reading communities that first forged and then continued to interpret the Hebrew Bible. Judaism has always intuited much better than Christianity how scripture solicits interpretation. It does not manifest meaning. While Christianity has often misrepresented itself to appear as if it only had one way of reading a story, Judaism encourages debate, discussion, and disagreement about textual interpretation. Through the rabbinic tradition of Midrash there is a robust tradition of textual wrangling and wholehearted engagement. Midrash affirms the polyvalence, the multiplicity of levels of meaning, that arise from the scriptural text. Rabbinic commentaries engage in seemingly endless debate and discussion.

MULTIPLYING MEANINGS

There have always been times when something similar was true within Christianity. Throughout the early centuries of Christian belief and through the medieval period, Christian readers were comfortable viewing scripture as inherently plural and capable of generating different interpretations. The fact that these are not better known makes it more critical that we examine them further.

The literal approach to understanding the scriptures was always found hand in hand with a variety of other approaches in the early church and its medieval successor. The apostle Paul was first to use the word allegory, but in the early centuries of Christian practice allegory became increasingly popular. Origen of Alexandria (c. 184–254) was one of the first theologians to articulate the idea that certain difficult passages of scripture did not easily give up their meaning if we restricted ourselves to a literal interpretation. These "stumbling blocks" were, instead, he argued, passages designed to alert the reader to a deeper spiritual (and non-literal) meaning to the text. By the third century Clement, also of Alexandria, was using allegory to interpret passages of the bible as pointing to timeless truths rather than their literal meaning.

By the fourth century, Tyconius was developing a fully-fledged interpretational strategy of his own. Although Tyconius was a Donatist (a group who disagreed with the Catholic understanding of the validity of the sacraments), his ideas were taken up and developed by one of the best known of all anti-Donatists: St. Augustine of Hippo. At much the same time, John Cassian (c. 360–435) constructs a fourfold way of interpreting, in which every piece of scripture is held to have four different dimensions of meaning: 1) the literal; 2) the allegorical; 3) the tropological, or moral; and finally, 4) the anagogical, or a level that signified things to do with the future. To translate one word "Jerusalem" into the fourfold, would be to interpret it to mean: 1) the actual city, 2) the church, 3) the human soul, and 4) the heavenly city, or our future home. Whether the text meant all four at once, or one of the four, or some other combination, was just one of the questions the early church wrestled with.

Cassian's fourfold would drive literalists mad. But it was just the kind of approach that was embraced wholeheartedly by the redoubtable creator of so much that is now appreciated as catholic orthodoxy. In St. Augustine's own words:

> Could God have built into the divine eloquence a more generous or beautiful gift than the possibility of understanding the same words in several ways, all of them deriving confirmation from other no less divinely inspired passages?[9]

Across the medieval period this delight in textual pluralism magnifies. Commentaries (or *glossa ordinaria*) are written that pull together the insights of the patristic period. They sought to expound on the text by gathering into one place all the interpretations of earlier writers. These are then followed by the development of *quaestiones*, or series of questions and answers, as theologians and scriptural commentators wrestled with the texts. These approaches did not seek to unlock a singular meaning to scripture. They were instead, like rabbinic midrash, ways of rejoicing in the multiplicity of scriptural meaning. All of this occurs as the medieval world creates a strong culture of writing, one in which the elevation of the written word (*locutio*) runs parallel with the elevation of the divine Word (also *locutio*).

Brian Stock has drawn attention to the interplay of "orality" and "literacy" as mutual moments within the formation of written textuality.[10] This textual development is part of the development from oral to written culture that has been extensively charted by other historians. M.T. Clanchy has examined this movement towards writing in detail.[11] Anselm of Canterbury, whom we encounter at key moments throughout this book, is on the cusp of this movement. Anselm is the first medieval cleric to fully press home the intellectual possibilities that arise within the textual revolution. In the words of Marcia Colish, Anselm was the "first thinker since the Carolingian age to make the patristic inheritance fully his own, to rethink it creatively, and to strike out in new directions."[12] Anselm stands as a symbol for the great flowering of subsequent writing: about God, about the scriptures, and about the ordinary implications of this within everyday life. Medieval culture saw a flowering of writing, understood as an inherently plural process in which a range of questions and interpretations multiply, apparently without limit.

Ivan Illich's illuminating reading of Hugh of St. Victor's *Didascalicon* analyzes in detail the practical aspects of the medieval sacred study of textuality.[13] Illich draws attention to the physical and visual dimensions of textuality that relate in turn to the incarnational status of medieval reading and writing. For Illich, textuality is intrinsically theological: "The Word becomes Flesh in the Book. Writing becomes an allegory for the Incarnation in the Womb of the Virgin."[14] Reading aloud in the monastic scriptoria adds another layer to this, with the written word retaining an oral dimension that connects in turn to the divine Word. For monks and nuns, the technological side of medieval textuality is always connected to the theological. Writing manuscripts was an important part of the monastic economy, and the circulation and devotional use of these texts was essential to their spiritual lives.

Half a century later comes the Reformation and its critique of such interpretative traditions. Instead, we move from a culture of writing to what Jacques Derrida and subsequent scholars have termed a culture of the singular Book. The invention of the printing press, and the rapid spread of this new technology, enabled new ideas to spread quickly. It also allowed the scriptures to be printed and bound in one volume for wider consumption. In the shift from manuscripts that were laboriously copied in monastic communities of prayer, new technology enabled the scriptures to become not simply accessible to a wider audience: they also became a commodity. Bound in one book rather than scattered over a library of scrolls or manuscripts, the bible becomes singular. It is impossible to underestimate the power of this physical move from multiplicity and variety within textual transmission to singularity. What used to be a library (*biblia*) becomes a book. And once everything is literally bound together, and translated in the vernacular, it is subject to new eyes and new singularities.

New ways of reading came to dominate. Gone is the "slow" theology of monastic contemplation and reading aloud in communities of faith. In comes the "fast" theology of individual reading and along with it new readers and reading sites. Like the democratizing effect of the internet, opening up the scriptures to a broader public did not always coincide with a deepening of reading habits. With even more disastrous effect in the early modern period, many approached the scriptures without the medieval intellectual reading habits that promoted multiplicity of interpretation. The vitality of Hebrew and medieval wrestling with a variety of interpretations degraded into a quest for one, increasingly literalistic interpretation. As Steinmetz summarizes:

> The medieval theory of levels of meaning in the biblical text, with all its undoubted defects, flourished because it is true, while the modern theory of a simple meaning, with all its demonstrable virtues, is false.[15]

Against the supremacy of the literal reading that dominates so many "modern" or literalistic ways of reading, the way of reading practiced by seekers of the *via media* has more in common with Jewish and medieval Christian practices. The Goldilocks approach to scripture knows that scripture will always generate plural rather than singular readings. Like the rabbis practicing midrash and medieval scholars searching for different levels of meaning, an honest spirituality fosters debate and disagreement. Miranda Threlfall-Holmes underlines this, showing how scripture is brimming with interpretational possibilities and identifying twenty-one different "nourishing ways" to read scripture. For those seeking freedom from stale literal readings, her work reveals the abiding freshness of a whole range of classic interpretational strategies.[16]

REIMAGINING THE STORY

In his informative exploration of American religious history, Peter Manseau explores both the diversity of American religious experience, and the hardship encountered by many adherents. Manseau offers a rich and complex series of vignettes describing the challenges faced by some of the most hidden figures of American life. In one of these, set at the time of the seventeenth century witch trials, Manseau examines the story of Tituba, an enslaved woman, possibly originally from South America.

Accused of being a witch at the start of the Salem witch trials, Tituba escapes execution. While two dozen of her contemporaries received the death penalty for their alleged role as witches, Tituba somehow survives. Manseau wonders what it was that enabled Tituba to escape. He suggests the answer may lie with the ability of Tituba, the "reluctant witch of Salem," to reframe the story of her witchcraft. Drawing on the work of Elaine Breslaw, we learn how Tituba's response to the charges was to "improvise an idiom of resistance" and "reframe her role in the drama." Unlike others who simply denied the story, Tituba became creative. She leaned into the story others had told, inhabiting it from within, even going so far as to supply details of the devil she was accused of consorting with. Rather than fighting against or rejecting the story, Tituba leveraged the story, creatively discovering meaning in it. Despite the treacherous role the story had assigned to her, Manseau concludes that she, "seems to have escaped execution at least in part because of her audacious attempt to control the story of which she had unwittingly become a part."[17]

If Manseau is correct, Tituba survived because she was able to creatively inhabit, and redirect, the story woven around her. She subverted the story and took control of it. Essentially, this is also what Manseau does with the conventional story of American religious history. In contrast to the notion that American religious history is the religious history of Puritan Christianity and its successors, Manseau gives voice to the full diversity of American interfaith experience. Introducing religion after religion, we encounter a plethora of different believers wrestling with remarkably different scriptures. Many of them were there right from the beginning, and some well before the start, of the colonial period. Native Americans, Chinese, Jews, Muslims, Sikhs, Mormons, atheists, and a plethora of others have wrestled with their religious beliefs on the American continent.

Tituba's story is a microcosm for how even the most powerless can embrace even a quite unpromising story and find redemption within it. Even those who are cast in the worst possible of roles, in her case that of a slave accused of being a witch, have the capacity to reimagine their stories. Tituba's retelling of the story others narrated opened up a new future for her. She did not remain a passive victim of the witch-hunters. Instead, she exercised her imagination to shape the story in a new way that leads eventually to her liberation.

Tituba's experience was remarkable, especially for someone subject to such prejudice. But the same essential dynamic is always at play when we encounter a story that puts us to the question. We can refuse to engage with the story. We can always deny it has any truth. Or we can try to glean some truth from it. This occurs when stories are allowed to be stories, and released from having a fixed content that is unchanging in all times and places.

POETIC LICENSE

This ability to imagine a wide range of meanings in the text is perhaps best understood by poets. Poets intuitively understand that words mean more than their face value. The Greeks viewed theology, reflections on the gods in their case, as a matter of *poesis* or poetic creation. It is no coincidence that many of the best-known writers in the Anglican tradition in terms of wider cultural memory have all been poets. John Donne and George Herbert were both poet-priests in the seventeenth-century Church of England who grappled openly with the divine. In the twentieth century, T.S. Eliot and R.S. Thomas did their own kind of wrestling, and have been hugely influential in shaping piety and poetry. As well as being perhaps the pre-eminent Anglican theologian of the twenty-first century, Rowan Williams is also a gifted poet. Louis William Countryman offers a sensitive and definitive reading of how this "poetic imagination" extends across the centuries of Anglican identity and tradition.[18] Another scholarly priest poet, Malcolm Guite, reaches back before the emergence of Middle English to remind us of the mythology and power behind even some of the most everyday words in this poetic imagination.[19]

From Guite's readings of the Anglo-Saxon poem *The Dream of the Rood* to his analysis of the poetry of Seamus Heaney, Guite reveals how theology grows out of the poetic struggle to respond to the mysteriousness of the divine. For those wishing to understand the sensibility of the classic Anglican *via media* the easiest way to experience its spirituality is to read poetry.

While the poet Mary Oliver has no declared religious approach, it is impossible to read her poetry without being led deeper into the spiritual. An explorer of the beauty, variety, and richness of nature, her descriptions of the natural also suggest ever fresh openings into the emotional world of the human heart. Oliver has an attentive eye for the mysteries, epiphanies, and tragedies of the natural world. In a sense her work is a kind of listening to what the medieval would have called the book of nature, the revelation that is woven into the tapestry of our environment. As she puts it, echoing one of the great insights of the mystics, "Attention is the beginning of devotion."[20] It is almost as if her poetry is saying how impossible it is to pay attention to the details, whether natural or human, and not begin to ponder more spiritual matters. And as we saw in chapter 3, the human capacity to wonder generates its own spiritual trajectory.

If the Episcopal and Anglican tradition learns anything from poetry it is that scripture is a *poesis* that has the capacity to intersect with, and shape, human experience. There is much poetry in scripture, and it is the more obviously poetic parts, such as the psalms, that are often the most spiritually generative. We need poets to show us how to imagine. Scripture certainly contains many different genres, and when it comes to reading scripture the best guides are poets. The notion that there is a final meaning to scripture is as patently silly as the idea that there is only one official reading of a particular poem. The poetic imagination is inherently hospitable to a diversity of viewpoints. It also encourages, and feeds off, the kinds of courageous struggles that are defining features of spiritual growth.

THE FREEDOM OF A CHRISTIAN

Martin Luther did perhaps more than any other individual to draw Christians back to the reading and study of the scriptures. For years he wrestled with the attempt to know God and to find out how best to respond to God. His breakthrough came when he realized that wrestling with the scriptures was ultimately about being open to receiving them as good news. The scriptures offered him a way to leave guilt and failure behind while embracing the knowledge that it is God alone who does the work of rescuing and restoring us. Luther's motto, *sola scriptura*, or by scripture alone, became one of the rallying cries of the Reformation. Along with *sola fide*, by faith alone, and *sola gratia*, by grace alone, Luther underlines how scripture, faith, and grace were the ways in which God rescues humanity from life and death struggles with meaning and salvation.

Luther's turn to scripture broke apart the Christian world, and few churches have been untouched by his insights. For Luther, the scriptures are where Christians experience the saving love of God, or "justification by faith." Without scripture the transmission of that knowledge is impossible. What is less well remembered is that Luther also had a profound understanding of just how alien the scriptures were. We already saw in chapter 2 how grace and faith were alien for Luther. Luther also experienced God's grace not through the knowledge *about* the scriptures, but instead through reliance on what he called the "alien Word" that is scripture.[21] The struggle for Luther was always profoundly existential. The true meaning of scripture is not discovered through scholarly debate, but in treating it as an alien Word that confronts and challenges our human wisdom. Like Tituba, Luther realized that he was already caught up in a story, and that the only way out was to creatively claim that story as one that provides liberation.

As Luther realized, it is because scripture is alien to conventional wisdom that it is worth engaging with and relying upon. The purpose of scriptures is not to be venerated or admired. Their purpose is to show the faithful, and the would-be faithful, the stories they need to wrestle with. Where do the stories challenge? How do they shape decision making in the present? What do they say about the purpose of life? These are not disinterested questions for others to answer. They may lead to agnosticism or atheism just as easily as to faith. Yet, for seekers the strange stories of the scriptures are gateways through which life's central questions are encountered. Adapting the words of Pope Gregory, Luther wrote, "An elephant drowns in this sea [of scripture]; a lamb that is looking for Christ perseveres, stands on firm ground and reaches the other side."[22] Lovers of the Goldilocks God share the concern that it is possible to drown in the scriptures. Those traveling on the *via media* also recognize that the remedy for drowning is to travel lightly, focused on the search for the presence of God in Christ.

Whether or not everything is "true" about the scriptural stories is of secondary importance to encountering through them the truth of God's forgiving love in Christ. Part of the purpose of scriptures is to dislocate and confound our ordinary interpretations. Elephants will always drown in them. Scriptures are not designed to be readily understood. Scripture instead speaks an "alien Word" that forces listeners and readers to wrestle with it.

Luther's 1520 manifesto, *The Freedom of the Christian*, addresses the paradox of how a Christian is always free, lord of all and a servant of none; and yet also dutiful, subject of all and servant of all. To be Christian is to be free. And yet to be free, as a Christian, is also to serve others. We are not free simply to do anything. We are free to serve God and our neighbor. And it is only because the faithful, and the would-be faithful, read about being beloved by God in the scriptures that they are able to receive this liberating knowledge.

One of the tragedies of Christianity is that for all his brilliance, Luther did not take his insights far enough. He recognized how the church of his day was holding people back and not helping them claim their liberation. And yet, when it came to interpreting the bible, he did not allow this liberation to be total. Luther was a man of his times. And so his reforming efforts did not usher in a new era of creative biblical interpretation. Instead, if anything, they ushered in a new form of orthodoxy: a fresh limiting of what the text might mean. So keen was he to distinguish reforming Christianity from that which went before that he did not extend Christian freedom to those who disagreed with him on how to interpret the scriptures. Luther's freedom for Christians was the freedom to be a very particular kind of Christian. The strange approach of those exploring the *via media* is different: to embrace both the freedom of the Christian, and the idea that others might construe this freedom in different ways.

WHY HERESY MATTERS

It is important to clarify that there need to be limits on this freedom if the *via media* is to retain integrity as a route to the divine. One of the great confusions within contemporary Christianity relates to the role of heresy in the early church. Today we conventionally use the word heresy, if at all, as a word that describes a belief that is so far outside of mainstream opinion as to be unthinkable. That was never the case in Christianity. Heresy was, rather, the word used to describe opinions that were too close for comfort to the mainstream. These were ideas that were so prevalent and so ubiquitous that they were identified as existential threats to the faith. They were not so much unthinkable ideas as ones that were constantly being practiced, often deeply rooted in the most active communities of Christian faith.

Part of the joy for students of early church history is discovering how almost every "heresy" of the first seven or so centuries is alive and well, flourishing somewhere today. And the reason is simple. The word heretic comes from the Greek for "choose" and literally means someone who chooses to hold fast to a specific belief about Christ. Heretics were not innovators or radicals. For most of the early church period the heretics were never unbelievers. It is only in the later medieval church that the label heretic becomes misapplied to those standing firmly outside the church (who, technically, never believing in Christ, could never be accused of choosing certain beliefs about Christ). Strictly speaking, a heretic is someone holding on too fast to something: not an outsider who believes something different, but an insider who has given up on listening to the constant stream of often quite innovative attempts to make sense of the Christian story.

In early church history a more helpful word, used with due caution, for the heretic could be "conservative." Heretics held diverging opinions, opinions that in many cases were the tried and trusted beliefs of the church. Heretics were never anti-Christian. In a remarkable number of cases, but not all, they were old-fashioned loyalists: the ones who resisted moving with the times.[23]

The birth of orthodoxy was a messy argumentative affair, challenging many conventional assumptions. In order to think through the logical implications, for example, of how God might be one but also three, a whole set of technical language is deployed from outside of scripture. The orthodox were in many cases innovators reaching for language outside scripture to press into service to explain the complexities of God's presence in the word. Orthodox innovators like Athanasius or Gregory of Nyssa pushed the envelope, forcing the church to think more deeply, arguing for a more expansive understanding of the Christian story. They did this not out of a desire to innovate for the sake of it, but out of a prayerful desire to understand and experience the divine life. The flip side of the history of heresy is that heretics were also deeply sincere believers, with a passionate commitment to one dimension of the Christian story.

This is where the metaphor of Goldilocks can potentially illuminate. Heretics were generally either too hot or too cold. Often they were fighting either for or against a particular understanding of who Jesus was. Some argued consistently against him being fully human in an effort to ensure his divinity. Others argued consistently against him being fully divine to guarantee the sovereignty of God or maximize the humanity of Jesus. Essentially, Christian orthodoxy emerges as a middle position that safeguards both positions. For example, in Christology, orthodoxy guarded both the insight that Jesus was fully human and the intuition that he was fully divine. What is fascinating is that there was in no sense a compromise between these two perspectives. Instead, a new position emerges that holds on to both critical beliefs at the same time. Intriguingly, it was only after first trying (and rejecting) the extremes of heresy that it becomes possible to create the Chalcedonian orthodoxy of 451. As so many have noted, Chalcedonian orthodoxy did not define exactly how the two natures (divine and human) are related. It simply stated full divinity and full humanity, leaving the details to the imagination. In this it was proto-Elizabethan. Unlike heretics who needed to reject other positions as wrong in order to hold onto their own belief, orthodoxy was more comprehensive. And more comfortable living within the uncertainty it created.

Those debates continue. The faithful are always engaging with new thoughts and developments in human understanding. Christian thinking occurs not by sticking doggedly to the insights of previous generations, but by struggling in each age with the questions of faith. As these debates grow out of the church's quest to grow closer to God, they often lead to the discovery of new middle ground.

Heresy continues to thrive where communities prefer to stick with what they know rather than engage with the challenge of locating God's presence in community with others. If truth is a matter of unforgetting and revealing, it can never simply be a matter of deciphering the notes of others. It must also entail rediscovering and reimagining the life of faith in the light of new insights. Wrestling is the action by which seekers overcome the basic human instinct to forget and ignore those who have struggled before them. It is how the faithful enter the interpretive community of people who continue to care enough about one another to take the time to disagree.

Disagreements allow travelers on the *via media* to write themselves into the story of Jacob and the angel. More important than false unity is the shared recognition that out of theological differences, and because of those differences, humans discover what it is to yearn for God. This is also why the chair breaking Goldilocks is such a good model for the spiritual life. For Anglicanism to continue to be a viable tradition that is hospitable to plurality and difference, new generations need to learn again the lessons of Chalcedonian orthodoxy. The middle way is not a compromise. Rather, the *via media* emerges when faithful wrestlers, who disagree profoundly with one another, commit to sitting at one another's feet.

NOTES

1. Salman Rushdie, *Haroun and the Sea of Stories* (London: Penguin, 1991).

2. David Steinmetz: "The notion that scripture has only one meaning is a fantastic idea and is certainly not advocated by the Biblical writers." in "The Superiority of Pre-Critical Exegesis," *The Theological Interpretation of Scripture*, ed. Stephen E. Fowl (Oxford: Blackwell, 1997), 31.

3. *New Revised Standard Version*, 1 Samuel 17:48–52.

4. David Gunn, "What does the Bible Say: A Question of Text and Canon," 242–61 in *Reading Bibles, Writing Bodies: Identity and the Book*, eds. Timothy K. Beal and David M. Gunn (London: Routledge, 1997).

5. Gunn, "Bible," 259.

6. R.R. Reno, *Genesis* (Grand Rapids, MI: Brazos Press, 2010), 245.

7. Genesis 32:27.

8. John Dominic Crossan, *Cliffs of Fall: Paradox and Polyvalence in the Parables of Jesus* (New York: Seabury, 1980).

9. Augustine, *De Doctrina Christiana*, trans. R.P.H. Green (Oxford: Oxford University Press, 1995), 169–71.

10. Brian Stock, *The Implications of Literacy: Written Language and Models of Interpretation in the Eleventh and Twelfth Centuries* (Princeton: Princeton University Press, 1983).

11. M.T. Clanchy, *From Memory to Written Record: England, 1066–1307* (Oxford: Blackwell, 1993).

12. Marcia Colish, *The Mirror of Language* (Lincoln, NE: University of Nebraska Press, 1983), 53.

13. Ivan Illich, *In the Vineyard of the Text* (Chicago: Chicago University Press, 1993).

14. Illich, *Vineyard*, 122.

15. Steinmetz, "Superiority," 37.

16. Miranda Threlfall-Holmes, *How to Eat Bread: 21 Nourishing Ways to Read the Bible* (London: Hodder and Stoughton, 2021).

17. Peter Manseau, *One Nation Under Gods: A New American History* (New York: Black Bay Books, 2015), 114.

18. Louis William Countryman, *The Poetic Imagination: An Anglican Spiritual Tradition* (Maryknoll, NY: Orbis Books, 2000).

19. Subsequent chapters will return to the theology of these connected topics: while chapter 8 investigates imagination, the question of myth is explored in chapter 10. See Malcolm Guite, *Faith, Hope and Poetry: Theology and the Poetic Imagination* (London: Routledge, 2016).

20. Mary Oliver, *Blue Iris: Poems and Essays* (Boston: Beacon Press, 2004), 56.

21. Heiko A. Oberman, *Luther: Man between God and the Devil*, trans. Eileen Walliser-Schwarzbart (New Haven: Yale University Press, 2006), 226.

22. Oberman, *Luther*, 309.

23. For an accessible introduction to the classic heresies see *Heresies: And How To Avoid Them*, eds. Ben Quash and Michael Ward (Grand Rapids, MI: Baker Academic, 2007).

Chapter Six

The Promise of the God Who May Be

We have seen how Queen Elizabeth was able to imagine a fresh path that did not fit neatly with the expectations of either her Catholic or Protestant subjects. She created new possibilities by reframing what was important about the spiritual practices and beliefs of her people. As we saw in the Eucharist, by avoiding taking a clear position on the most controversial theological issues of the day, Elizabeth and Hooker invented fertile space for others to create their own spiritual possibilities. Keeping her options alive was also the key to Elizabeth's marital situation, deferring a choice, playing suitors off against one another. It was also the essential plank of her domestic and international policy, as she allowed others to take the risks, refrained from grandiosity, and was careful never to overstretch her means.

A.N. Wilson describes how Elizabeth responded to her advisors demands that she should be Catholic or Protestant, marry, fight a decisive war in Ireland or the Low Countries: "In almost all cases, Elizabeth had dithered, Hamlet-like; and dithering had been if not the right policy, then at least not the wrong policy."[1] This strategic capacity to dither, what could also be called the ability to keep the future open, is a classic example of the neologism "possibilizing," the activity of creating, and keeping open, a wide range of possibilities. Dithering does not lead inexorably to the fate of Hamlet. For Elizabeth it was quite the opposite. Her wavering was a conscious policy of maximizing life-giving possibilities. It may also be interpreted as a sign of spiritual creativity.

The last two chapters focused on two fundamental spiritual and religious experiences: God's presence in the world through Eucharist, and acts of wrestling with the scriptures. Both are key spiritual practices which open up the future for their practitioners. Yet, what is missing to this point is how the spiritual life receives propulsion and purpose not solely from an encounter with the past but also the future. Presenting, and keeping alive, a multitude of possibilities is not simply good strategic policy. It is also excellent spiritual advice.

The quintessential sacramental Christian experience of possibilizing is baptism. In baptism Christians make promises, choosing God's grace, forgiveness, and love as the pattern for living. Baptism also forms a natural counterpoint to the sacramental remembering of Eucharist. Understood as the point of initiation into the body of Christ, baptism operates in a nonlinear way. Christians return to, and renew, their vows throughout their life's pilgrimage. With every baptism, the baptismal vows of the faithful are re-energized. Baptism cannot be lived without Eucharist or wrestling with the scriptures, just as Eucharist cannot be isolated from baptism.

To better understand the question of divine possibilizing, this chapter will explore a constellation of three elements. First, we will address the possibility that is spiritual and theological power, noting the difference to secular construals of power. Second, we will uncover how worship, in the performance of liturgy, creates possibilities. Third, we will analyze baptism in the light of these two explorations: as a sacrament of potentiality that opens up possibilities that are, strictly speaking, beyond imagining. Baptismal faith as the ability to entertain the possible, and to practice the habit of possibilizing, joins all three elements together. What emerges from these explorations is a way of approaching and responding to God not as an object, but as a giver of possibilities. The picture of God that emerges from this investigation owes a great deal to Richard Kearney's theological work, in particular his analysis of "The God Who May Be."[2]

First it is helpful to remember how language about God is always bound up with the concrete experiences of those who encounter God. Reflecting on the question of theological language, Rowan Williams quotes the Australian cartoonist Michael Leunig on how he first learned to use the word God:

> I have come to regard God as a one-word poem—probably a folk poem. I learnt it from my parents when I was a child, as they wandered about the backyard or in the house. My father might say rather despairingly, "Where in God's name is the bloody hammer?" and my mother might answer "God only knows."[3]

From these humble beginnings, Leunig delves into how problems of talking about God persist. As we saw in the first chapter, in struggles over apophatic and cataphatic language, spiritual cartographers are like the father who has lost the hammer. Leunig recognized how it is not always clear what religious language is saying. Language for God is always part of something else. It is always elusive as we fail to understand what we mean by our words. Analogies and metaphors always break down.

Which is a very good thing. It is because words are not fixed to a clear and unchanging reality "out there" that they are so good at generating meaning. As we saw with scriptural interpretation, texts make more sense when they are allowed to generate multiple meanings. This begs the next question: if that is true for scripture, could it not also be true for human lives? The spiritual life is not a track that leads inexorably in only one direction so much as an adventure with different trajectories.

THE POWER OF POSSIBILITY

Just as Leunig's "folk poem" God has many different interpretations, so there are different ways of thinking about divine power. The Greek New Testament word for power is *dunamis*, giving us the words dynamic and dynamo. If someone is dynamic we are saying they are full of power and energy, often of the rhetorical kind. To call someone a dynamo is to point out that they are the kind of person who gets things done. They are probably not literally making electricity. Helpful as these words are they obscure as much as reveal. The *dunamis* of the New Testament is something different from electrical, motive, or even rhetorical power.

When Paul talks about the power of God, the *dunamis* of God, he means a qualitatively different kind of power. It is not even the worldly power of a mighty President or Monarch. Instead, for Paul, God's power is revealed in weakness and powerlessness. This *dunamis* is seen in its sharpest form in the crucified One, who Paul terms a stumbling block to the Jews and foolishness to the Greeks. This is the scandal of the cross of Christ encountered in Eucharist. As Kearney puts it, "By choosing to be a player rather than an emperor of creation, God chooses powerlessness."[4] Christ's power is not a power that rules over others. Instead, Christ's *dunamis* subverts human power structures. Christ's *dunamis* is the power of things that are impossible for us but possible for God. The power of the powerless.

One of the problems with translating *dunamis* is that, strictly speaking, the Greek can be understood in two ways. It can mean *dynamic power*. But it can also mean *dynamic possibility*. Once we start to read *dunamis* as dynamic possibility this takes us in new and important directions. This understanding of possibility emerges from Kearney's exploration of God as possibility itself. Marking a break with traditions of philosophy that seek to circumscribe God as Being or within some philosophical schema, Kearney engages philosophy with the scriptural experience of God. For Kearney, the God who emerges as *posse* (possibility) rather than *esse* (being) is a God who is much more tentative than the domineering God who exerts power over others. This God "who may be" also bears comparison with the trajectory of Jean-Luc Marion's phenomenological approach to God without Being.

Kearney points us back to Nicholas of Cusa, the first theologian to describe God not as actuality but as possibility. Cusa reacted against conventional medieval understandings that reached back to Thomas Aquinas and Aristotle. Against them, Cusa mints the word *possest* combining *posse* and *esse* to express how God is the possibility to be.[5] Kearney echoes this by reimagining God as "The God Who May Be." Like Marion, Kearney argues for a God enclosed not by metaphysics but by an essential unknowability that nevertheless allows for self-disclosure at key moments: "In the circular words, I-am-who-may-be, God transfigures and exceeds being. His *esse* reveals itself, surprisingly and dramatically, as *posse*."[6] Kearney's tentative possibilizing God neither rains down fire and brimstone nor wages triumphalist battle against infidels and non-believers. This God is not the toxic domineering God. Instead, this God of possibility is revealed in the powerless. Here divine power is experienced in hospitality to strangers, serving the weak, healing the sick, and helping the vulnerable.

This approach to God's power not only combines the postmodern (Kearney) and the medieval (Cusa). It is also deeply Eucharistic and scriptural. The passage in which Kearney describes this strange possibilizing power also has key poetic resonances:

> this God is much closer than the old deity of metaphysics and scholasticism to the God of desire and promise who, in diverse scriptural narratives, calls out from burning bushes, makes pledges of covenants, burns with longing in the song of songs, cries in the wilderness, whispers in caves, comforts those oppressed in darkness, and prefers orphans, widows, and strangers to the mighty and the proud.[7]

The possibilizing power of God is something feminist theologians and mystics have pointed to for some time. In later chapters we shall explore how, for both groups, longing and desire manifest the essence of God.

Carter Heyward also saw the *dunamis* of Jesus as revealing what she called "the possibility of our own godding."[8] For Heyward, the verb godding reveals divine possibilities to be closer to us than we imagine. Relationality is an intrinsic part of this. We are not observers or supplicants to God's power. Godding is instead about connecting and relating our capacity for relationship to God's. This relationality is something theology and philosophy have not always understood. Often obfuscated by patriarchy, God's possibilizing power is better understood not as a kind of neutral mathematical theory so much as an invitation to embodied relationships.

Heyward's godding and Kearney's tentative God "Who May Be" both help frame how God may be encountered not simply in scripture, but also in the liturgical experience of Christian worship. While liturgy is a tradition inherited from the past, it is even more a way of becoming entangled in the divine. Liturgy makes it possible to have an embodied encounter with the divine that is deeply relational. While liturgy does not encapsulate all of the possibilities of godding, worship is where the wrestling started by scripture is woven into the longings of the human heart.

To speak of a spiritual thermodynamics in this context is to name how divine power is seen in possibility, relationship, and powerlessness. It is to remember again the aspect of Elizabeth's story in which the relatively powerless island Queen faces down the overwhelming might of the Spanish Armada. Ranged against the mighty forces of Philip II, king of a colonizing Spain whose empire stretched across Old and New worlds alike, the powerless Elizabeth opened up possibilities by prevaricating and playing for time.

PERFORMATIVE POSSIBILITIES IN THE LITURGY

Worship shapes how hearts, minds, and souls encounter the power of God's relational possibility in the middle of everyday life. So what can the performance of liturgy reveal about God's possibilizing power? Part of the purpose of liturgy is to provide language for engaging with God that others have found successful.

This is not to have romantic notions about the chorus always being in tune or correct. Worship so often misses the mark, with moments in which worshippers feel like Leunig's father: wondering where the bloody hammer is. Yet this wondering is also an essential part of liturgical life. It does not diminish the potential power of liturgy. Rather, it reveals the depth and breadth of the power of liturgical language.

Human language and intellect will always fail to make sense of the possibilities of God. Liturgy is the ancient and ongoing way that humans are shown there is no shame in this. We do not *have* to make sense of God. The power of liturgy is found partly in acknowledging how this trickiness constitutes the horizon upon which encounters with God may occur. Humans enter the Wittgenstinian "language game" of worship precisely because it gives them access to something far beyond individual comprehending.

My soul doth magnify the Lord. The difference between reading those words and worshipping *with* those words is not a minor difference of context. It is more like the difference between watching the World Cup and playing soccer with friends. One's soccer skills may be poor. Yet, in playing even the most halting form of soccer, we are closer to experiencing the truth of soccer than when we watch a team win the Premiership. Participating, however poorly, fleetingly or fitfully, in words of prayer and worship creates intimacy with the divine.

Outside the liturgy, words (sacred or secular) describe truths that may or may not be objectively true. Inside the liturgy, the same words describe potentialities and possibilities that can also be subjectively true for us. This is part of their power to make things possible, to possibilize. There is also another aspect to the performative power of liturgical prayer. It is not simply that words have a new context. There is also the matter of where these words come from and where they are going. Words of worship situate us as being addressed *by* the divine. To experience the liturgy is to be addressed not just by human words, but also by a divine Word. And to be called to respond. This is partly what Marion sees in the Eucharist, one aspect of why it is the preeminent site of theological fertility. And yet, it can also be true of other liturgical experiences.

The divine Word, in Greek the *Logos*, is another way of describing God as the creative principle that orders all life. Through the person of Christ, we are asked to imagine the somewhat outlandish possibility that this divine intelligibility was manifest, incarnate, in one particular person. To believe that this Word was made flesh, the incarnation, is to believe that God was possibilized in the person of Christ. To inflect it with Heyward's language, Christ is the supreme instance of godding. Yet this is not the only way in which the Word is possibilized. It also occurs in the words of the liturgy, when the divine Word is spoken by human beings, pronouncing God's possibilities in the here and now. Worship makes the Word real again. It makes Christ present. And that presence constitutes new trajectories of spiritual possibility.

Liturgy and worship are how we hear tell of these possibilities, some of which are past "mighty acts" of God in the world. Still other possibilities are promises made by God to those who believe. Faith, hope, and love are recurring themes within these divine possibilities. Liturgy names them, requiring both assent and response. We also hear the challenge of their implications. Liturgy is qualitatively different from scripture in that it is not simply a description of action. It is also an embodied performance that generates a new future for its participants.

While liturgical performance follows a scripted pattern of call and response, its power is in the unscripted movements of the heart that flow from this. Keeping the back and forth of dialogue alive was central to so much pandemic worship. Despite the challenges of unstable WiFi and the cumbersome choreography of unmuting, the dialogical nature of worship became even more precious and even more sacred. Liturgy makes it possible for participants to find themselves spoken into being. It does not simply put us on the spot or tell us things we already knew. It also shows us ways of living into the mystery of God.

We have not yet touched on how this mystery is inextricably woven into the mystery of God as Trinity. The Trinitarian mystery and the three Persons of the Trinity constitute the heart of the drama of Eucharist and worship alike. While chapter 8 explores the Trinity in more detail, for now the key dynamic concerns how mystery leads into Trinity, and vice versa. Without Trinitarian mystery, the fullness of Eucharist and liturgy cannot be experienced or conceived. In his famous analysis of the Trinity the *Monologion*, Anselm of Canterbury attempted to explain why the Trinity is necessary. After spending a considerable amount of time arguing for why the Trinity is rationally necessary, Anselm offers the following:

> It seems to me that the mystery of so sublime a subject [*tam sublimis rei secretum*] transcends [*transcendere*] all the vision of the human intellect. And for that reason I think it best to refrain from the attempt to explain how this thing is.[9]

This echo of apophatic method appears to beat the retreat for Anselm from further exploration of the Trinity. However, as it turns out, it is simply the spur for Anselm to try and decode and explain, using reason, the nature of Trinity with even more fervor. Anselm's reluctance to explain the Trinity is entirely genuine. At the same time, Anselm shows how *even* when we cannot understand the Trinity, something drives us to do precisely that. What Anselm says about the secret of Trinity may also be said about liturgy. It is best to refrain from attempting to explain it, *even* as we are drawn deeper into its possibilizing power.

Liturgy can feel like being grilled by a stickler for grammar: unpleasant, rigid, and soul destroying. It can also feel like having a chat with an old friend. In answering the gentle prodding of a companion there can be revelatory moments when one discovers, as if for the first time, what we *really* feel about something. Liturgy also has the capacity to reveal possibilities that we could never have entertained or come up with alone. It is not that the liturgy itself comes up with them. Instead, there is an oscillating movement between the words of the liturgy and the hearts and minds of those praying.

This possibilizing power of the liturgy can also be like drama. Not sentimental or melodramatic, but the kind of genuine drama that drives a stake through one's heart. The Greek *drama* literally means action, and it is in this active mode that liturgy creates possibilities. Something *has* to happen. Good drama does not deliver meaning intact or pre-prepared. It invites those watching to make something for themselves of the story unfolding before us. It might even be asking those watching to find their own place within the story. Rowan Williams describes how this happens even when we follow a very well-worn and familiar storyline (which is, of course, what liturgy becomes for those who return to it again and again):

> [And,] while we may watch a drama whose plot we know perfectly well, so that the outcome is not in doubt, we shall still be attending with the same intensity to see better how *this* moment opens and closes possibilities for the next (and beyond), hoping as we attend to see something of how it is that people "go on," follow what is said and done. We are hoping to understand human agency and interaction, hoping to see more clearly how and why this leads to that and so to become aware of larger possibilities for our own "going on."[10]

Discovering one's own "going on" is simply another way of describing the liturgical experience of possibilizing. The script becomes familiar with use. And yet, we still watch for what hints it provides about the way we might be "going on" outside of the script as well.

This is the generative power of worship. People worship because they are hoping to see more clearly. A liturgy becomes good where it engages the entire being of those participating. It draws them into the story. It makes it possible for them to ponder how the words connect with their individual lives. It offers what Williams calls the possibilities for "going on." People of every religious tradition turn to familiar words to help them discover how they will go on, and the full extent of the possibilities that God holds open for them.

The "going on" of Williams evokes again the language of Nicholas of Cusa about potentiality, the possibilities that lie ahead. As we saw in the dialogue between the Australian wondering where the hammer is and hearing the reply "God only knows" this is only part of the encounter. The letteral meaning of this dialogue does not encapsulate the totality of this exchange. The greater language game has us starting to wonder where the hammer might be.

BAPTISM—BACK TO THE FUTURE

The starting point for how Christians are equipped to face the future and receive God's possibilities is through the sacrament of baptism. Baptismal promises embrace a future that is life-giving. In baptism the fallen are made one with Christ, and shown what it means to be Christlike. In this sense, baptismal promises alert the would-be faithful to their inner potential. In baptismal promises the baptized receive the good news of God's love and forgiveness. In return, they claim the unique possibilizing power to be the person God would have them be.

The Italian philosopher Giorgio Agamben explores the theme of human potentiality in great depth. Agamben underlines how Western philosophy has not always been good at thinking through potentiality. Instead, it concentrates either on looking backward, at what has happened, or else on the present situation, at the "is-ness" of how things are. Since Aristotle first examined the question of potentiality, Western philosophy has privileged existence over potentiality. Agamben turns the focus instead onto the phenomena of potentiality associated with the experience of being human. Like Cusa, Kearney, and Heyward, Agamben affirms how possibility constitutes human experience.

Agamben recognizes that human potential is more obvious in the young, particularly infants. No one would dream of judging an infant for its achievements. We recognize that infants have enormous unrealized potential. It is entirely unremarkable to nourish that potential and avoid defining an infant by her past. Even the most myopic observer realizes that the future life of an infant will not be the same as her present. And yet, as people age humans stop marveling at their potential and instead fixate on what they are or, worse, what they have achieved. "Infancy" is the term Agamben gives to the significance of potentiality for human living and thinking.[11]

Theologians might add to this that baptism is God's way of revealing the horizon of human potentiality. And in baptism we claim the infancy that is our true calling. In the eyes of theologians, the potential and the reality of every person who is baptized is to be a saint. One of the reasons for baptizing infants is that infants reveal God's potentiality much better than adults. Babies cannot but help signify untold possibilities yet to come.

From a cognitive standpoint, infants who have been baptized do not know God in a rational or intellectual way. They have no understanding of creeds, sacraments, or scriptures. Nevertheless, none of this is the same as saying that they have no knowledge of God. And it would not be to say that God has no knowledge of them. A baptized infant belongs to, and is part of, the mystical body of Christ. God, through the wider community, makes it known that an infant (like every member of the baptized) becomes part of Christ not through any merit or achievement of her own. That is the fundamental point of Christian baptism. In this light, infant baptism may be a more powerful symbol of Agamben's infancy (of potentiality) than anything.

It is easy to forget that all children, young people, and adults have the same theological potentiality for goodness as a new-born. While there are those who think infants are born with indelible sin that needs to be washed away, this is not the prime function of baptism when understood as a sacrament of potential and promise. Baptism is not predominantly the removal of all stain. To be sure, the baptized are not miraculously free of failure or sin. Baptism is instead a reminder of how God's grace always precedes. By becoming part of a baptismal community, the baptized are reminded that the potentiality for goodness is never forgotten.

Jesus seems to have had a very strong sense of this. On several occasions, he is recorded as celebrating the potentiality of children. In one story he points out how the route to him passes through children: "Truly I tell you, unless you change and become like children, you will never enter the kingdom of heaven . . . Whoever welcomes one such child in my name welcomes me."[12] Jesus's emphasis, analogous to Agamben's affirmation of infancy, points to an essential dimension of Christian transformation.

It is not the individual's possession of faith that makes them faithful. Instead, it is God who makes people faithful by helping them perceive the world through the lens not of adult "knowledge" but rather the perspective of childlike trust, imagination, and curiosity. Political scientist and philosopher Jim Murphy's thoughtful exposition of the interrelationship between childhood and adulthood is instructive.[13] Murphy illuminates how important childhood is for understanding Christian theology. For Jesus, childhood and adulthood are not simply chronologically disparate or successive stages. They remain profoundly interconnected throughout our lifetimes. By combining this insight with Agamben's vision of infancy we begin to see the profound importance of locating baptism within a context of human potentiality.

In baptism the would-be faithful come to belong to a God who is all-loving and all-forgiving. It is a natural part of this belonging for Christians to move from seeing themselves at the center of everything to recognizing their dependence on the divine. In baptism, through no action of their own, the faithful (all of them, strictly speaking, "would-be" believers) are submerged in the depths of God's grace. This is a drowning of the old self, and a discovery of the new self, the potential self "to be" who is no longer distracted or disturbed by past failures.

Once experienced, Christians retain their baptismal knowledge. In keeping their promises, individuals find not only the full potential of their own lives, but, more importantly, they discover the potentiality of others. Baptism is never a sacrament of self-help. It is, rather, the sacrament of discovering how to extend grace to others. In baptism the community of faith discerns the action of God's grace in building the body of Christ with bodies of individuals who are far from perfect. The theological alchemy of baptism is to transform those who fail into people of the kingdom, people of the bread who feed others.

One of the reasons Kearney's theology of the God Who May Be is so deeply appealing is that the God Who May Be is found in this spirit of kingdom service. In discussing the resurrection appearances, Kearney locates Christ in a series of encounters with those on the margins:

> The post-paschal stories of the transfiguring *persona* remind us that the Kingdom is given to hapless fishermen and spurned women, to those lost and

wandering on the road from Jerusalem to nowhere, to the wounded and weak and hungry, to those who lack and do not despair of their lack, to little people "poor in spirit."[14]

Baptismal promises impel their bearers to imitate the One from whom they received their future. In return, God promises that humans will reach their full potential: "Beloved, we are God's children now; what we will be has not yet been revealed. What we do know is this: when he is revealed, we will be like him, for we will see him as he is."[15] In acknowledging how we are God's children the scriptures anticipate Agamben's infancy, not to diminish, but to affirm human potential. Part of the Christian reading of this potential is that the baptized will eventually realize their full potential. The kingdom, the power, and the glory constitute both the words of the doxology (in which the baptized praise God), and the promise of what lies ahead.

As a child I enjoyed playing the fantasy game *Dungeons and Dragons*. Made recently famous once again by the streaming hit *Stranger Things*, *D&D* is one of those wonderfully old-fashioned things: a role-playing game that requires one to be in the same physical space as fellow players. It also requires players to use their imagination to populate and explore dungeons full of treasure and danger. At the heart of *D&D* is the excitement of never quite knowing what will happen next. Thanks to the random chances of twenty-sided dice, no player knows how any given encounter will turn out.

The drama *Stranger Things* was successful, in part, because it understood this dynamic of close-knit community forged in make-believe. Generally, the baptized do not encounter too many fire breathing dragons, necromancers, or mercenary trolls. Yet, as part of trying to keep baptismal promises the baptized are asked to resist evil in other forms. Whether you think of them as evils, vices, or particularly virulent heresies, some beliefs and practices are firmly outside of the scope of Christian behavior. Cruelty, sexism, racism, xenophobia, and homophobia have thrived in every age. As have the seven deadly sins, or cardinal sins. Lust, gluttony, greed, sloth, wrath, envy, and pride are rarely topics of Episcopal or Anglican instruction, yet these traditional vices are a clear expression of what baptismal vows require the faithful to resist. Ignoring or pretending them away does not limit their power. And part of baptism is about working with others to defeat them.

Baptism names the worst sins explicitly as evils. Evil is always seeking to limit the possibilities for others. This is true of evils as varied as hunger, poverty, war, educational inequality, lack of healthcare, homelessness, and unemployment. These are all profoundly constraining. Theologians have long understood evil as the Augustinian *privatio boni*, the deprivation of the good. Through the lens of potentiality, we might add that part of the deprivation of the good is always a deprivation of the potentiality for further good. One way that we recognize evil is by its effects: and its tendency to limit human flourishing.

THE POSSIBILITY OF BEING KNOWN

Baptism asks those who would-be faithful to imagine a future that is held in common with others, and not simply those with whom they readily identify, whether religiously, culturally, or socially. Perhaps the most radical thing about baptism is that it asks humans to live *as if* God's kingdom has already arrived, when it is through keeping baptismal vows that the kingdom grows near.

If Eucharist is how God re-members the faithful, baptism is how God makes believers into one body in Christ, with the potential to be faithful. In baptism, seekers after God are literally made into the family of God's people, the communion of saints.

The suggestion of this chapter is that baptism is also the sacrament of divine cognition in which humans discover the full range of life-giving possibilities. It is not, as is perhaps more popularly imagined, a sacrament of limitation that defines who is inside or outside. Rather, it is the way the Christian church resists those who would seek to place limits on human flourishing.

Becoming a member of the baptized is about receiving God's promise that, in the name of the Holy Trinity, one's future belongs with Christ - and to Christ. After the gift of life itself, it is the most significant gift any human being can ever receive. This is why the believer's promises are substantial. Baptism is not a credential that can be pulled or not renewed at a later date. In baptism, God promises to the seeker that she belongs to God forever. This is also why it makes theological sense to allow Eucharist to prepare would-be believers for baptism, rather than only the other way around.

Clergy frequently hear from those worried about whether they believe enough propositions about Christian faith to be baptized. Others worry about whether they believe intensely enough to be baptized. It may be freeing to be reminded that baptism is not about interior belief. Baptism is instead about belonging to the family of God, the community to whom God delegates the work of loving and forgiving. The mistake of toxic Christianity has been to assume that God obsesses about mental states. I trust the reverse to be true: God does not desire intellectual assent. God wants us to sit down and share our porridge with others.

Baptism is how Christians begin. The spiritual thermodynamics of Goldilocks remind us that this beginning has little to do with our own action or intellect. Baptism is instead how the possibility of God's grace reaches out to proclaim God's forgiving love in the life of a sinner. There are traditions that proclaim the necessity of baptism to save souls from eternal hellfire. The perspective of those who seek the Goldilocks God is slightly different. Baptism is, indeed, a matter of life and death. But it is as much about life before death as the afterlife. God does not love the baptized any more than God loves the unbaptized. What makes the baptized different is that they have been chosen to be instruments of God's loving forgiveness this side of eternity—in the world. With that comes responsibility and accountability.

Baptism is how those who would-be faithful set sail on a lifetime journey home. Ever since Plato human beings have been aware that the world is not their home. Early Christians, following the death and resurrection of Christ, also experienced what the Swiss theologian Hans Urs von Balthasar calls "homelessness." Having lost Jesus twice, once in death, and once after the Ascension, the early church was bereft: "No longer at home in the world and not yet having reached their home in heaven."[16] Jesus had been their home, but with him gone, they set about finding their way home together.

What is fascinating about the early church is how the spiritual experience of homelessness did not drive the disciples to give up. As Balthasar notes, the promise of heaven spurred the earliest church to a ceaseless activity of making God's love present in the world. Keeping baptismal vows is strictly speaking impossible, as they create commitments that can never be entirely kept. Yet, they also reveal a possible future that would otherwise be impossible to imagine.

This forward facing dimension is also part of the efficacy and experience of Eucharist. Marion draws attention to the phenomenon of *epektasis*, first expounded by Gregory of Nyssa. *Epektasis* describes the straining forwards that is experienced in Eucharist. Although Eucharist is a sacrament of memorializing and remembrance, it also points believers forward: straining towards a new potentiality. As Marion explains: "The future as *future*, governs, runs through, and polarizes the eucharistic gift, thus 'straining [*epekteinomenos*] toward that which is coming to it (Phil. 3:13).'" He goes on to clarify that it is an "eschatological *epektasis*" that is experienced in the gift of the Eucharist, and made sacramentally present. What he means here is very similar to what Balthasar means by drawing attention to the yearning for a heavenly home. In this reading, Eucharist is an embodied sign and first fruits of the potentiality we have been exploring. For Marion, "The Eucharist anticipates what we will be, will see, will love: *figura nostra*, the figure of what we will be, but above all ourselves, facing the gift that we cannot yet welcome . . . In this way, 'sometimes the future lives in us without our knowing it' (Proust)."[17] Or to put it more simply, Eucharist is where we are made most aware of what we may yet become, even when we are unaware of it.

Within the *via media*, baptism is not primarily concerned with propositional belief or what happens after death. It is instead the mechanism by which fallible people experience and share the transforming potential of the love of God for all people. Christianity maps that love out, releasing believers from past failures to imagine better futures for themselves and others.

THE POSSIBILIZING POWER OF PRAISE

To recap briefly, we have explored the possibilizing *dunamis* power of the New Testament, Nicholas of Cusa, Richard Kearney, and Carter Heyward. Theological power is quite different from the power of the state to command armies or enforce laws. Instead, we have noted how theology imagines divine power as a *dunamis* of powerlessness, relationality, and possibility. Structurally and performatively, we have seen how liturgical performance conveys the possibilities for reimagining life. We also have seen how baptism, read through the lens of Agamben's understanding of potentiality, magnifies the possibilities of human flourishing.

The constellation of power, liturgy, and baptism arises out of promises humans make in response to the original promise of a God "who may be." Baptism is the site where human potentiality intersects with God's own promise of love and forgiveness to humankind. In baptism seekers are initiated into a spiritual adventure in community with others. To be baptized is to be grafted into a community responding to God's preferential love for the weak, the oppressed, the stranger, the immigrant, the alien, the widow, and the suffering.

Without hearing the possibilities of godding raised by the God Who May Be individuals struggle to discover their vocation to be the person they may be. Christian theology is always an interplay of the "always already" of divine presence and the "not yet" of eschatological becoming. Liturgy and baptism also inhabit this dynamic, revealing God's power in the unlikeliest of places: the lives of fallible human beings. The kingdom comes not at some distant future point far off, but in lives of prayer, service, and sacrifice. The God Who May Be is always already found by followers Who May Become.

All these factors are present in Frances Hodgson Burnett's classic story *The Secret Garden*. Mary and Colin both become whole through their willingness to explore and connect with the possibilities ahead of them. Their imagination awakens as they encounter and start to "like" others around them. This in turn connects them to a frequently recurring "magic," that somehow arises out of the natural world and the world of human connection. This magic is simply a metonymical substitution, another way of naming, the possibilizing, or godding that we have been exploring. Burnett makes explicit how this magic is not a relic of paganism. Rather, it has a profound connection to Christian worship. We see this where the two children link their "Magic" to its source in

God by exulting in the singing of the doxology. As Colin observes: "Perhaps it (the Doxology) means just what I mean when I want to shout out that I am thankful to the Magic . . . Perhaps they are both the same thing."[18] Within the current context, we might agree. The praise of doxology relies on a glory that is sourced beyond. At the same time, that glory, *á la* Marion, resides in, and springs from, those who are formed by the *imago dei*, the ones doing the praising.

We do not know whether Goldilocks was baptized or attended worship. We do know that in trying what was in front of her she embraced possibilities and echoed the psalmist's instruction to "Taste and see." It is here that the analogy with baptism and liturgy is strongest. If we are to find that sweetness where things are "just right" we need to be open to possibilities that are not so rewarding, whether too hot or too cold. The central promise from God to the baptized is that everything will, eventually, be all right. The Eucharist provides food for that journey, propelling the faithful who strain toward the kingdom.

In 1476 a Medici politician, Pier Filippo Pandolfini, evokes the purpose and motion of this route forward (to members of his Corpus Christi confraternity) in his description of Eucharist: "Our travel-fare to lead us to the real and true confines of the celestial land where he who is alive reigns."[19] The promises of God in baptism are what equip the faithful for this forward propulsion. Nowhere is it promised that it will be comfortable and easy. Instead, the baptized are told that to inherit the fullness of God's promises they will need to embrace their own powerlessness. Baptism is not about recollecting Christ's life, death, and resurrection. It is an invitation to become entwined in Christ.

On returning home Odysseus is not recognized by any human: none of his retainers, friends, or even his wife. Argos alone, his faithful dog, is able to recognize him. Even though he has made it home, he has not yet come into the power or the glory of reunion with his wife Penelope or his kingdom. Argos recognizes him but is too weak even to get up and greet his old master. Before he can take back all that is rightfully his, Homer has Odysseus lose everything, including faithful Argos who dies before Odysseus can greet him properly. It is at this very point, when all is lost, that all is also possible.

After Argos's death, it seems as if Odysseus could not be further from reaching his potential. Before Odysseus can recover all that is rightfully his he will yet need to demonstrate great cunning, enormous physical strength, and a dose of inside knowledge. But at his lowest point, immediately before he wins Penelope back, Odysseus is in complete solitude. The spiritual life entails similar dynamics of isolation. It also manifests the power of other possibilities that were simply not available to Odysseus. Certainties are rare for those drawn to the God Who May Be. God does not require the baptized to stand heroically alone against the world. Baptism enacts a shift in the center of gravity for the baptized. They are no longer simply pulled into the orbit of God. They also find themselves pulling onto, and being pulled into, one another. How this occurs is the subject of the next chapter.

NOTES

1. A.N. Wilson, *The Elizabethans* (New York: Farrar, Straus and Giroux, 2011), 371. Quoted in Gaddis, *Strategy*, 147.

2. Richard Kearney, *The God Who May Be* (Bloomington: Indiana University Press, 2001).

3. Rowan Williams, *Edge,* 4.

4. Kearney, *God Who*, 108.

5. Kearney, *God Who*, 103.

6. Kearney, *God Who*, 37.

7. Kearney, *God Who*, 2.

8. Carter Heyward, *The Redemption of God: A Theology of Mutual Relation* (Lanham, MD: University Press of America, 1982), 47.

9. Anselm, *S. Anselmi Opera Omnia*, edited by F.S. Schmitt. (Edinburgh: Thomas Nelson and Sons, 1946), Vol. I, 74–75; *St. Anselm Basic Writings*, trans. S.N. Deane (La Salle, Illinois: Open Court, 1962), 173–74.

10. Williams, *Edge*, 84.

11. Giorgio Agamben, *Potentialities: Collected Essays in Philosophy*, ed. and trans. Daniel Heller-Roazen (Stanford: Stanford University Press, 1999).

12. Matthew, 18: 1–5.

13. James Bernard Murphy, *Your Whole Life: Beyond Childhood and Adulthood* (Philadelphia: University of Pennsylvania Press, 2020).

14. Kearney, *God Who*, 51.

15. 1 John 3:2.

16. Hans Urs von Balthasar, *Prayer* (San Francisco: Ignatius Press, 1986). I am grateful to Angus Ritchie for drawing my attention to this reference.

17. Marion, *God Without*, 174.

18. Quoted by Gillian Adams, "Secrets and Healing Magic in the Secret Garden," in Frances Hodgson Burnett, *The Secret Garden,* ed. Gretchen Holbrook Gerzina (New York: W.W. Norton, 2006), 311.

19. Quoted in Rubin, *Corpus Christi*, 215.

Chapter Seven

Forgers of Holiness

Vittorio Gallese is an Italian neuroscientist who revealed for the first time the profound interconnections between human beings. Researching the human brain using MRI scans he and his colleagues discovered that when someone communicates a particular emotion to another person, the same areas of the brain light up in both individuals. In an encounter with a friend who is looking sad, the same neurons that fire up in the friend's brain also engage in our own. What is truly remarkable is that I do not even need to *feel* sad for this to be true. I simply need to witness the sadness—or joy, or whatever the emotion is. Simply seeing or hearing the emotion of another person affects our brains in the same way as the person we are observing. Gallese and his colleagues termed this effect "mirror neurons."[1] The implications of this for our understanding of the interplay between human psychology and neurobiology are enormous.

Mirror neurons provide another layer to place alongside that of Augustine and Kierkegaard in understanding how the human self emerges in relationship. Mirror neurons reveal how intimately human brains are connected to others. Part of what makes telling stories such an effective way of communicating is that the storyteller and the listener or reader experience this neurological mirroring. Whether we inhabit the active or passive part in the telling and hearing of a story, our neurons will be doing the same thing. Emotions literally join us together.

Something similar was seen in a study of the friendship networks of an entire cohort of graduate students.[2] Asking students to identify their friends provided researchers a map of nodes showing the friendship proximity between the members of the class. The students were then presented with a series of video images, which researchers described as like watching television while someone else channel surfs. As they watched, the students' neural reactions were recorded by functional Magnetic Resonance Imaging (fMRI). After correlating the fMRI results with the social network results, researchers concluded that close friends tended to have more similar reactions to the video images than people they were not close friends with:

> These results suggest that we are exceptionally similar to our friends in how we perceive and respond to the world around us, which has implications for interpersonal influence and attraction.[3]

Parkinson, Kleinbaum, and Wheatley are clear that "homophily," liking those who are the same or similar, is a constituent feature of human friendship. Their research shows how this operated all the way down at a neural level. The brains of friends are similar in the way they respond to similar stimuli.

In the light of his earlier research, Gallese coined a new term to describe human beings as "we-centric."[4] After preaching about Gallese an elderly parishioner reminded me that for centuries mothers have known the same thing. Children from an early age mirror pretty much every behavior they encounter. And often to hilarious effect. The results of mirroring are all around us, as we learn from our earliest experiences to copy those around us. Gallese's genius lies in adding a layer of scientific detail to quantify the depth of this mirroring.

One of the most disturbing things I have ever watched was a brief video called the "Still Face Experiment."[5] The subject of research by Edward Tronick, director of the Child Development Unit at Harvard, the video shows a caregiver together with a very small child. Only, instead of mirroring the child, the caregiver maintains a neutral and emotionless gaze. Even though the child was far too young to speak, it only took a few seconds for the child to pick up on the caregiver's lack of interest. As the seconds ticked by the video gets progressively more difficult to watch. The absence of reciprocity with the caregiver seriously disturbs the child, and any viewer with a modicum of empathy.

Within a relatively short time the child is angry, doing everything possible to draw an emotional response, or indeed any kind of reaction, from the emotionless caregiver. Every second that the caregiver remains impassive stretches like an eternity as the distressed child, experiencing no mirroring and no empathy, demands attention. Eventually, thankfully, the caregiver returns her attention to the child and the recovery is almost immediate. It is a haunting video that reiterates the power of mirroring and connection. Even before humans develop language to understand or articulate our need for human connection the need and desire for connection is there.

NO MAN IS AN ISLAND

It is impossible to overstate the significance of this to the spiritual life, just as it is impossible to be an individual without healthy relationships. Human growth requires individuals to have positive experiences that they can mirror. Whether we like it or not, the encounters of our lives are always being mirrored within us at the deepest levels of our being. As we age, we continue to require positive interaction with others to be whole. When the seventeenth-century poet and priest John Donne wrote, "No man is an island," he was drawing attention to the fact that emotional and spiritual health depends upon community with others. Humans cannot thrive alone.

Donne's view was more than a recognition that humans need social interaction and community. His insight that we are not isolated monads was tied to an understanding of the significance of a relationship with the divine. As humans cannot flourish alone from other people, neither can they flourish apart from God. Throughout his life Donne wrestled with the pains and hardships of staying in relationship with God. Yet, even at his most anguished he maintained a connection with the divine.

Donne understood the experience of alienation perhaps better than most. Nevertheless, he also experienced a range of other emotions as he attempted to relate his life to the divine. Joy, sadness, awe, wonder, melancholy, fear, doubt, anger, and faith are all equally present in his poetry. Malcolm Guite observes, "Emotional, imaginative, sexual and spiritual insights are all integrated and interlinked in Donne in a way that is perhaps unequaled in any other writer."[6] Donne's poetic range reveals a soul unafraid of externalizing his most intimate, and potentially embarrassing, failings. Somehow, something of God suffuses even the darkest and most anguished of his poems. For even when others are absent, Donne is never truly alone.

Donne is a quintessential example of someone who sought God in the middle ground of the *via media*. Rising to become one of the most senior clerics of his era, as Dean of St. Paul's Cathedral, London, he was a lifelong member of the Church of England. He was also one of the most resonantly poetic voices of the English language. His poems are not always easy to appreciate as the writings of a prelate in the established church, riven as they are with great personal revelation and honesty. Donne's emotional honesty reveals a God who does not have to be kept at arm's length from the hardest of life's questions.

Perhaps the hardest and most nonsensical part of Christian belief is the suggestion that God entered the world as a human in order to redeem it. Translated into Gallese's language, we might say that God mirrored to humans something of God's own humanity in the person of Christ. The idea of the incarnation, that God became human, is the strangest idea to have taken root in monotheism. The monotheism of Jews and Muslims is much more logical and sensible. The idea of a person who had both human and divine natures is certainly counterintuitive, and remains a legitimate stumbling block for many trying to comprehend Christianity. Yet, it also indicates how God shares in Gallese's we-centricism.

Many Anglicans have been deeply uncomfortable with the intellectual framework of incarnation. The writings of theologians John Robinson, John Hick, Don Cupitt, and Maurice Wiles a generation ago sought to recover some sense out of what seemed metaphysically suspect. Following in the steps of Rudolf Bultmann and Paul Tillich, some embarked upon the work of demythologizing the scandal of the incarnation. Nevertheless, for the broader Anglican tradition, the incarnation is often held up as the quintessentially Anglican doctrine. I think that this is no coincidence. Anglicans know incarnation is essential. Demythologizing for some led away from the uniqueness of Christ, and for others away from Christ entirely. For others demythologizing has been replaced by a re-enchantment with the mystery of God made human. The advantage of this re-enchantment is that we are not always terribly sure about how it plays out. Demythologizing flattened the paradox of the God human. Re-enchantment, like its earlier predecessor Chalcedonian orthodoxy, leaves more to the imagination.

Anglicans remain perplexed by the mystery of the incarnation, but particularly drawn to the imaginative resonances of living in the light of the incarnation. It is because of the incarnation that Christians are able to speak of God anticipating and mirroring human behavior. Incarnation opens up a window onto human and divine life that can be seen through from both sides. An icon would be a better description. Instead of opposing God to humanity, incarnation proclaims the possibility that the two are profoundly interconnected, right in the middle of ordinary life.

Through incarnation, seekers are given an icon in which to seek the face of God. As Jean-Luc Marion underlines, the icon is not simply something we look at. In the light of the experience of the child and the carer, Marion's theory of the icon makes this face-to-face encounter even more critical. Icons are how God summons us. Just as Emmanuel Levinas grounds the relationship with the other in the face, so Marion notes how the face of the icon grounds our relationship with the Infinite:

> The invisible summons us, "face-to-face, person to person" (1 Cor. 13:12), through the painted visibility of the incarnation and the factual visibility of our flesh: no longer the visible idol as the invisible mirror of our gaze, but our face as the visible mirror of the invisible.[7]

In contrast to the idol that simply retains our gaze, the icon gazes out at us, bringing the divine into the world. In the icon of Christ's incarnation, God gazes back at us. This is the essence of Christian uniqueness. It is not perfectly rational, nor does it make intuitive sense. Yet the claim that there is something distinctive about the person of Christ is one of few constants in the two-thousand-year experience of Christian belief.

Marion reminds us that the questions of human experience and divine experience are profoundly interlinked. It is not simply the gaze of the icon that connects the divine life to the human experience of God. The *imago dei* in humankind is also a point of connection. For Marion this image and likeness is a reminder that both humanity and the divine share a certain incomprehensibility. Along with Socrates, theologians are agreed that we do not know who we are. Marion pushes this further: if we *did* know who we are then that would destroy the image and likeness of God within us. For if the divine nature of God is essentially incomprehensible and unknowable, then so too is our human likeness. Marion quotes the medieval theologian John Scot Eriugena: "If in any way man could understand what he is (*quid sit*) he would necessarily deviate from the likeness with God (*a similituduine Creatoris deviaret*)." In turn, Eriugena directs readers back to the theory of the icon found in St. Gregory of Nyssa "On the Image."[8] Marion traces these reflections on the icon all the way back to St. Paul, and his description of Christ as the icon of the invisible God.[9] This affirmation of the Greek iconological inheritance by the Latin tradition is one that has often been overlooked in recent centuries. These reflections on Christ as icon remain the paradigmatic place where we see both the divinity of God being revealed *and* the impossibility of truly representing or comprehending that divinity. It is another pointer to the centrality of the paradox of how the divine simply cannot be understood (and yet calls forth a response).

THE BURNING QUESTION

The incarnation reveals God was human all the way down. A living, breathing human being whose neural pathways fired up in telling stories just the same way ours do when we hear his story. The central challenge of Christianity is how to follow, and imitate, this first-century Galilean preacher-healer. In copying and mirroring Christ, Christianity projects the presence of the divine into each generation.

The Northern Irish theologian Peter Rollins has written widely about the radical nature of the Christ event. Rollins invents the word "pyrotheology" to describe how theology needs to consign parts of Christianity to flames. To truly follow Christ, to imitate Christ, requires burning away some of the religious trappings that we have inherited. At the same time, his pyrotheology is far from destructive. Instead, it is a generative fire produced out of the radical proclamations of the person of Christ. Rollins affirms how the church needs to engage with "the white-hot fires of a fundamental question" that reveals the "revolutionary event" of Christ's Crucifixion and Resurrection.[10]

Too often the cardboard Christ who is held up as worthy of imitating is only a partial Christ: the teacher of morals is separated from the prophet who forces us to reappraise our deepest values; the forgiver of sinners is distanced from the preacher who proclaims the imminent arrival of the kingdom; the religious revolutionary is distanced from the reinforcer of the covenant between God and humanity; the rabbi teaching the return of the prodigal son is distanced from the one who promises to divide families in his name. By contrast, a fuller understanding of incarnation requires us to be seared by the white-hot heat (and contradictions) of the Christ event.

Faced with these challenges, it is reassuring to discover others trying to mirror the white-hot Christ event. God is not solely encountered through baptismal promising, Eucharistic remembering, and scriptural wrestling. We also experience the divine through the souls of others. We may not be terribly clear about the complexities of the doctrine of the incarnation, but it is possible to become quite adept at learning to look for the *imago dei* in others around us. In the next two sections we will explore two saints, and the very different ways in which they mirrored Christ.

THE MIRROR OF FRIENDSHIP: ANSELM OF CANTERBURY

Saints are people drawn to gaze through the looking glass at the image of God that lies within every human being. It is instructive to remember that the inventor of Alice in Wonderland, the heroine who peers through the looking glass, was an Anglican canon. Charles Lutwidge Dodgson, better known as Lewis Carroll, is said to have been inspired by a visit to Ripon Cathedral. Under the nave there is an Anglo-Saxon crypt to St. Wilfrid, which pilgrims enter through a small aperture down a steep stone staircase. This narrow entrance to the saint's chapel later achieved literary immortality with Alice's disappearance down the rabbit hole. Without St. Wilfrid, Alice's story would have been different.

The origins of the cult of saints are as a movement from below, a flowering of devotion by the faithful. Peter Brown has shown the uniqueness of Christianity's treatment of the bodies of its saints, cultivating practices around them quite unlike that of their pagan neighbors. Rather than hiding them away or keeping them at arm's length, Christians venerated and visited their saints. They built basilicas and churches around them. The saints were never simply dead and gone; they remained active members of the community.[11] Over time, the authorization of sanctity becomes centralized and ritualized to a high degree. For many centuries the saints, and certainly the most popular ones among them, were simply the people the Christian community most identified with. Historian Robert Bartlett has explored how these cults of sanctity flourish and develop through the medieval period. Cults of saints showed remarkable adaptability, and depended heavily on the adoration and investment of both laity and clergy. Over time, geography and vocation there is an enormous breadth and scope to the saints:

> Just as the saints were universal and local, so they were present but also transcended time, and they were often imagined as a glorious company in heaven, apostles rubbing shoulders with medieval bishops, virgin martyrs with saintly queens. They have shaped the lives and imaginations of millions, and still do.[12]

This imaginative dimension is central to the ability of saints to make neural and theological connections across both generations and culture.

The workings of this imagination are particularly apparent in hagiography, the writing of the holy. Hagiography develops as a literary genre to spread the knowledge of those popularly believed to be worthy of imitation and devotion. Hagiography often receives attention for its focus on the more extraordinary aspects of saints' lives. St. Francis's ability to speak with animals, commanding in one instance birds to obey him in order that he could worship, is probably one of the more famous hagiographical stories. Hagiography is also notorious for stories of strikingly unnatural interventions, often in the form of tall stories of healing and protection.

Through hagiography, the church telegraphs the possibility of imitating in real life. Hagiographers reflect the concerns of the age in which their stories were being consumed. The more hagiography one reads, though, the more we discover that for every astonishing tale, the vast amount of hagiographical literature is remarkably prosaic and ordinary.

We see this in the *Vita* (the life) of Anselm, the eleventh-century Archbishop of Canterbury and theologian. Like Hildegard, Anselm was an influential figure whose counsel and insight were sought out by his contemporaries. Frequently asked to write to explain the mysteries of faith, or simply to encourage others, Anselm has left behind a significant theological and literary output. Eadmer, a contemporary of Anselm who knew him well, sought to bear witness for posterity to the fame and sanctity of his friend. In Eadmer's hagiography, one of the clearest and most recurring signs of Anselm's sanctity were his amazing, yet robustly human, gifts of conversation and friendship. While there are, as the genre requires, occasional instances of the miraculous, it is the warmth, and what we would call charisma, of Anselm's conversational and teaching gifts that pervades Eadmer's writing.

In addition to being an influential theologian, Anselm was an important political figure in the challenges faced by the English king in conflict with the Pope. And yet, while these aspects of his life were important, Eadmer focuses his readers on Anselm's more everyday human gifts. The key to Anselm's holiness, at least according to Eadmer, lay in his eloquence:

> For it seems to me impossible to obtain a full understanding of the tenor of his life if only his actions are described and nothing is said about how he appeared in his talk.[13]

Eadmer goes on to tell various tales in which Anselm counseled the perplexed, responding to doubts, confusions, and frailties of others both near and far. Anselm imitated and mirrored the love of God, through speech and letter writing, building others up to the point where they might also be strong in God's love. Through the written word Anselm's spiritual friendship circulated beyond simply the monastic communities. Mathilda, Countess of Tuscany, was one of many women recipients of these letters, and probably responsible for ensuring that they were widely disseminated.[14] Letters in the medieval period were not simply private documents. They were also designed to be read aloud and shared.

Some commentators have been stunned, if not embarrassed, at the depth of feeling Anselm could express. Anselm cultivated friendship as a deliberate strategy for drawing others to God. He was an inveterate correspondent, and hundreds of his letters to monks, nuns, lay people, kings, queens, and popes remain. Anselm believed in the ideal of monastic friendship as part of how humans could attain union with God. While this was a matter of both faith and intellect, he delighted in expressing this affection in language that continues to jump off the page. Take this extract from a letter to fellow monk Gundulf:

> Since your soul and my soul can never bear to be absent from each other but are incessantly entwined together, nothing of ourselves is lacking in the other except that we are not present to one another physically.[15]

Although penned sometime before 1077, more than one modern reader has been led to wonder whether this says more about Anselm's sexuality than his spirituality. The consensus of the vast majority of historians is to echo Eadmer's original understanding. Anselm's dramatically emotive language was all part of how Anselm conveyed his fundamental trust in God's love.

To search for God is to enter into the possibility of spiritual union not just with God but also with others on the way. When we explore the Trinity in the next chapter we will examine in more detail the fundamental reality of desire within the Christian life. Letters like the one to Gundulf were personal, but they were never meant to remain private. They illustrated the dynamic of the Christian life, and the vocation of Christians as fellow lovers, souls entwined with one another, to be entwined with God. Medieval historian Richard Southern explains:

> That is why he wished letters which superficially seem embarrassingly intimate to be read by readers other than their recipients: in speaking of friendship, he was making statements about eternity.[16]

It was a very Goldilocks way of proceeding. Anselm cultivated friendships to introduce others to the sustaining love of God. The overwhelming evidence of this saint's sanctity is not found in miraculous suspensions of the laws of nature. Eadmer's account and Anselm's letters themselves leave readers in little doubt that being a patient teacher and eloquent friend were the primary ways that Anselm mirrored Christ to others.

Anselm's friendship was wholehearted: and he literally showered friends with love and kisses. In the monastery, as in wider feudal society, a kiss was not a romantic gesture. Instead, it was what Southern calls the "crowning act" in various sacramental practices: when new monks were professed, abbots elected, penitents reconciled, the dead commended to God, and as objects or buildings were set aside for sacred use. Many priests still kiss their stole or the altar linen as part of their personal devotions. These religious kisses were ways of being joined to the holy, and at their most profound, they represented union with the Holy Trinity. In the Hebrew scriptures there are only two people, Moses and Abraham, who are described as friends of God. Anselm, like a many of the saints, represents a universalizing of the potential for friendship with the divine.

As Brian McGuire explores in considerable detail, Anselm intensifies the conventions around the monastic cultivation of friendship. Quite literally, "the sweetness of his talk made men love him."[17] The emotionally freighted language of love and kisses is difficult for modern readers to entirely comprehend. Yet, it shows how vital friendship was for Anselm for imitating and mirroring Christ. Like Augustine before him (and Marion after him), Anselm saw the human mind as a mirror of the divine. His words of love are always mirroring the divine love that formed the basis of both his friendship and his desire to write.

Anselm was passionate, truly, madly, deeply, for God. We have not explored his explicitly theological works for which he remains most famous, but it is important to note how his passion for God appears even there. In the *Proslogion*, his meditation into the nature of God that created an "argument" into the nature of God as "that than which nothing greater can be thought" that continues to be taught in the academy, what is generally not taught is the expression of desire for God that saturates the text of this "argument." The following extract is illustrative of the general tone of the text of the entire *Proslogion*, which deserves to be prayed as much as studied:

> O Lord my God,
> my Creator and my Re-creator,
> my soul longs for you.
> Tell me what you are, beyond what I have seen,
> so that I may see clearly what I desire.[18]

Friendship was simply one way in which Anselm revealed his own desire for God. In turn, others recognized how this passionate Anselmian friendship had a divine origin. As Hugh, Abbot of Cluny, wrote in a letter to Anselm, "Who could ever be so inhuman that after he had experienced the sweetness of your talk, he would not receive and venerate you as the angel of God?"[19]

THE LITTLE SAINT: FOY OF CONQUES

At the heart of the tiny medieval village of Conques in the South-West of France lies an enormous basilica. Named after the shape of a conch shell, the village nestles precariously on a mountainside. Conques is so inaccessible that when I arrived after a long drive alongside twisting rivers and deep mountain passes, a helicopter was dropping off building supplies. The village is tiny, but the basilica that was built around the relics of St. Faith (Foy in French) is huge. Precipitously located and enormously solid at the same time, it seems to defy gravity. Like hundreds of thousands before me, I had come to pay my respects to the "Little Saint," in Hannah Green's evocative phrase.[20]

Defying gravity and ignoring the constraints of physical limitations seem to have been defining characteristics of Foy. Over the centuries she developed a reputation for being both a bit of a trickster and a lover of gold. Foy's legend anticipates Goldilocks. Although she died in the fourth century, it is not simply her original story that captivates. She had no contemporary like Eadmer to record her conversation. Instead, it is the later medieval stories about her as much her original life that ensured the flourishing of her reputation. Pilgrims came to her shrine from far and wide in search of healing and many of their stories were collected. Numerous stories of miraculous healings and liberations of prisoners have survived, many of which were compiled in the middle of the eleventh century.[21] These narratives reveal a saint whose posthumous influence was larger than life. The architecture of her basilica and relics studded with gold pay testimony to how grateful her people were for Foy's patronage and intercession.

St. Foy, like St. Lucy of Syracuse (another fourth-century martyr whose memory remains strong in Italy and Scandinavia), died young. But it is the central reason for her martyrdom that is perhaps the most inspiring part of her ongoing influence in the church today. The story is told of how she got into trouble with her pagan father for taking food to hungry and persecuted Christians. Keen to evade the pagan authorities, she hid food under her cloak. Accosted by her father, she was forced to reveal what she was hiding. Lifting up her cloak for inspection, anxious that he would catch her red handed, Foy was taken aback to discover that the contraband bread had turned into flowers.

St. Foy was revered for the practical compassion and care she gave to the needy. This faith expressed itself in actions that set her up for conflict with her own family and the government of the day. Refusing to sacrifice to the pagan gods, she dies for the faith that gave her name to her. Centuries later dozens of stories continue to be told of her influence as patron, helping those who turned to her in prayer. Some of these became popularized in songs that circulate, spreading her fame and influence. While she not die near Conques, she was brought there in the ninth century in what has all the appearances of a carefully planned classic "relic theft." Saints were never stolen in the medieval period, but when they were being ignored, their movement to a more welcoming place was a common phenomenon. These transitions ensured they might be given more veneration and attention. This phenomenon is described in wonderful detail by Peter Geary in his analysis of relic circulation and movement. In the case of Foy, Geary notes how the theft from Agen helped bolster the power of the monastery of Conques. One of their monks went undercover to Agen and one night, when he is left alone with the treasures, he is able to steal Foy away to Conques.[22] As the guardian of her relics Conques gains prestige, becoming the center of an active cult. Through the power of trust in Foy, Conques became a major center of pilgrimage, as well as a significant stop on the way to other shrines. Built on the grateful devotion of her many pilgrims, and countless stories of sickness healed, Foy's mountaintop retreat becomes famous both for its stories of a plucky young girl, and for its riches.

Foy's most famous hagiographer, Bernard of Angers, was one of the first to compile a book of the interventions of Foy in the eleventh century. Like many hagiographers, Bernard is keen to explain his motivation for writing about her miracles:

> Partly because it seemed to be the common people who promulgated these miracles and partly because they were regarded as new and unusual, we put no faith in them and rejected them as so much worthless fiction.[23]

Clearly skeptical, Bernard nonetheless concocts a plan to visit Conques to learn more about this saint. Delayed for three years in Angers ("I wasted time there that should have been used for study on behalf of stupid good-for-nothings") he eventually arrives in Conques where he describes his investigations into Foy's wonder working:

> Since the time of my arrival here I have begun to inquire diligently about Sainte Foy's miracles. Such a great number of miracles have poured forth from various narrators that if my mind had not been burningly eager to hear them my brain would have been overwhelmed with weariness.[24]

From there Bernard goes on to compile what is, by any standard, a fearsome number of miracle stories about Foy's continuing involvement in the lives of her people. He even attests to having seen with his own eyes some of the people who the saint has healed.

For all his initial skepticism, Bernard goes out of his way to record only recent miracles ("only those not older than our own time, and whose eyewitnesses told me not an invented tale but the clearest truth"). Although many of the miracle stories that follow his introduction reflect clear *topoi* of other miracle collections, Bernard is keen to claim authenticity for the material he narrates. He concludes:

> I have very diligently investigated to determine the inviolable truth of these miracles. Because there is nothing truer, I implore you to bring faith wholeheartedly to my narration so that later you will not regret that you disparaged a holy martyr.[25]

In prefacing the collection with these remarks, initially addressed to no less an individual than Bishop Fulbert of Chartres, Bernard is keenly aware of the need to defend the veracity of his collection. The fact that miracle stories are often not believed is a subtext that Bernard is acutely aware of. In their analysis of the miracle collection, Kathleen Ashley and Pamela Sheingorn read this skepticism as a way of allowing Bernard to "rehearse" arguments that will persuade other skeptics.[26] Usually a collection like this would have been recorded by the keepers of the shrine, in this case the church of St Foy in Conques. As an outsider who was trained in the arts, Ashley and Sheingorn also suggest that Bernard brought a greater level of sophistication to the conventions and dangers of writing miracle stories than might have been found in Conques. At the same time, coming from outside the monastic community that kept Foy's shrine, he may also have had more critical distance, even as he preserved her stories. Either way, he offers a unique window into the local community's perceptions of this saint and how her people experienced her presence.

And what a set of experiences those are. Restoring a certain Guibert's eyes after they were torn out by the roots; reviving a mule from death; how a man was killed when attacking one of Sainte Foy's monks; how divine vengeance acted against those who wanted to steal the monks' wine; celestial vengeance striking a man who attacked Sainte Foy's pilgrims; how a man who was slandering Sainte Foy was destroyed by the sudden collapse of a roof. These are just half a dozen of the thirty-four miracles contained in the first book, and the collection extends to four books. With the distance of a thousand years it is harder for Bernard to overcome our skepticism than that of Bishop Fulbert. However, the level of detail in these stories, and Bernard's presumption that he needs to underline the veracity of them, make the rhetoric of the community's trust impossible to ignore.

The Foy that Bernard and his successors write about takes her patronage and protection of her people extremely seriously. When she is not smiting enemies or defending her people, whether monks or pilgrims, Foy is somewhat impishly collecting (on occasion, practically extorting) gold to adorn her monastery. Whatever one thinks of the miracles themselves, the picture that emerges is of a saint who was meeting the socioeconomic needs of both her monastic community as well as a remarkable cross-section of society who sought her blessings.

Foy's miracle stories show how saints are always we-centric. They emerge within a community. Often long after they are dead, a community will find new meaning and hope in its patron saint. To study any one of the saints who has been around for more than a century or so is to discover how the stories of saints are changed in the telling. Hagiography is as much about the needs of the writing and believing community as it is about the original saint.

While we know relatively little about the fourth-century life of Foy, we know a lot about the challenges facing pilgrims to her shrine in later centuries. Bernard's writing reveals as much about everyday life as supernatural intervention. Wrongful imprisonment, various forms of sickness, brutally oppressive knights, dozy monks, and cheating merchants are all to be found in her stories. But, by far the most important character is the saint herself. Even in the eleventh century, she remains larger than life in her interventions in the middle of the ordinary lives of supplicants and malefactors. Appearing in dreams, arguing for the rights of monks and pilgrims, berating slackers, and enacting revenge for wrongs, Foy intervenes again and again to improve life for her flock. Without Bernard we would know little of the detail. Foy sought to imitate Christ in life and, should Bernard be believed, beyond death. By keeping her memory alive Bernard made sure of it.

The faithful need saints to inspire and imitate, and in every generation what they need from them is constantly evolving. Foy's posthumous movements and interventions are very different from Anselm's spiritual conversation and professions of friendship. While Eadmer focuses on the influence Anselm had during his lifetime, Bernard's Foy is very different. When much of medieval Europe was dangerous and lawless it was not surprising to see saints fill the void as bringers of justice. In a world of the most basic healthcare, saints like Foy often made up for medical deficits. Like the mirrors of divine love they aspire to be, saints are those others both project onto, and turn to, for assistance.

Saints are never stable. Throughout the medieval period, healings were relatively common, and shrines places where the faithful gained access to both the holy and much needed hope. In the absence of a strong central or regional government, even the divine revenge meted out by Saint Foy was as near as peasants, monks, and merchants could get to justice in the face of the ravages of errant knights.

To this day, to encounter Foy is to be swept off one's feet. Green's modern hagiography provides an astonishingly beautiful and moving account of her own pilgrimage to Foy's church. At the heart of this remains her Treasury in which her treasures (including a remarkable three foot statue of the little saint), continue to be revered. In writing about the time she spent living alongside Foy and the community that continues to keep her, Green conjures an extraordinary vision of a saint who remains powerfully present. For all that she is a diminutive figure, Green explores the huge influences that Foy's cult has on the people of the Rouergue region.

At the entrance to Foy's basilica there is a beautiful stone tympanum above the western door. Green describes it as:

> One of the four marvels of this world, a Last Judgment completed most probably between 1135 and 1150, and almost perfectly preserved. Even the colors still cling to the stone in places and grow luminous in that hour just after the sun has gone down—the blue on the robe of Christ the Judge in Heaven seated in His almond-shaped glory, His mandorla.[27]

Quoting the townsfolk who interpret the tympanum for her, Green relays their reading of how Foy appears in this, "represented not in heaven, but *here, at Conques here in her church*, fallen on her knees praying for her people, praying for the souls of the dead, still, on the last day in time; and the hand of Jesus reaches out, down through the cloud waves of heaven, to touch, to almost touch, her head."[28]

As if this stone presence was not enough to convince pilgrims entering her church of the ongoing power of the saint, Green offers another connection between the figures in the tympanum and the work of the saint. Green identifies 126 figures in the tympanum, from Jesus, and the saints, to angels and archangels, blackened demons, strange animals, wicked hunters, and poor condemned souls. These carved faces in the tympanum are faces that continue to be seen in the Rouergue. Mary, mother of Jesus, has a face that is "solid yet shining, a country face with the fine clear features of this region, lit by the glow of heaven within her—the wide high forehead, the straight long nose, the curved lips, the cleft chin, the direct, clear gaze . . . Charlou, Rosalie's husband, could be descended from her, I think, for his face is her face."[29] Just as the face situates the ethical encounter for Levinas, so these faces situate and invite a response. There is also a fruitful analogy to be made here with Marion's reflections on the living gaze of the icon, and how it sees us and summons us "face to face" into the divine.[30] The figures in the tympanum are not static and passive. Their faces look out at pilgrims not simply from stone, but also from the people of the Rouergue, showing pilgrims the complex human tapestry that both creates and recreates Foy's community in every generation. This is not to romanticize Foy. It is simply to note how, like Anselm, she continues to inspire adoration. Where Anselm's letters and writings lead readers deeper in their quest for friendship with the divine, Foy does the same through the material culture with which others celebrate her abiding presence.

SAINTLY HABIT LOOPS

Anselm and Foy point to the power of habit, and how those habits can be sustained across generations. Charles Duhigg has explored how habits are created and sustained, identifying habit loops. A loop involves a trigger or a cue, the routine or habit itself and then a reward. Cues or triggers are what initialize or produce the routine while a reward is what closes the loop. The difference between a good habit and a bad habit has nothing to do with the structure of the habit. Both kinds of habit share alike this configuration of cue, routine, then reward. By identifying the common structure that all habits share, Duhigg hopes to intercept bad habits with interventions at the trigger stage. Duhigg's model also explains how to create good habits by being mindful of these cues and triggers. Understanding triggers and cravings makes it possible to create prompts that will lead in more positive directions. Once the structure of habits is exposed, it becomes possible to form and reshape them.[31]

Creating good habits is why saints exist. Saints are those who have internalized loving habits into what has the potential to be a second nature. Eadmer could not stop writing about his beloved friend Anselm. Green visited Foy over a period of twenty years for months at a time to inculcate the habits of the heart that eventually manifest themselves in her lyrical testament to the little saint.

Imitation is how the would-be faithful develop and deepen life-giving habits. Saints are human triggers of positive habit loops for the faithful. Saints are not exclusively remembered for their achievements. They are, instead, people around whom the baptized build "habit loops" of generosity, love, sacrifice, forgiveness, and service. Understanding the power of habit involves recognizing how we are always relying on cues and triggers, even when these are unconscious ones. For millennia, wearing the symbol of a saint or keeping a relic or picture of a saint was a way of triggering the memory and example of saintly inspiration.

When others are practicing desirable habits it is much easier to emulate those habits. Good habit formation is hard to do alone. As Duhigg recognizes: "Belief is easier when it occurs within a community."[32] Community provides both accountability and support for creating mutually positive habit loops. While Duhigg's examples come from the worlds of commerce and sports, the dynamics are remarkably similar to the stories told by medievals and moderns alike.

One of the most remarkable of Duhigg's examples is coach Tony Dungy, who realized that the key to coaching winning teams lay in changing players' habits.[33] Dungy wanted players to respond *without thinking* to situations in the game. The removal of decision making, and the creation of instinctual patterns of reaction, helped him to turn dismally performing teams around. From coaching one of the worst teams in the NFL, he eventually took the Colts to Superbowl victory in 2007. Dungy's success rested on an awareness of cues, triggers, and routines that helped his players respond automatically to conditions on the ground. Just as Anselm's letters and conversation helped to lay down routes to the divine for his listeners and readers to make their own, so Dungy created pathways for players to achieve their own objectives. Dungy's coaching builds on Gallese's original insight. Humans are profoundly connected when they share experiences. Together the insights of the coach and neuroscientist show how exposure to Anselm's friendship or Foy's stories allow their holiness to live on inside of us. Christianity anticipates the shared wisdom of neuroscience and athletics in forging habit loops that are accessible, practical, and repeatable.

Spirituality is all about imitating the grace-full habit loops of others. To be inspired by holy women or men is also to be inspired to become a saint of one's own. In the words of Blaise Pascal: "Grace is indeed needed to turn a man into a saint; and he who doubts it does not know what a saint or a man is."[34] The purpose of hagiography is simply to make it easier for this transition towards sanctity by way of grace. Bernard of Angers and Eadmer of

Canterbury were doing the same thing as Coach Dungy. They were modeling what others could emulate.

Hagiographers have always deployed every kind of trick imaginable to help them. To write about holy lives was never an act of reportage. It is always a deeply creative act. As Green experienced so profoundly, hagiography channels emotional connection; it is not a neutral discourse. In every time and place, saints imitate the divine in ever-changing ways. Hagiography simply highlights what the community of the day needs to see. In her ground-breaking study on cults of the royal saints in Anglo-Saxon England, Susan Ridyard examines how important hagiographical bias is:

> A saint who specialised in doing battle with serpents and sorceresses was clearly a very different creature from a saint whose principal function was to strike fear into the hearts of the invaders of monastic property.[35]

Even hagiographers whose raw material was found at the intersection of Germanic heroic warrior culture and Anglo-Saxon royalty had a range of different types of holiness to choose from. Hagiography is easily mocked for stock portrayals, repetitious themes, and conventional descriptions of holy living and miracle working. Hagiography can perpetuate, or less kindly, recycle a fairly limited set of hagiographic *topoi* that may have had little historical relationship to their subjects. Nevertheless, hagiography is always working carefully within the expectations of the day concerning what it takes to be holy. And expectations had to be met. They also had to be elevated, transformed, or redirected for the purposes of the community generating the hagiography. In Green's writing we see a new level of psychological intensity of feeling committed to the genre. That she is writing about a saint and a community largely untouched by the innovations of late twentieth-century modernity at the time of her writing is not irrelevant. This is hagiography as an escape from secular evasions of the holy, a return to a time when generosity towards the holy formed and elevated culture.

Hagiographers certainly made an awful lot up as they drew attention to their subjects. Osbern of Clare, an eleventh-century hagiographer, seems to have been adept at creating the source material to back up his hagiography. In Ridyard's analysis he was: "not only a controversial prior and a prolific hagiographer; he was also one of the most successful forgers of his time."[36] Eadmer and Bernard may not have been forgers in the literal sense of the term, but along with Osbern they deployed their literary imagination to great effect. The forging of Green is entirely different. Her literary artifice is on full display, and yet it would be the surliest and most cynical of readers who could not be captivated by what is patently genuine devotion. Green erases the false modern distinction between hagiography as it is so often depicted, a crude genre, and the literary creativity of our most celebrated contemporary writers. Her carefully crafted words reveal both the artifice and literary merit of hagiography.

Neither historians nor recording angels, the work of hagiographers is infinitely more important. They forge stories about how real people had imitated God. Their creative tellings of the stories of their saints act both as windows onto God and portals through which readers can pass. The literary creators of saints knew that the stories they told would do more than simply inspire. In telling of the exceptionally holy, hagiography supplied precious fuel for reinvigorating and sustaining spiritual habits. The sometimes aligned, sometimes competing, desires of popular and official devotion, ensured that there was always a demand for these storied saints.

Saints were not simply to be imitated. They were a continuing presence: a shrine to go on pilgrimage to, an intercessor in heaven to pray to, a patron to turn to in times of crisis. As Eadmer eagerly persuades us, Anselm's status as saint grew out of his remarkable gift for conversation and friendship. Anselm's writings on friendships and theology provided other points of access to him that would sustain, and enlarge, his reputation across time. Accessibility, the ability to visit with, and talk with the saints, and their willingness to be friends with the perplexed and the suffering were two of the most important ways in which saints imitated God. It was also how saints remained active in the world, able to meet the needs of future generations. Caroline Walker Bynum notes that in the medieval world, the activity of the saints, and the associated miraculous materiality that went along with it was never in question. This was a world of bleeding hosts, weeping statues, and miracles of healing:

> To oversimplify a bit, one might say that to a modern theorist, the problem is to explain how things "talk"; to a medieval theorist, it was to get them to shut up.[37]

While Bynum is referring to talking statues, she might as well be referring to talkative saints like Anselm or mischievous saints like Foy.

The medievals approached the holy as an active and ever-present feature of ordinary human life. Over time their stories grew ever more elaborate in the telling because they continued to show the rest of us not simply *how* to live, but *with whom*. Megan McLaughlin in her work on the saints of early medieval France has a beautiful turn of phrase for this: "consorting with the saints."[38] Lay people sought contact with the saints as a way of navigating both life and death. The saints had a much more expansive and interconnected role in culture here than is often realized. They were not simply turned to in moments of great need or to solicit favor for the afterlife. Even when arranging prayers for the dead, these requests turn out to be as much about forging relationships in the present as any concern for what lay beyond death.

Saints invite fellowship. To gaze on the tympanum in Conques is to find inspiration in the communion gathered on display. Saints are those, living and departed, who reveal the light of God's love. Green recalls beings a "stranger to saints" before she encountered Foy. She becomes enthralled, and ends up entrancing her readers with Foy's golden presence. In recent decades there has been a flowering in the number and diversity of saints entered into the official church calendars. Fifty years ago lists of Episcopal saints remembered in prayer were predominantly male and European, now they include Native Americans, African Americans, indigenous peoples, as well as women and men from across the globe.[39]

A significant proportion of medieval saints were deacons, priests, bishops, monks, nuns, missionaries, and mystics. However, in the last twenty years the saints who are being commemorated are more likely to include other members of the baptized: nurses, workers for social justice, artists, musicians, educators, poets, writers, environmentalists, and people who gave their all in service to their fellow human beings.

Many of the saints included in the last one hundred years deserve to be better known. New Hampshire Episcopalians are justly proud of Jonathan Myrick Daniels, a seminarian who was training for the priesthood and was active in the Civil Rights movement. As a young man, aware of his white privilege, he traveled to Alabama to join with African American brothers and sisters in their marches for freedom, integration, and equal civil rights. One day a construction worker and county deputy aimed a shotgun at Daniels and his companion Ruby Sales, an African American who was 17 years old. Daniels reacted by shielding Sales with his own body, taking the full force of the shotgun blast. He was only 26 years old when he died protecting her on August 20, 1965. By 1991 Daniels had been officially designated as a martyr in the Episcopal church. His selfless heroism reminds us that the path of imitating Christ continues to lead to sacrifice. Sales went on to seminary, and has devoted the rest of her life continuing the work of the Civil Rights movement through the SpiritHouse project. While the cultural reach of Foy and Daniels is vastly different, they have this in common: they continue to draw admirers and devotees. And as we learn their stories, we find ourselves yearning to follow in their footsteps.

NOTES

1. Gallese, Vittorio, Luciano Fadiga, Leonardo Fogassi and Giacomo Rizzolatti. "Action Recognition in the Premotor Cortex." *Brain*, Vol. 119, 2 (1996), 593–609.

2. I am grateful to Nicholas Christakis for introducing me to this study.

3. "Similar neural responses predict friendship," Carolyn Parkinson, Adam M. Kleinbaum, and Thalia Wheatley. January 30, 2018. Accessed September 24, 2021, https://nature.com/articles/s41467-017-02722-7.

4. Gallese, Vittorio. "The shared manifold" hypothesis: From Mirror Neurons to Empathy." *Journal of Consciousness Studies*, 8 (2001), 33–50.

5. "Still Face Experiment," Edward Tronick, Accessed March 28, 2021, https://thepowerofdiscord.com.

6. Malcolm Guite, *Faith, Hope and Poetry: Theology and the Poetic Imagination* (London: Routledge, 2016), 105.

7. Marion, *God Without*, 22.

8. Jean-Luc Marion, *Negative Certainties*, trans. Stephen E. Lewis (Chicago: University of Chicago Press, 2015), 39.

9. Marion, *God Without*, 17. Here Marion refers to Paul's letter to the Colossians 1:15.

10. Peter Rollins, *Insurrection: To Believe is Human, to Doubt Divine* (New York: Howard Books, 2011), xi.

11. Peter Brown, *The Cult of the Saints: Its Rise and Function in Latin Christianity* (Chicago: University of Chicago Press, 1982).

12. Robert Bartlett, *Why Can the Dead Do Such Great Things?* (Princeton: Princeton University Press, 2013), 637.

13. Eadmer, *The Life of St Anselm*, trans. R.W. Southern (Oxford: Oxford University Press, 1972), 36.

14. Richard Southern in Anselm, *Prayers,* 9–10.

15. Anselm, *The Letters of Saint Anselm of Canterbury*, trans. Walter Fröhlich (Michigan: Cistercian Publications, 1990), Vol 1, Letter 41, 144.

16. Richard Southern, *St. Anselm: a Portrait in a Landscape* (Cambridge: Cambridge University Press, 1990), 159.

17. Brian Patrick McGuire, *Friendship and Community: the Monastic Experience, 350–1250* (Ithaca: Cornell University Press, 2010), 227.

18. Anselm, *Prayers*, 256.

19. Quoted in McGuire, *Friendship*, 227.

20. Hannah Green, *Little Saint* (New York: Modern Library, 2000).

21. *The Book of Sainte Foy*, trans. and introd. Pamela Sheingorn (Philadelphia: University of Pennsylvania, 1995).

22. Peter Geary, *Furta Sacra: Thefts of Relics in the Central Middle Ages* (Princeton: Princeton University Press, 1991), 58–59.

23. Sheingorn, *Sainte Foy*, 38.

24. Sheingorn, *Sainte Foy*, 39.

25. Sheingorn, *Sainte Foy*, 41.

26. Kathleen Ashley and Pamela Sheingorn, *Writing Faith: Text, Sign and History in the Miracles of Sainte Foy* (Chicago: Chicago University Press, 1999), 56.

27. Green, *Little Saint*, 39.

28. Green, *Little Saint*, 40.

29. Green, *Little Saint*, 44.

30. Marion, *God Without*.

31. Charles Duhigg, *The Power of Habit: Why we do what we do in Life and Business* (New York: Random House, 2014).

32. Duhigg, *Habit*, 89.

33. Duhigg, *Habit*, 60ff.

34. Blaise Pascal, *Pensées*, introd. T.S. Eliot (New York: E.P. Dutton, 1958), VII (508), 139.

35. Susan Ridyard, *The Royal Saints of Anglo-Saxon England* (Cambridge: Cambridge University Press, 1988), 14.

36. Ridyard, *Royal Saints*, 24.

37. Caroline Walker Bynum, *Christian Materiality: An Essay on Religion in Late Medieval Europe* (New York: Zone Books, 2011), 283.

38. Megan McLaughlin, *Consorting with the Saints: Prayer for the Dead in Early Medieval France* (Ithaca: Cornell University Press, 1994).

39. This can be tracked in The Episcopal Church in the expansion from *Lesser Feasts and Fasts* (New York: Church Publishing, 1980) to *Holy Women and Holy Men* (New York: Church Publishing, 2010), and *A Great Cloud of Witnesses* (New York: Church Publishing, 2016). The rate of saintly additions to the church's official liturgical calendar is presumably set to accelerate in the future. A similar phenomenon of exponential saintly multiplication began in the Roman Catholic church in the twentieth century.

Chapter Eight

The Gift of Desire

While the pervasive reach of hagiography in Western culture has diminished, the emotive power of its step-child, fiction, has grown. Fiction is a gift which exposes the movements of God in the world in acts of giving and givenness. This chapter will explore something of the web that connects gifts of fiction to the divine Giver. Fiction both reveals and revels in the mystery of God. Despite having even less of a purchase on reality than much hagiography, fiction is perfectly suited for trafficking spiritual insights. In spite of, or perhaps because of, the secular spirit of the current age, fiction has not inoculated us against the charms of the fantastic, the sacred, and other discourses that resist reduction to purely practical categories. Like poetry, fiction discloses truths that are hard to fathom.

The writer Charles Dickens knew this well. Living at a time of great scientific advances, he understood the abiding importance of fairy tales. Bewailing their rewriting into tales of moral instruction, he berated the tendency of his day to modernize them and strip them of their strange charm:

> In a utilitarian age . . . it is a matter of the gravest importance that fairy tales should be respected . . . they must be as much preserved in their simplicity, and purity, and innocent extravagance, as if they were actual fact.[1]

With secularity also comes a yearning for the sacred, or at least mysterious and foreign worlds. Instead of suppressing hagiography or fairy tales, citizens of modern democracies require new genres to do their work. It is not that we no longer crave the inspiration of heroic individuals. We simply look for them in different places. Marvel's *Agents of S.H.I.E.L.D.* or *Jane Eyre* may not have much in common with Foy of Conques, but each holds up a mirror to us, reflecting possibilities for living. While Stan Lee and Charlotte Brontë have different cultural contexts and authorial intentions, both had an astonishing ability to create characters that reach across generations. Like Bernard of

Angers their stories deepened our understanding of the tribulations and joys of being human.

Chronologically midway between Bronte's 1847 novel and Marvel's twenty-first century cinematic reboot we find Elizabeth Goudge's children's story *The Little White Horse*. Published in 1946, its influence has been broad and significant. J.K. Rowling cites it as one of her favorite books, acknowledging its influence on the Harry Potter books. Populated with some of the most charmingly conceived characters it combines many of the cultural traditions of *Jane Eyre* with the imaginative overload of Marvel. There is a merry uncle, a truth-telling minister, a mysteriously appearing and disappearing young boy, and a clan of ne'er do wells.

The heroine, Maria Merryweather, is perhaps the most lovable of them all. A young orphan girl who has been transplanted into an unfamiliar community, she has an unusually open heart. In the tradition of both St. Augustine and Brené Brown, Maria is a restless soul whose wholeheartedness leads her to search out the truth of her new surroundings. Maria's inquisitive spirit leads her on a series of literal and metaphorical journeys. Naturally curious, Maria also has visionary gifts, seeing things the adults around her miss. At first we think Maria is simply imagining things, but as the narrative unfolds the truth of her visions becomes clear.

One of the most remarkable things about Maria is that she is more than usually attentive to others. In one instance, Maria quite literally blunders into the village's Old Parson. A delightful individual with an oversized heart, he takes her under his wing. Like Maria, he is a visionary who insists on telling everyone everything as he sees it. Even when he happens to be speaking from the pulpit. Old Parson tells the truth in love in such a straightforward way, calling his flock out by name, that wrongdoers have no option but to make amends. As a strategy for contemporary preaching, Old Parson's example is best avoided. Better homiletic advice is found in Emily Dickinson's insight, "Tell all the truth but tell it slant." Nevertheless, Old Parson is adored by his people with almost hagiographical devotion.

Through her attentiveness, Maria eventually discovers that centuries ago her family took possession of a hill from the church. Known as Paradise Hill it had the best grazing land, and for centuries it was the site of a monastery. Under the grasping machinations of her ancestor, Sir Wrolf, the monks were evicted and the land turned to pasture for grazing sheep. Confronting her guardian about this centuries-old injustice, Maria is rebuffed. The land is amongst the best on the estate and surrendering it would be far too heavy a price to pay.

Fortunately, Maria is not deterred in her quest. Maria persists in her oft repeated desire to "give Paradise Hill back to God." Eventually, and in no small part to her pleading, Paradise Hill is gifted to the successor to the monks, the local church. The seemingly impossible is achieved. This one act of radical generosity becomes the symbolic turn in the book. This costly gift is simply the first of many *volte faces*, as relationships that were fractured become amenable to repair. Paradise Hill stands as a metaphor for other radical changes that Maria's loving attention arouses in those caught up into her orbit. Through gifts, large and small, Maria's intervention makes it possible to overcome estrangement and effect reconciliation. Even after generations of mutual suspicion, discord, and constant harassment, this singular and costly act of giving breaks open a new future. The cycle of giving Maria unleashes is even more miraculous than the eponymous white horse.

WHY DO WE GIVE?

Elizabeth Goudge was a lifelong Anglican, and her other novels often include selfless acts of generosity. She also had an unerring ability to see human brokenness and failure. Giving is not a universal feature of the condition of every human individual; but it is a universal feature of our societies, especially when they thrive. Some interpreters of scripture believe that every blessing is a sign of being rewarded by God, chosen by God, and deliberately preferred by God over others. Such interpretations might struggle with the story of Paradise Hill. For Goudge the rich blessing of the hill is not something that the Merryweathers deserve. It is not rightly theirs. Instead, it is a possession that calls to be given away. The anthropologist Marcel Mauss explored how gifts in ancient societies require reciprocity, creating and strengthening ties within ancient cultures. Gifts in this reading are not freely given, they create ties of what Mauss calls "reciprocating generosity."[2] There are always good societal reasons to give. The nature of giving (including the possibility or impossibility of a "true" gift) has been taken up by many others.

The literary theorist Jacques Derrida's analysis of the nature of the gift remains one of the most fascinating accounts. Although Derrida begins from a perspective that has more in common with atheism than religion, he quickly finds himself embroiled in an extended reading of theology and faith. The thorny question of the gift, and whether it can ever be truly given, leads him into dialogue with Kierkegaard's classic exploration of Abraham's faith in *Fear and Trembling*.[3] Derrida's reading treats the gift as a question that is not easily resolved, and we will return to this in chapter 11. The human experience of gifts involves us in an endless cycle of reciprocity. But might there also be another way (a more theological way) of conceiving of the gift? Through all the detours Derrida takes us on we discover how thinking the gift, and what it means to give a gift, is always to enter the realm of the possibility of a more original experience of the gift, and not simply a reciprocal giving.

Gifts call to mind givers. They make us wonder what kind of giving might constitute an exception to Mauss's cycle of reciprocal generosity.

The urge to give seems innate to life, and as individuals our thriving is closely connected to our ability to give. Numerous scientific studies have shown support for the notion that altruism is its own reward. One medical study saw how positive emotions can benefit an individual's physical health. Increased joy and happiness were also seen to contribute significantly to an extended lifespan.[4] The altruism of generosity does not simply feel good, it also has discernible health benefits. Taking all this several steps further, physician and sociologist Nicholas Christakis has studied the evolutionary biology of how human communities are created, and what makes them tick. He makes a powerful case for a "social suite" of characteristics that are encoded into the human genetic blueprint. These are social skills found across cultures, a set of universals that our genetic inheritance passes on:

1. The capacity to have and recognize individual identity
2. Love for partners and offspring
3. Friendship
4. Social networks
5. Co-operation
6. Preference for one's own group (that is, "in-group bias")
7. Mild hierarchy (that is relative egalitarianism)
8. Social learning and teaching[5]

In the light of our discussion of Anselmian friendship and Foy's protective social network, it is interesting to reflect on how much of the social suite appears within the construction of the communion of saints. Taken together these eight elements constitute an argument against the notion that genes push us towards being naturally selfish. Quite the contrary, "Our evolutionary past compels us universally to make a basic, obligatory sort of society."[6] Mauss would say a society of reciprocal giving. It is also worth observing just how many of these eight parts of the social suite are core to the construction of Christianity. These basic building blocks make us human. They also explain the genetic preference for why people might be drawn to a community of faith.

Christakis is acutely aware of the difference between theology and evolutionary sociology. Yet, his research points to a fundamentally positive way of looking at human nature: "The project of evolutionary sociology in which we have been engaged reveals that humans everywhere are pre-wired to make a particular kind of society—one full of love, friendship, cooperation, and learning."[7] This is a remarkably Anselmian statement, one that would have resonated with other medieval readers who shared his Augustinian view of humanity mirroring the divine. Anticipating and echoing this science, people of faith recognize this obligatory society. We become our better selves by letting go of some of the things that are most precious to us. And we are drawn to develop friendship and cooperative networks with others—including those who are in "out" groups.

The virtuous cycle of giving is one that enriches both the recipient of the gift and the giver. Givers are enriched spiritually, and one of the most obvious signs of this is in their capacity for wonder, love, and joy. Giving in response to the needs of others allows the cultivation of increased gratitude for our own blessings. The opposite also applies. Faith that does not cost deeply is not really faith. Kierkegaard's disturbing reading of the story of Abraham and Isaac on the journey to Mount Moriah makes this clear. The spiritual choice is always between practices that cost nothing and lead nowhere, or habits that cost everything and lead one deeper into relationship with others. To at least this native of the United Kingdom, generosity also seems to be a particularly American phenomenon, one that presumably reflects greater levels of religious belief. While the British economy is about 15 percent of the size of the US, charitable giving is about three quarters smaller in proportional terms than one might expect.[8]

TRINITARIAN GENEROSITY

If Christakis is correct, the impulse to generosity is in the DNA of the faithful and the unfaithful alike. At a deeper theological level, all is gift. Faith receives one's humanity as a gift. We are not the author of our own creation. As Marion reminds us, we did not choose this life. We are instead, those who have been given life. All that has gone before us to bring us to this point is also a gift of God. This is not to ignore the scientific account of the complex processes by which we understand biological life to have evolved. Rather, it is to affirm that there is not one atom, molecule or quark that lies outside God's extravagant gifting. Adelard of Bath, the "first" English scientist, wrote in the twelfth century how everything created has two reasons for its existence: God as ultimate providential creator, and a natural scientific reason. For Adelard the identification and comprehension of natural reasons was coterminous with God's role as creator (and vice versa).[9]

In giving to others, humans respond to something within their nature. We experience the cycle of gifts that have gone on not just for the millennia of recorded history but for millions and billions of years. It is also in God's nature to give. God gives not because God wants something from creation. Rather, God creates because God desires to share the abundance of the divine life with others. To share in the *imago dei*, the "image and likeness of God," is to share in divine creativity.

Giving requires a theological account of who the giver is. The prime giver is always the God who could not stay alone and disconnected. This is why any account of giving within a Christian framework will always lead into a reflection on the nature of God. The doctrine of the Trinity shows how at the core of God's very being God desires community with others. In the language of Sarah Coakley, the Trinity entangles us in God's desire.[10] To embark upon the search for the *via media* is to seek a God who grew so tired of human failure that God gave once again in a surplus giving: a new creation in the person of Christ. Without an account of the Trinity we have no way of hoping to make sense of the nature of that giving. The spiritual thermodynamics of the search for God is in this account thoroughly Trinitarian. It names a constant experience of receiving and reciprocating giftedness.

Every search for God enfolds us in Trinity. At the same time, the Trinity is manifested in the gift of God's self, a full and equal member of the Godhead in the Son, the Word. Only because we believe Christ might be God do we begin to posit that God might be triune. Without Christ, there would be no need to breach monotheism. It is also no coincidence that the story of hospitality experienced by Goldilocks is also the story of receiving sustenance from a community of three. There is something triune to the good life.

Imagery evokes this better than words. Coakley focuses on an image of hope from the poet, printmaker, painter, and spiritual revolutionary William Blake. Tenderly drawn, "A sketch of the Trinity" shows three people: Christ in the shape of a cross, embraced by his Father.[11] Coakley writes:

> Christ is veritably leaping into the Father's arms, in an ecstasy of simultaneous joy and costly gift. And because the vibrant presence of the Spirit [hovering above] . . . so exactly emulates the shape of the Son's outstretched arms, the viewer experiences the movement of death precisely as a leap into life.[12]

Pondering the mystery of God's giving renews our appreciation for the mystery of God's involvement in the world. The Trinity also reveals how the presence of the Spirit continues to entangle us. God is not an absent God who wrought creation and left it to its own devices. Trinity speaks instead of the ways in which God may be encountered in cycles of giving and receiving. Part of what Trinity provides is a model of giving and receiving within the Godhead that also foreshadows giving and receiving in the human community. Theologians have always argued with intensity about just how the Father, Son, and Holy Spirit are related. And yet, a remarkably stable part to so many of those arguments is the notion that the three are dynamically interrelated in the form of gift.

The question of how that gift operates is behind one of the most fundamental divisions in the Christian world. Latin, Hebrew, and Greek all give various words and concepts for approaching the divine. The Cappadocian fathers (Basil the Great, his younger brother Gregory of Nyssa, and Gregory of Nazianzus) were the fourth-century Greek theologians and bishops who advanced an experience of the Trinity that depended upon specific Greek terminology (*hypostases*) for different "persons."

For the Cappadocians, the dance of relationships that energizes and connects these persons is fundamental to the Trinity. The Greek *perichoresis*, quite literally, is an encircling of a shared territory. But *perichoresis* may also be understood as how Trinitarian love mutually interpenetrates, encircling and drawing together the three persons of God. Christians have always wanted to add that this Trinitarian love also encircles and entangles the wider human community. Such love is freely given, and participation in it is not out of a sense of obligation but out of the dynamic of grace. God's love is not simply deeply personal, revealing our truest selves, it also shows us the purpose of personhood. To be persons is to be in communion with other persons. As the contemporary Orthodox theologian John Zizioulas explains: "The Life of God is eternal because it is personal, that is to say, it is realized as an expression of free communion, as love."[13] To experience love, then, is always to be in fellowship with the persons of the Trinity.

The prayerful approach to the Trinity by the Eastern church also offered a way out of the false polarity between spiritual and erotic desire. For Gregory of Nyssa, like Anselm and so many others after him, the desire for God is a response to God's desire for us. Sarah Coakley encourages us to "reverse the modern shrinkage of thought about desire" by recovering Nyssa's entwinement of physical and spiritual desire. For Gregory the desire to know the Trinity is a refraction of divine desire in which humans are caught up in both moral and eschatological goals (which reach their apogee in the Trinity). Intellectually, the Cappadocians could not have envisaged their Trinitarianism without help from both scripture and Greek philosophy. Coakley sees Gregory effecting a "*rapprochement* between Plato's views on *eros* and biblical teaching on love and desire."[14] Against certain streams of thought that sought to radically separate the philosophical (of Platonism) from the theological (of scripture), the Trinity draws the two together.

Less than a century after the Cappadocians, Augustine attempted to comprehend the essentially incomprehensible Trinity for himself. Writing in Latin, and perhaps because his Greek was not as good as it could have been, he develops an understanding of God that leads in part to the split between Western Christianity (Latin speakers) and Eastern Orthodox Christianity (Greek speakers) that still abides. Following Augustine's Latin, the Western church added the *filioque* to the Creed, reframing the Holy Spirit as proceeding from the Father *and* the Son. By contrast, the Eastern, originally Greek-speaking, church has continued to teach how the Holy Spirit proceeds from the Father. The salient point is that both Greek and Latin speaking churches, and their descendants, continue to see the Trinity as an embodiment of the dynamics of gift. While theologians debate the relative merits of either position, what has not always been understood is the way in which *both* "positions" can only be made sense of through lived experience, rather than philosophical analysis. The Trinity is not an object to be studied. It is the energetic self-revealing of God's action in the world.

Jean-Luc Marion's investigation of Augustine underlines this sense in which the Trinity is less an object of philosophical speculation and more of a gift. Distancing Augustine from his latter-day interpreters, both scholastics in the tradition of Thomas Aquinas and philosophers like Martin Heidegger, Marion shows the centrality of the category of gift for understanding the Trinity. The Trinity for Marion is not a form of metaphysical speculation in which God is identified with Being. Rather, Marion's Augustine reveals God as a giver of love. God is the way we both discover and are enfolded into that gift. In discovering that we are the recipients of that love we are opened to the reality of God:

> Thus it is necessary for me to enjoy what I love in order to know that I loved it and that in fact, knowingly *or not knowingly*, I desired it beforehand. I am always late to the event and the last to know what I love. The will therefore follows what I love, and what I love precedes my will. I do not find myself there where I am, or where I am thinking, but there where I love, I desire and enjoy.[15]

In this reading of Augustine, the search for God is always a response to God searching out for us in love, and our desire to respond to that love. Until we respond to that gift of love from God, we do not even know who we really are. God's love gives us our sense of self, and draws us into the Trinitarian life.

The Holy Spirit has been described as a bond of love (*vinculum caritatis*), tying the Trinity together. A better locution for this essential act might be gift (*donum*). The Spirit is the gift of love that not only joins the Father and Son together, but also connects human beings together with God. In recognizing this donation we become entwined in the life of God. As shown in the last chapter, Anselm made this possible through practices of friendship as well as theological exploration. Like the Cappadocians and Augustine, he also did this in prayer. In his third Prayer to St. Mary, mother of Jesus, we hear Anselm's prayerful evocation about this gift of love. The same love that enfolds him in the Trinity, also makes him long for union with Mary and all the saints:

> Let me rise up to your love
> Desiring to be always with you, my heart is sick of love,
> my soul melts in me, my flesh fails.
> If only my inmost being might be on fire
> with the sweet fervour of your love,
> So that my outer being of flesh might wither away.

The faithful are marked by their recognition that the gift of love lies at the heart of the Christian experience of God. Part of the need for a doctrine of the Trinity is to underline how God's gift is premised on a desire for communion, seeking no reward other than the forging of the kind of mutual affections that we saw so vividly with Anselm and Gundulf.

There are, of course, traditions that do not appreciate the dynamics of Trinitarian gift. Theologies of thralldom lie at the beating heart of toxic Christianity. In them, God is feared as a capricious and overbearing patriarch or puppet master, pulling the strings of both humans and other Persons of the Trinity. It is no coincidence that sectors of the church that inhabit this theological model frequently end up privileging white male heterosexuals. They have misread Trinity for patriarchy. By contrast, if we begin with Trinity and follow its movements into the world, we will find ourselves tracking the self's desire for God, as well as uncovering a more prayerful and positive account of physicality.

The church was moved, in part, to create the doctrine of the Trinity to help explain the way the humanity and divinity of Christ are part of the divine life. Trinity is also an attempt to show how God's love is manifest and involved in the world. Trinitarian entanglements reveal God disrupting and overflowing the barriers we try to place between God and ourselves. Intellectually, Trinity is, also faith's way of maintaining the divinity of Christ while adhering to a strict monotheism. To this we also need to add how the three Persons of the Trinity represent a spiritual diversity drawn together by reciprocal givings of love.

The Trinity is a precipitate of the Christian community's attempts to understand the mystery of God. It is a prayerful rejoinder to centuries of argument and disagreement within Christianity. Equally, it is a reminder of the community of persons within God's very being. As part of their pre-*filioque* experience of the divine, the Orthodox retain a powerful sense of the threefold communion of three distinct persons at the heart of the God: "True being comes from the free person, from the person who loves freely."[16] What this means for Zizioulas is that our understanding of personhood itself is also ineluctably bound up with theology (and its understanding of the three persons of the Trinity).

There is also a connection here between the nature of an icon, and how the face is a window onto the divine. The *prosopon,* the face of the Person, is what guarantees an integrity to the personhood of each Person of the Trinity (in the same way human faces are how we situate a unique identity to the *imago dei*). There is not some abstract "Being" before personhood. The inner life of God (which is also connected to the outer experience of God in the world) is found in personhood related through love. Marion also echoes how this perichoretic life (of the Trinity) is constituted in a freedom of giving.[17] Paradise Hill is not just a symbol of this giving, it also points to how gifts freely given draw us into the divine life.

The network of Trinitarian loving is always about two interrelated communities. It is about the community of the God who is somehow, mysteriously, three persons in one communion, constituted by a dance of interpersonal relations. It is also about the community of those who have heard the story and are willing to respond to the mystery of God's gift of love. For Augustine, Zizioulas, and Coakley, the Trinity is best sought within the context of Christian prayer, Eucharist, and communal practice. This is perhaps why Trinity has been so resistant to "modern" rationalistic understandings, and so friendly to more "postmodern" understandings that celebrate broader ways of knowing. While the Trinity has a fearsome reputation as an intellectual puzzle designed to confuse, it is better approached as bottom up kind of belief. It emerges from believers wrestling, praying and working with the story of God's love in their lives. In trying to comprehend the Christian story, the faithful discover the Trinity as a mystery to join in fellowship with, rather than a riddle to be solved.

DIVINE *JOUISSANCE*

The French word *jouissance* provides another hint at the personal nature of this fellowship of love, both divine and human. *Jouissance* cannot be properly translated into English. The nearest word we have to it, "enjoyment," is only a pale shadow of the original French. *Jouissance*, by contrast, means a capacity for enjoyment that is excessive, including sexual delight. *Jouissance* denotes an ecstatic form of pleasure, and along with it a crossing of boundaries and a redefining of the self. The joy of *jouissance* cannot be easily described or easily contained, which makes it a fitting analogue for Trinitarian love. Just as God cannot be contained in a singular identity, overflowing into community, so God's love is irrepressible.

The French writer Hélène Cixous heightens the spirit of *jouissance* in the poetry, fluidity, and energy of her writing. Language for Cixous is deeply carnal, with great potential to be incarnational. A prolific author, playwright, poet, literary theorist, philosopher, feminist, and theorist, Cixous writes as if her life depends on it. Writing is not an optional extra. Writing is instead a way of loving in the world. Like the medievals before her, writing opens up the inexpressible. Cixous is steeped and immersed in language in a way that is playfully iridescent. For Cixous language is not simply a vehicle that has to be navigated to get somewhere. Language is a gift to enjoy and savor, an endlessly creative experience with which to be swept off one's feet. Cixous knows how language "englobes us and inspires us and launches us beyond ourselves, it is ours and we are its, it is our master and our mistress."[18] This could just as easily be a description of Trinitarian love.

The Trinity could be approached as both an example of, and an invitation to encounter, *jouissance*. Trinitarian spirituality through the lens of Augustine, Gregory of Nyssa, or Sarah Coakley delights in a love that is superabundantly giving, a plural love that is also singular, one that overflows and cannot be contained. To experience the Trinitarian gift of love is to experience multiplicity and interconnectivity. Cixous again seems to echo this:

> Everyone is nourished and augmented by the other. Just as one is not without the other, so Writing and Loving are lovers and unfold only in each other's embrace, in seeking, in writing, in loving each other. Writing: making love to Love.[19]

This also recalls Ivan Illich's description of medieval writing. It is almost impossible not to see resonances here with the giving of the Word that is made flesh in the prologue to John's Gospel. The Trinity names this loving not simply as a relation to one apophatically undefinable (Holy) Other, but as God who is specifically revealed in three persons, as well as in the community beyond the divine life. Cixous is frank about the way she is driven by immense desire to write. A similar intensity of desire informs the writings of the mystics in describing their own yearning to experience the joy of the divine life. It is a yearning that has frequently been mistaken for something else.

The sexual dimension to this *jouissance* is not something to ignore. Luce Irigaray, the French feminist psychoanalyst, reminds us that there is something intrinsically triadic about sexual love at its best. It is not egological or even an intertwining of dualities, rather it is an ecstasy of transcendence: "In this relation we are at least three . . . you, me, and our creation of that ecstasy of ourself in us (*de nous en nous*) prior to any child."[20] Pointing to Irigaray, Coakley wants to recover the sense in which *eros* will always be deeply entangled in Trinitarian desire. Sexuality in this reading becomes not a barrier to the divine, but a *vestigia*, an imprint of the divine that humans carry.

In chapter 4 we encountered Augustine's triadic understanding of the Trinity as memory, intelligence and will. Anselm of Canterbury, the ardent scribe of divine desire, repeats this psychological mapping of these *vestigia*. For Anselm, the human mind mirrors the divine through the intersection of memory (*memoria*), intelligence (*intelligentia*), and love (*amor*).[21] The human mind for Anselm is an expression of the divine mind, which is an original organizing principle. The only way that humans have rational thought is because they mirror the original intelligence of the Father (memory), expressed through the Son (intelligence) and the Spirit (love). Within this intellectual experience, Anselm is clear that love is critical. For him there is nothing more "delightful" than that the Father and Son share this "mutual love,"[22] which is how Anselm interprets Augustine's *filioque*. Love proceeds from both Father and Son. Yet, it is the psychological and erotics of desire that is even more interesting. Like Anselm, Coakley knows that the *vestigia* of desire (*eros*) works both ways: "if human loves are indeed made with the imprinting of the divine upon them—*vestigia* of God's ways—then they too, at their best, will surely bear the trinitarian mark."[23]

These erotics of Trinitarian giving-which-is-loving fly in the face of attempts to rationalize. Such a divine erotics breaks apart singularities and closed systems of thought or action. The dynamic of love cannot be understood by appeal to intellect alone. Instead, they demand to be experienced as a form of divine *ecstasis* or *jouissance*, a mode of experience beyond simple rational comprehension. In his exploration of this desire, Marion draws attention to how Denys, author of the mystical text *Treatise on the Divine Names* understood divine desire (*eros*) searching out creation: "God himself 'charms' all beings at once by 'goodness, charity and desire . . .' since he loves 'with a beautiful and good *eros* of all things, by the hyperbole of desiring goodness, *erotike*.'"[24] (We will return to this question of desire in the final chapter.)

The goal of Christian life is to be caught up into union with this ecstatic love-saturated Trinitarian life. As Coakley emphasizes throughout her work, this union occurs when an individual practices both a life of prayer *and* an awareness of the gendering of desire. Pneumatology, the way we experience the movements of the Holy Spirit, is at the heart of Coakley's exploration of the Trinity. God is not a remote or foreign object, so much as: "a life into which we enter and, in unbreakable 'union' with Christ, breathe the very Spirit of God. Such is the goal of a life animated from the start by *desire* for Christ." She concludes that those who enter into this desire will end up experiencing, "fascinating shifts in perceptions of (both worldly and unworldly) understandings of 'gender.'"[25] Again, this is a theology that depends on understanding the importance of personhood (including its gender dynamics) in the heart of the Trinity.

Like the Hebrew wisdom tradition out of which it emerges, the Christian experience of the Trinity veers toward a complexifying of gender and sexual difference. Trinity resists singularity and the idolatry of uniformity, offering a much richer way of imagining gender differences beyond fixed binaries. There is an antiquity to diversity in the Trinitarian life as much as in scripture. Even Anselm, a male monastic, reflects on this ambiguity of gender, naming Jesus as both mother and father:

> And you, Jesus, are you not also a mother?
> Are you not the mother who, like a hen,
> Gathers her chickens under her wings?
> Truly, Lord, you are a mother;
> For both they who are in labour
> And they who are brought forth are accepted by you.[26]

This Trinitarian gender pluralism invites shifts in the way we relate to our deepest longings: an invitation to embrace mystery and fluid boundaries. It also reinforces the inherent unknowability of God. Cixous suggests as much when she notes the mystery of not being able to understand the beings that she loves the most. Loving, and being loved, ushers in mystery. Like Anselm and Augustine, Cixous knows that the inability to comprehend the mystery of those she loves, "does not prevent me from either loving them or understanding them: what I do not understand is their own mystery, which not even they themselves reach. But I know their incomprehensibility well."[27] Once again, it is noteworthy how this secular thinker repeats a classic theological insight: the God who is divine Love is incomprehensible. Cixous illuminates the incomprehensibility of the doctrine of the Trinity, and its resistance to comprehension. The Trinitarian mystery could be described as a theology of falling in love. And the way we fall in love is through the Holy Spirit.

DETECTING INSPIRATION

Dorothy L. Sayers was a writer of detective mysteries as well as a near contemporary of Elizabeth Goudge. Both women were daughters of Anglican priests, growing up in learned environments. Sayers's father taught her Latin at age six, while Goudge's father went on to become Regius Professor of Divinity at Oxford University. While Sayers is beloved for her Lord Peter Wimsey detective books, she was also a dramatist, poet, and advertising copy writer. Yet her religious writings and translation of Dante's *Divine Comedy* are, perhaps, her most enduring legacy. She did not simply write mysteries. Sayers also wrote about the nature of mystery, something the Archbishop of Canterbury recognized in offering her a Lambeth Doctorate in Divinity in 1943 (which she refused).

Combining her two lay vocations as a writer and a theologian, Sayers argued that the uncertainties of the authorial process mirror the mystery of the Trinity. In each she saw an act of creation, the process of giving life, as the central mystery. Making an analogy between an author and God the Father, she saw that the offspring (whether the story or the Son of God), was connected to the author/Father—while still remaining free and unique. In order to realize the story, the author has to grant freedom to the characters to achieve their possibilities. Good writing for Sayers was always Trinitarian in that the characters and text need, and achieve, some form of independence. They cannot simply be controlled or dominated by the author. Characters needed to have their own identity, something that could not simply be contrived. In Sayers's language, the Idea had to be Realized. Analogous to the possibilizing power of the liturgy, stories gain their power when their characters claim and experience their own potential.

Writing is about Realizing the Idea, and allowing the Idea to take flesh in a way that was not forced. But this is not the entirety of the creative or Trinitarian process. Sayers believed that inspiration was also necessary to make the idea real. Inspiration, what theologians would call the breathing in of the Holy Spirit, is how the Father and Son are connected. As the Latin *in-spiritus* makes clear, to be inspired is at its most basic to be in the spirit. Inspiration is also how an author turns an original idea into a reality. Sayers believed firmly in this analogy. The Holy Spirit connects humans to the divine life of Father and the Son. Which is why the Holy Spirit is frequently so hard to make sense of: "We cannot really look at the movement of the Spirit, just because It is the Power by which we do the looking."[28] If one takes Sayers seriously, her theological explanation of the authorial process helps us understand both the complexity of the Trinity and the enduring power of fiction. The creativity of fiction, its "made-up ness," reveals something essential about the relationship between a gift and a giver. Fiction is a pure form of gift. It comes out of nowhere, at least nowhere apparently beyond the author's imagination, and yet it fills entire worlds. Fiction is successful when it exhibits all the characteristics of being inspired (as colloquially understood)—something that deserves admiration and elicits recognition. Inspiration is less about veracity of historical or scientific fact, and more about how the trajectories and entanglements of the characters reveal truth.

Inspiring stories in this sense also tend to efface signs of authorship. There is nothing stirring about stories when the author's machinations are too visible, clunky, or contrived. Narratives and characters easily fail to come alive or inspire. For Sayers this is because there is not a true connection between the Idea and its Realization. The missing connection is, of course, that elusive quality, inspiration. By contrast, when stories succeed in stirring their readers or viewers, regardless of the absurdity of their premises, it is because they have disclosed and inhabited freedom and integrity. For an idea to be properly manifest, the author needs to remain hidden.

This is all very evocative of Zizioulas, Marion, and Coakley. The creation is God's text, the medieval book of nature, and humanity provides the characters and narrative threads. Despite a history of being implicated by some of the most devoted adherents as a little more than a badly written check-out aisle thriller villain, God is no puppeteer or contriver of false human emotion. Rather, God withdraws from creation in order to allow the diversity of human lives to find unique expression. Just as characters in a novel rarely comprehend being written into being, so the same is true for humanity. What matters is that fictional lives and real lives have this in common: they seek a pattern of their own, searching for meaning on the horizon of their potential.

Sayers shows both how the writing process can shed light on the Trinity, and how the Trinity enhances our understanding of creative writing. The mysteries and complexities of the creative process are real. So real, in fact, that they are almost supernatural. Even some of the most dedicated atheist authors testify to varying forms of superstition as they try to better channel or control the indescribable forces of inspiration. The resolutely rationalist author of magical fantasy Philip Pullman admits (with admirable courage) to having "plenty of superstitions, which are my own and no one else's," from using worry beads to writing with only a particular type of paper and pen.[29]

Writers are rarely conscious of where ideas or inspiration come from. It just happens. Or, in Trinitarian terms, it is simply given. Faced with the ephemerality of inspiration, it makes sense to follow Pullman and create habits to grant at least some control over the inherently uncontrollable. Yet, the mystery discerned by Cixous and Sayers may also be approached with an openness to fluctuations of the divine life. To exercise creativity is to be opened to the deepest of God's desires. Marion has a deep sense of how the gift of Trinitarian love works: "To return the gift, to play redundantly the unthinkable donation, this is not said, but done. Love is not spoken, in the end, it is made."[30] Trinity is an invitation to participate in making love in this way.

The Japanese artist Makoto Fujimura terms artists who break down disciplinary barriers "border-stalkers." Like Coakley, Fujimura also finds inspiration in the figure of William Blake, a prophet of imagination who saw deeply into the heart of things. For Fujimura, the work of the artist is to "train our imagination" to see beyond the tribal divisions society depends upon, and reveal a broader cultural ecosystem. To create art is to enter into divine love by practicing "culture caring." As we saw with Sayers, Fujimura recognizes how the human capacity to create is where we share a common characteristic with God. In human creativity, and in the inspiration of making art, we manifest the divine. Like Marion and Sayers, Fujimura connects being creative with humanity's status as creature: "We are *Imago Dei*, created to be creative, and we are by nature creative makers."[31] Reflecting on the artistic practice, Fujimura explores further parallels between human creativity and divine creativity. Art in its very superfluity and lack of utilitarian necessity can open us to the theological: "Jesus's tears are gratuitous, extravagant, and costly. My art imitates this, through the use of expensive minerals, gold and platinum and a reliance on a slow process that fights against efficiency."[32] If God is the first artist/creator, then for Fujimura, the work of human creators is always entering into and pointing back to this original gratuitous creativity.

To describe love as God's Trinitarian gift is to recognize something inherently supernatural about all inspiration and creativity. It is possible to create conditions congenial for inspiration. However, it is not possible to predict the arrival of inspiration any more than it is possible to anticipate the coming of the Holy Spirit. One of the things that is frustrating about so many religious accounts of the Holy Spirit is that they proceed as if God's Spirit were an obedient pet, capable of being called from one room into the next. If the Holy Spirit is the gift of love, then that gift is a wild *jouissance* or *ecstasis* that cannot be channeled or constrained. It will arrive unexpectedly, and cannot be domesticated. Yet, we can create the conditions under which it may be welcomed. Fujimura describes his visits to the nonrepresentational paintings of Mark Rothko and sitting in front of them for about fifteen minutes, waiting for something to emerge:

> Most of the time, we are trained not to see, but to categorize and move on. It's our basic survival mode. But if you allow yourself to simply sit and stare, the eye can open up to take in beauty in a way that is rarely experienced in life. Rothko painted in layers, and each layer, it seems, comes alive to our eyes after a while.[33]

This training of the imagination is not easy. Yet it is just this kind of receptivity that draws one into the divine life.

Oikonomia (economy) is the Greek for the exchange of love for love in which no party seeks reciprocity or a return on their investment. Like the secular economy, the divine economy connects everyone together, one with another. Unlike the secular economy, this divine *oikonomia* is a communion that does not depend on rational exchange. The divine *oikonomia* is structured instead by love calling forth an overflow of love. This economy is one of superfluity and abundance, generosity, and profligacy. In Kierkegaard's poetic metaphor, love is a lake, fed by a hidden spring: "Just as the quiet lake originates darkly in the deep spring, so a human being's love originates mysteriously in God's love."[34] The economy of this spring-fed divine gift of love is boundless. It is extravagant, profligate, and reckless. The spring, the source of this love, is also well-hidden in Kierkegaard's metaphor.

In *The Little White Horse* Maria opens up new economies of giving. She helps people to look again at one another, and be willing to give ground on grudges and resentments. Like Old Parson she brings out the best in others by granting them her full attention, and then inspiring them with new hope. This relational giving is the most transformative aspect of the book, with Maria helping her elders substitute affection for enmity, and reconciliation for hatred. We might call it everyday inspiration.

To journey into the zone of the Goldilocks God is to discover the transformative reality of Maria's giving for oneself. Being human is being surrounded with gifts that we do not always appreciate. We rarely stop to think about their point of origin. For seekers of God, what matters is whether we can learn to practice a Franciscan counterintuitive habit of giving freely without counting the cost. Giving is its own reward. To give to another is to open oneself up to the mystery of that other. It is also to experience the *jouissance* of Cixous, to be decentered and taken one out of oneself.

Jean-Luc Marion has spent an entire academic career charting the phenomenology of giving. Like Martin Heidegger and Edmund Husserl before him, Marion recognizes how central the experience of the gift is to human experience. Whether encoded in the German "it gives" ("es gibt") or in the French "there is" ("il y a"), this fundamental giving is prior to metaphysics. As we saw in the second chapter, philosophers have always been astounded by the fact that there is something rather than nothing. Marion shows how this something to be amazed at is *not* a thing, so much as a phenomenological experience of being given. He also rephrases the experience of fundamental giving in the French from "il y a" ("there is") to "cela donne" (his preferred translation for the German *es gibt*, "it gives").[35] This change highlights the *donne*, the gift at the center of reality. The complex byways and detours of phenomenology in its twentieth century to twenty-first century iterations need not detain us. What Marion is really marking, however, is a shift from a metaphysics of being and Being as the fundamental questions of philosophy or theology, to the significance of givenness and gift. The encounter with the given, and the realization of being given, constitute the nature of reality.

For Christians this entry point is also named as love. Christian giving will always involve both inspirational and sacrificial elements. This is the way giving is experienced in the life of Christ. Christ dies that we might experience love and forgiveness. He dies for others, even going so far as to forgive his betrayers and accusers. His death is holy not because it is somehow free of pain or trauma. Rather, it is holy because it leads to life, a death brimming with potential. As William Blake's image reveals, it is only in the cross that we may begin to see the Trinitarian reality of resurrection hope.

This is the story J.K. Rowling gives to the orphan Harry Potter, saved by the love of his mother from the dark magic of Voldemort. Love defeats evil. Which is the story Rowling found in *The Little White Horse*, where Maria Merryweather creates community, overcoming enmity with the inspiration of love. Each story builds on the one before it, all the way back to the primal story, the gift of life by God to Adam and Eve. These stories are not simply feats of heroic imagination. Nor are they fantasies that have nothing to teach us about real life. As Sayers theorized, the truth is more complex. The creativity of these imaginative fictions draws us deeper into experiencing the full giftedness of life. Their imaginative overload shows us that there is more than we can comprehend or master. Forcing us to give up our efforts to distance or to rationalize, they urge us instead to give something in return. Mauss was correct: society is premised on the desire to return, to reciprocate the gift. Theology differs only in reminding us that this desire for reciprocation is as essential to human flourishing as it is impossible to accomplish. The Trinity shows what this impossible flourishing always looks like. Both a symbol of God's mystery, and an intimate gift given to us, Trinity is how our desire finds its origin.

NOTES

1. Charles Dickens, "Frauds on the Fairies." *Household Words. A Weekly Journal. Conducted by Charles Dickens.* No. 184, Vol. VIII. 97–100 (London: Bradbury and Evans, 1853).

2. Marcel Mauss, *The Gift: The Form and Reason for Exchange in Archaic Societies* trans. W.D. Halls (New York: W.W. Norton, 1990), 83.

3. Jacques Derrida, *The Gift of Death*, trans. David Wills (Chicago: University of Chicago Press, 1995).

4. Barbara L. Fredrickson, "The Value of Positive Emotions: The Emerging Science of Positive Psychology Is Coming to Understand Why It's Good to Feel Good." *American Scientist,* 91, no. 4 (2003): 330–35.

5. Nicholas Christakis, *Blueprint: The Evolutionary Origins of a Good Society* (New York: Little Brown, 2019), 13.

6. Christakis, *Blueprint*, 16.

7. Christakis, *Blueprint*, 418.

8. Different tax codes, cultural assumptions, and ways of funding education and healthcare make direct comparisons difficult. Americans gave away $449 billion in 2019 (on GDP of $21.4 trillion), a figure that has been steadily increasing in recent years. "Charitable Giving Statistics," National Philanthropic Trust, https://www.nptrust.org/philanthropic-resources/charitable-giving-statistics/. Comparing with the UK shows a very different landscape of giving. The total given in the UK for 2018 was around £10.1 billion (on GDP of $2.8 trillion), or about $13 billion. "CAF UK

Giving 2019," Charities Aid Foundation, https://www.cafonline.org/docs/default-source/about-us-publications/caf-uk-giving-2019-report-an-overview-of-charitable-giving-in-the-uk.pdf, both accessed February 19, 2021.

9. A.C. Crombie, *Robert Grosseteste and the Origins of Experimental Science 1100 – 1700*, (Oxford: Oxford University Press, 1971), 12.

10. Coakley, *God*.

11. William Blake, British Library ADD.49460 fo. 53v. Reproduced on the cover of Coakley, *God*.

12. Coakley, *God*, 255–56.

13. John Zizioulas, *Being as Communion: Studies in Personhood and the Church* (Crestwood, NY: St. Vladimir's Seminary Press, 1985), 49.

14. Sarah Coakley, *The New Asceticism: Sexuality, Gender and the Quest for God*. (London: Bloomsbury, 2015), 7.

15. Marion, *Self's Place*, 184.

16. Zizioulas, *Communion*, 18.

17. Marion, *God Without*, 78.

18. Hélène Cixous, *The Hélène Cixous Reader*, ed. Susan Sellers (London: Routledge, 1994), xix.

19. Hélène Cixous, *Coming to Writing and Other Essays*, ed. Deborah Jenson (Cambridge, MA: Harvard University Press, 1991), 42.

20. Lucy Irigaray, "Questions to Emmanuel Levinas," in *The Irigaray Reader*, ed. Margaret Whitford (Oxford: Blackwell, 1991), 180.

21. Anselm, *Opera*, Vol. I, 51; *Basic Writings*, 141.

22. Anselm, *Basic Writings*, 159.

23. Sarah Coakley, *Asceticism*, 97.

24. Marion, *God Without*, 74.

25. Coakley, *Asceticism*, 126.

26. Anselm, *Prayers*, 153.

27. Cixous, *Reader*, 95.

28. Dorothy L. Sayers, *The Mind of the Maker* (San Francisco: Harper, 1987), 115.

29. Philip Pullman, "Why we Believe in Magic," *The Guardian*, September 1, 2018, https://www.theguardian.com/books/2018/sep/01/the-limits-of-reason-philip-pullman-on-why-we-believe-in-magic, accessed September 8, 2018.

30. Marion, *God Without*, 107.

31. Makoto Fujimura, *Art and Faith* (New Haven: Yale University Press, 2020), 14.

32. Fujimura, *Art*, 12.

33. Fujimura, *Art*, 120.

34. Søren Kierkegaard, *Works of Love*, trans. Howard V. Hong and Edna H. Hong (Princeton: Princeton University Press, 1995), 10.

35. Jean-Luc Marion, *Being Given: Toward a Phenomenology of Givenness*, trans. Jeffrey L. Kosky (Stanford: Stanford University Press, 2002), 33ff.

Chapter Nine

Transfiguring Touch

Many years ago I found myself standing by the font, in this case a large stone basin often mistaken for an enormous flower pot. Fonts symbolize eternal life in Christ, taking their name from the Latin for well, fountain, or spring. Sources of the spring-waters of baptismal love that are poured over initiates into Christian community, fonts are gateways into the community of faith. Familiar waypoints in the lives of the faithful, on this occasion a large group waited to receive the coffin of their loved one.

It was an unusually tragic death. A young mother had died of cancer leaving several young children. Her large extended family, mostly from Quebec, had traveled down for the funeral. Encircling the font were several children whose mother tongue was French. One of them, a niece who cannot have been more than nine or ten years old, suddenly stretched out her arm to touch the gold leaf of the prayer book I was holding. Full of marvel, her eyes shining with wonder, she spoke, "C'est tres jolie." "*It's very pretty.*" In the midst of her grief that simple prayer book communicated something to that young girl that no words could. And for some reason, perhaps unknown even to her, she needed to touch it.

The need to touch the holy is primal. Spirituality is also about the human need to be touched *by* the holy. Central to the Christian story is God's desire that God's very self might be made subject to human touch. God becomes human in the person of Jesus in order that humans can touch God more easily, and also learn what it is to be touched by the holy. God touched humankind through incarnation, taking human DNA and human spirit. Incarnation demonstrates God reaching out to touch creation, quite literally, in an embodied life. So many of the New Testament stories involve touching, whether of a metaphorical or literal kind. And the touching goes both ways. Jesus touches people, but he is also one sought out to be touched.

This is particularly evident in the story the apostle Thomas, colloquially dubbed "doubting Thomas." Not present when Jesus appeared to the other disciples following the resurrection, Thomas doubts their story. Naturally enough, he wanted evidence for his own eyes. Thomas needed to see to believe. He also wanted to touch the Risen Christ for himself. In being honest about his doubt, Thomas gives the church an enormous gift. His story is a powerful reminder that words and sight alone cannot touch us. We also need physical evidence. The Gospel of John places Thomas's words to Jesus, "My Lord and my God," as the culminating point to the narrative. The apostle's words of recognition are at the climax of the Gospel, the first time we learn who Christ truly is.[1]

To a greater or lesser extent all human beings are like Thomas. The story of Thomas makes it clear that it was because Thomas doubted that Jesus appears to him, even going so far as to invite his touch. We do not know whether Thomas *did* actually touch Jesus. Nothing is said of it in the Gospel account. The Episcopal collect for St. Thomas stresses the fact that Thomas believed. While that is true by the end point of the narrative, it seems a little obtuse to place the focus there. The Church of England collect is more pastorally honest, celebrating God for allowing Thomas to doubt the resurrection. Thomas is not unique for believing. Rather, he is unique for being openly honest about his doubts.

St. Thomas's feast day, December 21, is by no little coincidence the shortest and darkest day of the year. The timing points to how the knowledge of God's love and light is most needed where life is at its darkest. In Christ's offer to let Thomas touch his wounds, seekers are also shown how the Christian God is unafraid of the darkness. God is fearless about being touched, being vulnerable and being radically present to those in grief and pain.

Touch has become a deeply contested and difficult reality, with boundaries that keep changing even as they are drawn even more firmly. Two millennia ago the situation was even more shocking. Some kinds of touch that now seem ordinary were then taboo. What is startling about Jesus is that he accepts both the most intimate and the most taboo forms of touch into the divine life: the nurturing touch of his mother Mary; the anxious and utterly taboo touch of the hemorrhaging woman; the grieving touch of the women who took his body from the cross.

The symbol of St. Thomas is the carpenter's square, a tool used for ensuring that right angles are square. It is hard to imagine that the carpenter's son, Jesus of Nazareth, did not use one from time to time. The carpenter's square is also a fitting illustration for the process of reaching the Goldilocks God. Shaped like a square "L" with equidistant sides, it is a visible reminder of how finding the square requires both the perpendicular and the vertical. To be upright in the spiritual life requires us to make the square our own: to be firmly grounded while also open to the transcendent.

The biblical world view, like its medieval successor, believed that the heavens were, quite literally, above. Metaphorically, the perpendicular always points away from the humdrum of ordinariness, and "up" to the infinite. The rest of this chapter is devoted to exploring what those perpendicular moments of intersection might be. What are those vertical moments that lift us up and point us "heavenward" towards God? As we shall see, they also require us to be rooted horizontally on solid ground, in the real world.

CYCLES OF PRAYER

Over the centuries prayer and worship have been the most common ways people have sought to touch, and be touched by, the holy. Some find prayer comes easily, while others, like me, do not. I have always been in awe of those who have an intimate relationship with God, treating the mysterious ground of all being as a friend who is instantly available to respond to one's every change of mood. I've always found God to be a lot more elusive. Worship and prayer are hard, if not actually the most difficult aspect of being faithful.

It is because prayer is difficult that I value the presence of others to show me the way. There may well be something of the divine in every human person, but that does not mean that we are all equally capable of finding it left to our own devices. There is much comfort in Bonhoeffer's insight that, "the poorest mumbling utterance can be better than the best-formulated prayer."[2] Prayer need not be perfect or poised. Its validity lies in the human heart responding to God. And yet, as Bonhoeffer also recognizes, prayers like the psalms are vital: modeling prayer and inviting us in. As Rowan Williams might say, they interrogate us, and shows us we are not alone. Without others pointing out the way, I would never have found a way of praying that worked. The wonderful gift of liturgical traditions is that they offer a helping hand to those of us for whom prayer is difficult and those of us who do not know where to start. Not everyone is a mystic lost in the depths of prayer and meditation, but we can all be carried by the prayers of others.

Within the traditions of the church there are many ways of praying to God that do not require an innate propensity for prayerfulness. Perhaps the best, and most accessible, is the service of Compline, a service that originated in the monastic prayers said before retiring for the night. Anyone can pray Compline, even alone. During the pandemic, Compline became a particularly beloved service for college students, many of whom were profoundly isolated with in person classes and activities suspended. Prayed at the end of the day before retiring for the night, it is a poignant and reassuring way of concluding the day and finding comfort and peace.

Christian prayer, like the Jewish prayer it emerged from, began by marking and celebrating the cycles of time that shape life. Prayer is structured and shaped by the different hours of day as well as the times and seasons of the year. With both an eye to eternity (the vertical), and boots on the ground (the horizontal) praying fluctuates, minute by minute, day by day, and season to season. The cycles of the agricultural year have always been significant for liturgical prayer. From the association of spring with Easter to that of autumn with harvest festivals like Thanksgiving, even modern city dwellers still inhabit parts of this agrarian-inspired cycle. Centuries ago the connection was even more explicit and universal. The medieval peasant kept track of daily time by the angelus bell and the bells announcing the services of the church. The passage of the seasons would have been marked by a plethora of feasts of saints and other holy days. Unlike the relatively small number of Federal holidays in America, many of which have almost no traditional activities associated with them, medieval people enjoyed what was both a much larger variety and a more public set of celebrations, traditions, and feasts. Feasts of the church were appropriately named as such, and these communal festivities spilled out from the church sanctuary. Saints days allowed the weary not only to rest from their labors, but to make merry and to be refreshed.

To this day, residents of the United Kingdom never go on vacation. They go "on holiday," a reminder that the original periods of rest and joy, the holy days, were times set aside by the church not purely for religious celebration, but also for rest and renewal. Feasts were just that: communal times of revelry when communities came together to experience abundance and extravagance. As well as shaping and responding to the season, prayer also shapes and responds to every human life. From birth and through all the possibilities of life and then on into death, the human life cycle forms the template for prayer's infinite variety.[3]

Just as habits of prayer evolved and changed across the centuries, so the same is true within an individual's lifetime. It would be ludicrous to suggest that a toddler, a new parent, and someone diagnosed with terminal cancer require the same prayer. We are not all touched by the holy in the same way, and yet we do all share something more elemental - our inability to grasp the holy. This inability is not a deficiency in us. It is part of why we turn to prayer in the first place:

> Rather, what is blanked out in the regular patient attempt to attend to God in prayer is *any* sense of human grasp; and what comes to replace such an ambition over time, is the elusive, but nonetheless ineluctable, sense of *being grasped*, of the Spirit's simultaneous erasure of human idolatry and subtle reconstitution of human selfhood in God.[4]

This contemplative insight is also what allows Coakley's theology of the Trinity to forge a more complex theological understanding of sexuality and desire.

In these repeated attempts to "reach" God in prayer we discover, instead, God's presence reaching out to us. It is also important to remember how this "being grasped" in prayer forms the heart of a tradition of "spiritual pragmatism" that goes on to inform and influence our action in the world. The seventeenth-century divine Jeremy Taylor's *Rule and Exercise of Holy Living* makes this fusion of prayer and action abundantly clear. Taylor was more interested in the moral behaviors that prayer sustains than an examination of theological concepts. Seventeenth-century texts frequently had very long titles, and it is worth quoting the original subtitle to Taylor's work (in updated English): "In which are described the means and instruments of obtaining every Virtue, and the Remedies against every Vice, and Considerations serving to the resisting of all Temptations Together with Prayers Containing the Whole Duty of a Christian and the Parts of Devotion fitted to all Occasions, and furnished to all Necessities."[5] Taylor locates the pursuit of the holy firmly in the real world and in the middle of the challenge of his day. *Holy Living* begins by offering advice on a whole range of ordinary topics: anger, sobriety, temperance in eating, sexual abstinence, widowhood, humility, modesty, contentment, one's duty to every relation or authority, fasting, wandering thoughts, and preparing for death (both our own, and others). Only then, towards the end of the book does Taylor more explicitly address faith, hope, charity "or the love of God" and the way that the Christian religion can be increased in us. It is not that prayer is an afterthought or optional extra for him. Rather, prayer saturates the entirety of this practical Christian wisdom.

One of the advantages of corporate prayer for those who are not naturally prayerful is that it helps one recalibrate and find perspective. The point of being steeped in liturgical prayer is that it is hard to ignore other people, and the myriad ways in which God has the capacity to touch us. Left to my own devices, my interior life is a pretty meager spiritual diet to live on. For all those times when I find it hard to pray, do not want to pray or struggle to focus, I need others to show me how, and to keep the rhythm going. One of the benefits of locating oneself in a spiritual community is that others experience the same poverty. Many of the great "experts" in the search for holiness have drawn attention to this. Abbot Dom Chapman of Downside Abbey acknowledges in his spiritual letters how difficulty in prayer is not simply for those starting: it is always part of the reality of prayer: "What I am writing about is a prayer of 'beginners': I know nothing about any other."[6]

One purpose of corporate prayer and worship is to experience transformation. Rote prayer can be off-putting. It is often critiqued for lacking "authenticity" and freshness, and it is true that rushed prayers gabbled without feeling can seem like just so much mumbo jumbo. However, it also works the other way. The more we pray the words of others the more we may find ourselves released from superficial concerns. The rhythms and cadences of familiar prayers shape one's heart, mind, and soul in deeper ways than mere conscious thought. Through exposure to the prayer of others, across both time and space, souls expand. There is nothing particularly intellectual about this. Rather, it is the feeling of being woven ever deeper into a tapestry more complex and more refined than anything one might create alone. To worship in language others have hallowed is to be touched by something of the mystery of God.

CHANGED FROM GLORY INTO GLORY

In the science-fiction series *The Expanse* we encounter a hard-bitten detective, Josephus Miller, who is determined to locate a missing woman, Julie. The television series is based on the novels of James S.A. Corey, the pen-name for collaborators Daniel Abraham and Ty Franck. Set in a future in which Mars and Earth are competing planetary systems of influence, Miller's search leads him to a shocking scientific experiment. When he eventually locates Julie he is too late. She is dead, her body laced with a strange crystalline alien infestation. Later, Miller returns to the site of Julie's inert body, only to witness a spectacular reversal. No longer dead, Julie is now alive, her body glowing with a luminescence that spreads throughout the space station. Julie has been so dramatically changed that her identity and the alien life form have fused. It is a visually spectacular scene: pinpricks of alien light flit like fireflies around Julie's radiant body. She quite literally glows. Julie's life force extends to become one with not just the space station, but eventually the asteroid that shelters it.

What is particularly moving about this scene is that while Julie has been transfigured beyond all seeming reason, she is subjectively unchanged. She wants to return home. She doesn't realize that in her transfigured state, fused with the asteroid, she can no longer return. Indistinguishable from billions of tons of space rock, going home would result in the devastation of her home planet. Displaying something of Brené Brown's courage, Miller ventures out to talk Julie down from this course of action. Making himself vulnerable to her, he removes his space suit to touch her. In this intimate manner Miller is finally able to reach the transfigured Julie: face-to-face. Revealing his identity, and reaching out in touch, Miller communicates with Julie in a way that words alone cannot. Her human consciousness reawakened, Julie diverts the asteroid to chart a new, safer, course.

This scene is eerily reminiscent of the biblical story of the Transfiguration in which Jesus climbs the mountain with Peter, James, and John. Jesus experiences the glory of God descending upon him and his disciples are overcome by emotion. We are told that Jesus's face shone like the sun, and that his face glowed. We are also told that he encountered if not alien life, then at least life that should not have been there. Matthew's Gospel narrates how two dead prophets, Elijah and Moses, join Jesus on the mountaintop. Witnessing this the disciples were, naturally enough, afraid. Jesus calms them not by talking to them but, again like Miller and Julie, by touching and reaching out with his transfigured body.[7] Like the Still Face Experiment and St. Paul's and Marion's reflection on the icon in chapter 7, these face-to-face encounters are moments of spiritual awakening that are not simply moments of passive adoration or recognition. It is not simply the glory that is beheld that is a subject for wonderment. The stories also reveal something profoundly revelatory to the way visitors to these sites of glory are enfolded in the glory of the one transfigured. As glory shines through the glowing face of Julie or Jesus, those beholding their transfiguration are also transformed.

Both episodes, one secular fiction and one sacred tale, are about seekers (whether the detective or the disciples) who experience the closest of encounters with a transformed body that is radically beyond one's normal ken. Such encounters are life changing, and lead to transformation. Miller and the disciples share the same vocation: they are metaphysical detectives. Their search for the truth leads them to stay close to the one wondrously transfigured, even when that means risking their own lives. It leads them to glory.

Glory (*doxa* in the Greek) is a recurring experience of Christian worship. Not simply found on mountain tops, it is encountered wherever Christians pray. At its most prosaic level, this is true in the doxology, a literary form that structures God's glory (*doxa*) in the deeply relational, personable, and social language of Trinity. Christians also ascribe glory to God in the Lord's Prayer, with its final acclamation found both in early Gospels and in most Protestant traditions, "For thine is the kingdom, the power, and the glory." Within the Orthodox church the two major feasts of the church remain the Epiphany and Transfiguration, celebrations which point to how the glory of God is decisively revealed in Christ.

For thousands of years hymns and words of praise have been directed to this divine glory. We continue to do this, even though theologians never cease to tell us that God has no intrinsic need of this praise. Yet, while God has no need of our praise, we are always being invited to ascribe to God not only praise, but also power and glory.

It is helpful to reflect on what this might signify. In Greek culture, Jewish and Christian scriptures alike, there is one recurring motif to which this glory is directed: a throne with no one sitting on it. In the psalms and in the book of Revelation, the throne is described as empty and awaiting the glory of God. The emptiness and majesty of the throne is what Agamben terms the "sovereign figure of glory."[8] Glory here is something different from activity. The throne symbolizes power but does not contain it. It is useful to ask what it might mean to approach the three chairs in the Goldilocks story as if they were thrones. It is their emptiness that allows Goldilocks to try them on for size, yet, as was true for so many rulers, these thrones do not fit. After rejecting two she breaks the third, literally revealing the inability of all of these thrones to do what they were designed for. The potential of the chairs to become a throne for her is never realized. In this failure to seat Goldilocks they anticipate a key part of Agamben's reflection on how the throne manifests glory.

Quoting from Augustine on the connection between glory and the Sabbath, Agamben interprets this supreme glory of God in the empty throne as a form of eternal Sabbath. It is an astonishing revelation to read in the work of a secular philosopher. As he explains:

> At the beginning and the end of the highest power there stands, according to Christian theology, a figure not of action and government, but of inoperativity. Glory, both in theology and in politics, is precisely what takes the place of that unthinkable emptiness that amounts to the inoperativity of power.[9]

What he is really saying here is that glory is both the site of ultimate power, and the site where this power is utterly inactive. Once again we see how the *dunamis* of God is radically unlike secular theories of power. This idea of inoperativity is much closer to the inaction or powerlessness of prayer than any human rendition of power.

Agamben's glory of "inoperativity" also sheds new light on something Christianity has more familiarly named as eternal life. Eternal life is not a place where something occurs. Although it has been portrayed as a bustling place of worship and praise, it can also be seen, quite literally, as an eternal sabbath. From a theological perspective, the inaction of glory and the empty throne is not something to be feared or rejected. It is instead the driving possibility of Christian life, an eternal life where action no longer matters. What Agamben names inoperativity the church names as the kingdom, the power, and the glory.

Eternal life read through the lens of glory is a call to embrace the inoperativity of the sabbath. The empty throne here is not simply a symbol of a meaningless void or nihilism. It is instead a symbol of the richness of unimaginable possibilities that lie ahead for what Agamben in other places calls the "coming community."[10] Once again we might wish to note how Agamben's language of the coming community is remarkably similar to the eschatologically forward-facing community that goes by a much simpler name: church. Or to give it its Greek inflection, *ekklesia,* a gathering of those summoned to a new potential.

To enter the liturgy is to become a part of this coming community, an extension of the divine life that allows us to touch, and be touched by, the divine. Theologically, the power of the liturgy resides in connecting us to God's glory. Worship does not require us to climb mountains or travel through space to experience this glory. The paradox of Christian worship is that there is nothing we need to do to experience this glory. We do not even need glowing lights. On the other hand, wherever we lift up our hearts and voices in praise and glory we are able to experience the glory of God for ourselves. This seems to be something musicians have always experienced more readily than others. As the hymn writer Charles Wesley put it, the goal of Christian life is to be "changed from glory to glory."

MATERIAL TRANSCENDENCE

As Jeremy Taylor's guide for holy living powerfully illustrates, the glory of God's eternal life is never something entirely removed from this life. Instead, it is a fullness of life that spills out and breaks into the ordinary. For this reason, the search for the transcendent also involves important questions of materiality. Just as the Trinity requires the construction of a theology of desire, so the life of prayer will cultivate greater intimacy and connection with those around us. Christianity has an unhappy history of presenting the search for the holy as a search that required a denial of the flesh or a fleeing from human touch. For centuries, to encounter the holy was only deemed possible if one decisively rejected the attractions of the physical world, especially sexuality. Monks and nuns were the ultimate spiritual warriors who alone were able to withstand the assaults of physical temptation. Lesser mortals were clearly second-class Christians.

The perspective of seekers of the Goldilocks God is different. Spirituality permeates materiality. It does not oppose it. To use classic Christian language, the material world is good because it has been created by God. So, to experience the material world is to be intrinsically connected to God. Encountering God is always a material, embodied, experience.

Makoto Fujimura understands this better than most. The Japanese art of Kintsugi is formed from the word *kin* for "gold" and *tsugi* "to reconnect." In the origin story for the art form, a warlord's broken pottery was made whole again using the *Urushi* Japan lacquer technique. Broken tea ware is bonded with lacquer which is then covered in gold. In this art form the mended pottery becomes even more invaluable than unbroken pottery: "Kintsugi does not 'fix' or repair a broken vessel; rather, the technique makes the broken pottery even more beautiful than the original, as the Kintsugi master will take the broken work and create a restored piece that makes the broken parts even more visually sophisticated." Fujimura views this restoring of tea ware as a foreshadowing of the New Creation, in which God restores humanity in Christ.

There is an obvious connection between brokenness and restoration (in Christ, or in Kintsugi). Visiting a Kintsugi master, Fujimura explores the broken shards collected by Nakamura-san, who hunts antiques for his craft. Holding one particular broken pot, Fujimura writes: "When I held it in my hands, it felt almost like a small soccer ball but had the warmth of rough-hewn clay."[11] In this particular case the fragment was from the Jopon period, and was probably 10,000 years old. Nakamura-San explains that the sixth dimension revealed by this object is its invitation not to be mended, but to be contemplated. While Kintsugi is an art of turning the broken into a new creation, it is equally an art of contemplation, an invitation through the touch and feel of the bowl to experience a "visceral communication spanning thousands of years."

These kinds of physical connection cannot but inform our understanding of the holy. Kintsugi and the raw materials used by its practitioners broaden what it means to be quite literally transfigured by touch. These tactile invitations to imaginative reflection also echo the work of the potter Edmund de Waal.[12] Inheriting a netsuke collection of 264 wood and ivory carvings, de Waal returns to the past to make sense of the family who collected them, before the horrors of the Anchluss ripped them apart. The story he tells of the netsuke reveals the history of the Ephrussis family. A professor of ceramics, DeWaal's narrative performs a kind of literary Kintsugi. Launched by the tactile experience of the netsuke he makes a new creation in which the tribulations of those who curated the netsuke are transfigured. As in the case of Fujimura, it is the physically experienced touch of the objects that spurs the moment of revelation and the quest to understand what they signify.

The physical is deeply spiritual. Even the apparent exceptions to this rule, some of the great ascetics of the early church, are themselves proof of the power of physical experience. A character like Simon Stilites seems out of this world to most modern people. Simon would sit on a platform at the top of a column for years at a time. In seeking to deprive himself of human contact and nourishment he was far from alone. History is full of stories about saints who attempted to draw closer to God by denying the demands of the flesh. Yet these spiritual athletes were also showing how impossible it is to set aside the human body. By virtue of their attempts to abase themselves through fasting or the denial of basic comforts, they testified to the profound interconnection of the spiritual and the material. Such practices may seem bizarre, but I would be the last to cast aspersions on St. Stilites. As someone who enjoys running, I recognize the elation, both physical and spiritual, associated with pushing one's body to its limits. Many continue to describe physical exercise in language redolent of spiritual experience. The ecstasy of physical exercise is one of the ways we come to "stand" outside of ourselves (*ek-stasis*). To run is to experience a form of transcendence, with the "runner's high" a form of addiction, tricking one's brain into running again and again as we crave elation. Spiritual people could also be said to be soul runners: people drawn to practices of transcendence that are ecstatic, taking them out of themselves.

How we touch, and how we are touched by the holy, are never simply spiritual issues. This is part of the problem of proclaiming oneself to be "spiritual but not religious." This phrase is about as meaningful as declaring oneself to be "human but not a person." To be a human being with any kind of self-consciousness is to be spiritual. All atheists are spiritual. Just as all agnostics are spiritual. To have any kind of recurring habits is to be religious. Whether one practices backhand on the tennis court or walks in the cathedrals of the California Redwoods, we are all religious, and we are all spiritual. Of course, to be "spiritual but not religious" is mostly a socially acceptable way of underlining one's autonomy and lack of need of institutional religion. But what of those who have routines, traditions, or experiences that they repeat to keep their spirits up? It does not seem extravagant to suggest that routines constructed to build up spirits are, at their most practical level, forms of religious life. And I have yet to meet a human being who has not mastered that particular skill.

Of course, theology wants to say a little bit more than this. Humans experience the reality of the divine not solely in our cerebral cortex or feelings of spiritual uplift. We also experience the reality of the divine in a spiritual network that connects us both with others and with the humdrum world in which we find ourselves. Materiality for Christians is not inert physical matter waiting to be shaped. Creation reveals the generous giving of God. Both sacred and good, creation points to its creator in the same way that human life signifies a divinity beyond.

Some places manifest the sacred with more ease than others. The tidal island of Holy Island, or Lindisfarne, entangles visitors with a sense of the holy, whether in the glittering water of the crescent harbor, the roar of the surf, the calls of the seagulls, or the gothic ruins of the abbey where monks once prayed. Although regularly cut off from the mainland when the tide is in, Lindisfarne has attracted pilgrims for centuries even after the closing of its monastery and the removal of the relics of its saints.

Like other "thin places" in remote locations where the veil between creation and heaven seems permeable, Lindisfarne is a spiritual home for those seeking isolation to draw closer to God. Holy Island's most famous resident was St. Cuthbert, living there as a hermit bishop. Cuthbert's desire to encounter God in nature was so profound, and his longing to be alone from others so visceral, that he ended up leaving Lindisfarne for the tiniest rocky islet just off the shore. No more than a couple of hundred yards long when the tide is out (much less when it is in), St. Cuthbert's Isle could not be a more inhospitable place to live. And yet, the memory of Cuthbert's prayerfulness on his Isle is strong on the island. It is impossible to visit and not marvel at the thought of Cuthbert praying in the middle of the roaring surf on his tiny rocky outcrop.

The story is also told of how Cuthbert would pray for hour upon hour simply standing in the sea, allowing otters to warm his feet. The strongest impression of my visit to Lindisfarne was standing on the beach on the feast of St. Cuthbert as the parish priest, teachers, and children from the local primary school led the island's celebration of Cuthbert.[13] Marking the shore with a stone circle, the children embodied the story of Cuthbert, telling it again, pressing Cuthbert's memory back into the sand. Juliana of Cornillon would have approved at how Holy Island continues to cherish the memory of their saint in public, even on a blustery day by the North Sea.

Despite the attraction of such places of great natural beauty and pilgrimage, the holy is not limited to them. The "common" of the church's prayer originally arose from the radical notion that the language of prayer should be in the language of the people. *The Book of Common Prayer* was designed for the *hoi polloi* or the commons: ordinary folk in search of the holy. Sacred places manifest how the experience of holiness can also be a part of a common geographical shared experience. These holy places may be rare, but they are not uncommon. Instead, they reveal how holiness has something to do with the common witness of people across time who have responded to a particular site with reverence, awe, or prayerfulness. Places as remote as Lindisfarne, Iona off the Scottish West coast, the Isle of May on the north of the Firth of Forth (on the other side of Scotland), or Skellig Michael off the South West coast of Ireland, are all magnificent to behold. They make us feel small, overwhelming us with their beauty and majesty. They demand wonder. They invite a sense of mystery.

Holy places answer the human desire to encounter the holy, and one of the ways they do this is by pointing back to holy people worthy of imitation. The human need to touch the holy is connected to the human need for exemplars like Foy, Hildegard, and Jonathan Daniels. To be human is to need to do something in response to the alienation and wonder that the universe arouses in us. Prayer, touching the holy in the middle of everyday life, is the primary way humans have done this for millennia. Holy places call forth the need to fall on one's knees and pay attention. They reward that attention by keeping traces of it long after those kneeling have left.

We do not know who built Stonehenge or for precisely what purpose, but it is hard not to be drawn into the mystery that there may be at least something sacred about the site. It seems hard to think of it solely as a Neolithic supermarket or trading center. We crave the idea that it might have had a more sacred function, and given what we know of its unique solar alignment we are probably not entirely wrong. Stonehenge clearly had a higher purpose.

The holiest sites are places that do the same possibilizing work of the liturgy. They are where prayer intersects with materiality. In the middle ages, the most famous and common of these were shrines. Host to the relics of saint, and often a great many saints, shrines were a common and embedded part of the religious experience. Shrines were then, and remain today, places to make contact with the holy.

There are as many reasons for visiting a shrine as there are people. Many have gone to be healed. Many go for deeply spiritual reasons. Some go to pay their homage or respects at the tombs of the saintly or the famed. One of the most popular "secular" pilgrim sites in contemporary England is the memorial to author Jane Austen, buried at Winchester cathedral in England at the tender age of 41. Some undertake visits to sacred places to honor a promise they made in a time of trial. Others are accidental pilgrims.

Shrines make it possible for us to be caught up into the presence of saints. For centuries the experience of pilgrimage was entirely ordinary and routine. It was not something only for one socioeconomic stratum of society, nor only something for the assiduously religious. The holy was all around, and unremarkable for its ubiquity. In recent centuries the popularity of pilgrimage waned in many parts of the church. Yet, over recent decades the numbers of people journeying as tourists or pilgrims to shrines is steadily increasing. More and more people are walking ancient pilgrim routes, with more and more of these routes being written about, redeveloped, or created in response to new needs.[14]

PILGRIM PEOPLE

In his wide-ranging exploration of the Anglican ethos across history, Frederick Quinn explores the influence of major figures across the centuries who did the most to shape the *via media*. For Quinn, to walk on this way is "to be a pilgrim."[15] Pilgrimage is a fitting metaphor for the spiritual life. It is also a powerful practice for those looking to ignite the embers of faith. Walking the Spanish pilgrim route with my family to Santiago de Compostela, the Camino de Santiago, it was impossible not to be struck by the demographics of fellow pilgrims. While many were of retirement age, a significant proportion were young, in their twenties or thirties. Few were as young as my daughters (ten and seven at the time), but there were also some babies in strollers. Most of the people we encountered on the Camino did not describe themselves as formally religious. Yet, even the most "secular" of these pilgrims on arriving at journey's end in the cathedral of St. James in Santiago would check in at the cathedral's Pilgrim Office.

Hikers and pilgrims alike show their stamped pilgrim credential to receive the compostela, a certificate marking completion of the pilgrimage. A compostela is only issued if the pilgrim credential can be authenticated, verifying that its bearer has completed a minimum of 100 kilometers of the pilgrim way. The Camino Frances, the most popular pilgrim path leading to Santiago across Northern Spain is a full 800 kilometers long, and yet many pilgrims complete the entire journey. The truly adventurous can begin in almost any European country and follow a local medieval pilgrim route that will eventually connect with the Camino.

Most pilgrims arriving in Santiago find themselves swept up in the excitement paying their respects to the statue and shrine of St. James in his cathedral. Situated immediately behind and beneath the high altar in a small crypt-like chapel the relics of St. James are held in a silver reliquary chest. Whether or not the bones of the Apostle James the brother of Jesus are contained in that reliquary, kneeling before them remains one of the most special, and yet profoundly ordinary, moments I have ever experienced. On leaving the relics, we walked around and up behind the high altar to embrace the larger than life statue of St. James himself, presiding over the cathedral. Adorned with gold and encrusted with large jewels, it is traditional to give the saint a hug or a kiss. Surrounded by crowds of others lining up to do the same, it was hard not to be affected by the experience. If the ultimate symbol of glory is the empty throne, the statue of St. James is a close second. Once again, touch mediated the holy. The very definition of Agamben's "inoperativity," the statue does absolutely nothing. Yet, by passively inviting reverence it does everything. It was a gift that invited response.

Pilgrimage changes the pilgrim. Some of that change occurs through the other pilgrims one encounters. Other change occurs through the experience of journeying through unfamiliar landscapes and places. Transfiguration occurs when we leave behind the familiar and encounter that which is other. Whether that alien encounter is with a gilded prayer book, a tidal island, a reliquary of bones, or a foreigner in a strange land, the effects are similar. The holy is by its nature unfamiliar, special, and hallowed. It is that which is not ordinary. And yet, paradoxically, it is in repeated encounters with the holy that we start to see the sacred all around. Before walking the Camino I had no particular interest in shrines, pilgrimage, or saints. These experiences helped me to understand what Coakley is getting at when she describes prayer as an adventure that sweeps us up into the Trinity:

> What we discover in the adventure of prayer ... is a gentle but all-consuming Spirit-led "procession" into the glory of the Passion and Resurrection, a royal road to "Fatherhood" beyond patriarchalism.[16]

She goes on to explain how this in turn connects inexorably to the Spirit and to the Son. Prayer sweeps us into relationship with all three Persons of the Trinity. Ordained a priest for fifteen years when I set out on pilgrimage, my initial interest was nevertheless purely academic. Visiting Cuthbert, Foy, James, and countless other shrines along the way, I found myself unwittingly entangled in the holy. This was not an intellectual awakening. Instead, I found myself changed by the devotion and faithfulness of the pilgrims who had gone before me, those who had built the way, as well as those, like me, who were not quite sure why they were walking on it.

Being touched by the holy is not reserved for those venturing out on special pilgrimages. It is part of ordinary life for the would-be faithful. At its core, being touched by the holy is the experience of being open to that which is other. The French mystic Simone Weil searched for God in the repetitive and mechanical work of a Renault factory as much as in Eucharist. She understood that creation offers *metaxu*—earthly blessings that offer deeper connections with the divine. For Weil it is the "essence" of created things to be intermediaries that lead to God.[17] Discerning where these bridges to the holy are and how to respond to them requires deep attention, something critically important for her: "the development of the faculty of attention forms the real object and almost the sole interest of studies."[18] Weil was a notoriously difficult character to be around (as so many of the saints), yet her wholehearted and deeply courageous life reveals an important corrective to a dangerous fantasy of prayer disconnected from life's hurly-burly.

As Geoffrey Chaucer's *Canterbury Tales* reveal, pilgrimages bring people of different ways of life together. Chaucer exploited with brilliant irony and satire the impure actions and motives of pilgrims. Yet, by participating, even the most impure were able to receive spiritual insights and benefits. Where shrines and pilgrimages "work" they foster new forms of attention to ordinary life. They shift the focus of the pilgrim from pure interiority to externality. Such encounters with strangers and unfamiliar places are at the heart of Christian life. We cannot be touched by the holy if we always remain alone. Transfiguration occurs in journeying away from the familiar and into the forms of community. Diana Butler Bass sees congregations as communities that nurture and sustain pilgrim practices:

> In an age of fragmentation, it may well be the case that the vocation of congregations is to turn tourists into pilgrims—those who no longer journey aimlessly,

but, rather, those who journey in God and whose lives are mapped by the grace of Christian practices.[19]

One person who shaped and enlarged my own understanding of this in no small part was lay Canon Judith Esmay. With an eye for detail and an ability to discern and magnify grace that would have caught Weil's respect, Esmay was a gentle, yet intellectually rigorous, shepherd of countless travelers into the labyrinth of Christian pilgrimage.[20]

Weil and Esmay understood that while pilgrimages invite adoration, they are arduous. They both worked hard to invite others into the mystery of the holy: but in very different ways. To sustain the hard work of touching the holy requires a certain lightness of heart. While Weil understood how the *metaxu* provide bridges from the ordinary to the holy, her "utopian pessimism" may not be the most helpful guide for lifelong growth into the grace of Christian practice.[21] Dying too young in Southern England, the testimony of her life makes one wonder whether she set the bar of gravity too high to experience abiding grace. While her life is only intelligible in its pointing toward God, she does not point as clearly toward the *via media.* By contrast, it is in the joy-filled lives of touchers of the holy like Esmay that we may better look to for sustenance for the long haul of everyday faith. Those who touch the holy also need to pull others in alongside them.

Every life is a journey from the source of life and back again. The points at which we discover how to touch the holy are anchors that allow us to turn our life's journey into a pilgrimage. While journeys have beginnings, middles, and ends that are set in advance, pilgrimages are more about the experience than the destination. To treat life as a pilgrimage is to learn to be comfortable with not always knowing where one is headed (or even where we might be sleeping that night). More significant is who one's fellow pilgrims are, and what one might learn from them. The little girl at the font was Foy-like in being touched by the glitter of the prayer book. Nevertheless, it was her curiosity and wonder in the face of trauma that have remained transfiguring for me.

NOTES

1. My gratitude goes to Stephen Rugg for helping me appreciate this.
2. Dietrich Bonhoeffer, *Life Together* (New York: HarperOne, 1954), 65.
3. Susan J. White, *Introduction to Christian Worship* (Louisville, KY: Westminster John Knox Press, 2006).
4. Coakley, *God*, 23.
5. The thirteenth edition consulted was printed in London, 1682.

6. Dom John Chapman, *Spiritual Letters* (London: Burns and Oats, 1935), 46. I remain indebted to Neil Heavisides for introducing me to this reference.

7. Matthew 17:1–8.

8. Giorgio Agamben, *The Kingdom and The Glory: For a Theological Genealogy of Economy and Government*, trans. Lorenzo Chiesa with Matteo Mandarini (Stanford: Stanford University Press, 2011).

9. Agamben, *Glory*, 242.

10. Giorgio Agamben, *The Coming Community*, trans. Michael Hardt (Minneapolis: University of Minnesota Press, 1993).

11. Fujimura, *Art*, 50.

12. Edmund de Waal, *The Hare with the Amber Eyes: A Family's Century of Art and Loss* (New York: Farrar, Straus and Giroux, 2010).

13. I am extremely grateful to Sarah Hills, Vicar of Holy Island, for her graciousness and hospitality towards me and the student pilgrims during our stay on Holy Island.

14. For an excellent overview of the major pilgrim routes in Britain see Emma J. Wells, *Pilgrim Routes of the British Isles* (Marlborough, UK: Robert Hale, 2016).

15. Frederick Quinn, *To Be A Pilgrim: The Anglican Ethos in History* (New York: Crossroad, 2001).

16. Coakley, *God*, 332.

17. Weil, *Gravity*, 132ff.

18. Simone Weil, *Waiting on God* (London: Putnam, 1951), 5.

19. Diana Butler Bass, *The Practicing Congregation: Imagining a New Old Church* (Rowman & Littlefield, 2004), 60.

20. Judith Esmay chaired the Diocesan Transition and Search Committee that elected V. Gene Robinson the IX Bishop of New Hampshire. For decades she mentored Education for Ministry groups and was a Spiritual Director. She was also Chair of the Planning Board at a time of conflict between the Town of Hanover and Dartmouth College. Esmay's attention to detail and knowledge of the Canons of the Church and the Planning Code of the Town were the stuff of legend. She provides another archetypical example of what the search for the Goldilocks God looks like. Esmay died in early 2020 as the Covid-19 pandemic lockdown was just beginning.

21. David McLellan, *Simone Weil: Utopian Pessimist* (London: Macmillan, 1991).

Chapter Ten

Why Do We Fall?

The Goldilocks story is on one level a story of failure. The tale of a young misfit who raids a well-kept home, leaving a trail of destruction in her wake. Without these breakages and failures, Goldilocks would never have enjoyed her porridge. Similarly, failure is an essential component of the spiritual thermodynamics of those seeking the *via media*.

My sociological suspicions are that this may be easier to grasp for those of experience within the Church of England than in the Episcopal Church. Both are gatherings of searchers for the Goldilocks God. Yet while America's culture of promise, hope, and success positively radiates Agamben-like potentiality this is less true in the United Kingdom. The British (Welsh, Scots, and Northern Irish included) positively adore failure. We thrive on it. We know it intimately, and there is no shame in the admission. National fiascos, particularly sporting defeats, give us a kind of visceral delight. From the tennis court of Wimbledon to the soccer turf of the World Cup or the various arenas of the Olympics, we revel in national failure. The British love to root for the loser, and braggers who flaunt their successes are not popular. In a culture that has historically prized eccentricity, failure is one of the common strands that binds us all together.

More than successful by any account, the actor Michael Caine recounts how he "became something of an expert in failure." Alfred Pennyworth, the butler he played in the movie *Batman Begins*, pastorally explains the importance of failure: "Why do we fall sir? So that we can learn to pick ourselves up?"[1] Failure shows us how to live. It has revelatory powers. It helps explain how people tick. And on occasion, defeat can be every bit as sweet as victory.

Failure also powers comedy (which shares a narrative ancestry with tragedy). Whether at the hands of Monty Python, *Saturday Night Live*, or the Greek comic writer Aristophanes, failure supplies a limitless supply of oxygen to creators of comedy. Comedy depends on falling short, and we laugh at the reversals it brings: the proud brought low, the humble exalted, the unexpected, and the unforeseen. Comedy evokes the truth of Mary's song,

Magnificat: "He hath brought down the mighty from their thrones and exalted the humble and meek." Just as society needs comedians to bring down the powerful and mock the serious, so the faithful need training in failure if we are not to take ourselves too seriously. Kierkegaard's *Practice in Christianity* could be read as a recognition of just this: "But woe, woe to the Christian Church when it will have been victorious in this world, for then it is not the Church that has been victorious but the world."[2] To practice the Christian story is to discover how failure is good for us. Failure is the primary mechanism through which humans grow and mature.

IN DEFENSE OF FAILURE

Failure requires that we make peace with disappointment and disaster. As Rudyard Kipling put it in his poem *If*, the key lies in recognizing that "Triumph" and "Disaster" are both imposters. The capitalizations are important. Kipling seems to be saying that nothing is truly triumph or unmitigated disaster. Life requires us to see the potential for both within each situation. Unfortunately, our age has forgotten Kipling's wisdom. In some arenas of life, naming even just a small "d" disaster has become almost taboo. The elimination of disaster has made triumph ubiquitous, ironically, stripping it of meaning. With the meanest features of ordinary life pointed to as triumphs, we find ourselves in a kind of double think where triumph is just as absent for all that it is constantly invoked.

By eliminating failure, or at least forcing it underground, we extend the thraldom of false triumph. The fakery of success, like the false praise of the cynic or hypocrite, is a cultural toxin. By contrast, we need to experience, and acknowledge, failure. At its heart Christianity is a story of how failure is redeemed, and how failures are called to the ongoing work of experiencing and sharing that redemption.

The divine has always been approached from within the context of a community forged out of failure. At their best, churches allow seekers to face the shadows and not allow them to dominate the future. Fear of failure is probably responsible for far more failure than anything else in human society. Dietrich Bonhoeffer reminds us that one of the worst dangers to the Christian church is believing in an ideal of spiritual community. By contrast, faith needs to interact with "ordinary" reality. Too often the search for an "ideal" leads to ignoring the tricky real bits. And then, as Bonhoeffer relates, all we have left is an idol of our own creation:

> By sheer grace, God will not permit us to live even for a brief period in a dream world . . . God is not the God of emotions but the God of truth. Only

that fellowship which faces such disillusionment, with all its unhappy and ugly aspects, begins to be what it should be in God's sight, begins to grasp in faith the promise that is given to it . . . He who loves his dream of a Christian community more than the Christian community itself becomes a destroyer of the latter, even though his personal intentions may be ever so honest and earnest and sacrificial.[3]

It is precisely a failure to live the "dream" Christian community or be the "perfectly" faithful person that guarantees spiritual vitality. Too often the faith found in churches has more in common with a narcissism that countenances no imperfection than the grace that always emerges in response to gravity.

Theologically, this is why Christians continue to direct their attention to the cross, the ultimate sign of failure. The symbol of Christian faith, the crucifix, is the symbol of legal execution. Humanly speaking, it is not a symbol of triumph. It is a symbol of abject catastrophe. Yet, this horrendous punishment remains at the core of Christian identity. Humans failed to love, and so Christ was sent to show us how to love. The fact that we crucified Christ, simply underlines the persistence of our inability to love.

Theologians have been discussing the theology of the cross for centuries. This is not simply because we believe in a God who was crucified and who rose again. The faithful return again and again to the death on the cross when confronted by failure and suffering. The cross reveals God involved in the harder parts of life. God suffering and dying is somehow worthy of belief and trust in a way that God avoiding all suffering or death can never be. Christianity's radical rejection of traditional monotheism reveals a suffering, vulnerable God who knew disappointment and bereavement from within. Without a Trinitarian understanding of God as the communion of three persons it is impossible to imagine the heartache of the cross. There are those who gloss over the cross as if the only thing that matters was the success of the resurrection. And many wish to defend the theological tradition that God does not actually suffer on the cross, that only the human nature of God suffers in Christ's agony. Wiser heads suggest that it is only because of the cross that there is a Christian story at all. The cross reveals that it is not simply humans who have experienced failure: God has also experienced failure, bereavement, and abandonment.

Crucifixion is not simply an event that happened long ago. It also represents what we do to our own highest aspirations and noblest hopes. We crucify them. Just as we crucify, mostly metaphorically—but sometimes literally—the prophets and visionaries who unsettle us and cause us to rethink our preconceptions. One of the ways failure can be spiritually generative is by acknowledging that the cross is not something others did to Christ. Spiritual maturity comes, rather, in finding oneself able to join the Palm Sunday crowd and hear our own voice join with their shouts of "crucify him, crucify him." The danger of not joining in with that cry is the danger of denying our own culpability and our own failures. We are all like Goldilocks, and spiritual health lies in being honest about our own shortcomings.

The cross neither condemns nor recriminates. Instead it reveals how love transfigures failure. Nevertheless, before we can understand how love can possibly do that, we need to acknowledge that failures are not simply an unparalleled good that draw us closer to God. Failures may draw us into God's grace: but only if we can acknowledge them for what they are, and repent. This is the work of both individuals and society. And it is in this spirit that we need to attend to one of the most endemic failures of contemporary life, within and without the church: the presence of racism.

A TALE OF TWO MINISTERS

The origin story of Dartmouth College is a cautionary tale that illustrates a wider narrative about the personal and institutional racism that shaped both America and its most venerable colleges of higher education. The first President of Dartmouth, Eleazor Wheelock, graduated from Yale in 1733. Wheelock was an academic high-achiever, receiving Yale's first scholarship. Known as the Berkeley grant, it was a scholarship reserved for the best students in Greek and Latin as well as graduate courses. It was also funded by the rents from a slave plantation that had been given to Yale by the Reverend George Berkeley, an Anglican minister who had profited from the slave trade. This was simply the first of many personal and institutional connections between Wheelock and slavery.[4]

Like so many graduates of the age, Wheelock went on to become a minister, in his case, a Congregational minister. Taking his learning out into the world, Wheelock's original plan was to found a school for the education of Native Americans. To support these efforts, in 1770 he was given three square miles of land to settle on in Hanover, New Hampshire. Craig Steven Wilder in his analysis of slavery in the Ivy League recounts how Wheelock was not alone:

> Rev. Wheelock set out for Hanover with a small group of students, his family, and eight enslaved black people: Brister, Exeter, Chloe, Caesar, Lavinia, Archelaus, Peggy and a child.[5]

Once in Hanover, Wheelock continued to acquire slaves as the newly founded College grew. Wilder estimates that there were as many enslaved black people as there were college students.

Wheelock sought resources from far and wide in his new endeavor, enlisting his friend and collaborator the Native American Samsom Occom. Occom was a Mohegan Indian and Presbyterian minister, formerly a student of Wheelock in Connecticut. He also has the distinction of being the first Native American clergyman ever to be published in English. The story of Wheelock's treatment of his former student and colleague in Christ illustrates the truth of Kipling's warning about the imposter's triumph and disaster. Occom knew both, being, in some ways, a perfect victim of his own success.

At Wheelock's request Occom traveled overseas to England preaching sermons all over the country to raise funds for the new school. Enormously successful in his fundraising, Occom's eloquence raised over 12,000 British pounds, including 200 pounds from King George III. The resulting 1769 royal charter that founded Dartmouth College bore the seal of the King and explicitly created a college ". . . for education and instruction of Youth and Indian Tribes in this Land . . . and also of English Youth and others." During all this, Wheelock remained in Hanover, having promised to look after Occom's family.

Thanks to the hard work of Occom gathering donors to support the new school, Dartmouth received both funding and its future name from William Legge, Earl of Dartmouth. Legge gave 50 guineas, starting a tradition of generous giving by wealthy donors to the College. It would be exactly fifty years later, in 1819, that this origin story would again influence not just the college, but also the rest of American civil and political life. Dartmouth's royal charter played another decisive role as Dartmouth fought to retain independence from the State of New Hampshire. In the lawsuit *College v. Woodward*, Samuel Webster successfully used the king's charter to defend Dartmouth's ability to govern itself as a private institution free from State interference. Thanks to Webster's powerful oratory before the Supreme Court, corporations were afforded rights of personhood, creating a significant precedent that continues to influence American public life.

There is no little irony in how the legal arguments of this revered son of Dartmouth used the seal of the king to free Dartmouth. In the process Webster provided the necessary legal precedent for subsequent centuries to solidify the rights of corporations to flood money into American politics. The Native American studies and legal scholar, Bruce Duthu observes how, by contrast, the rights of American Indians were nowhere to be seen during this period. Webster was heavily involved in creating the myth of American history that placed its inception at Plymouth rock. Representing not simply his *alma mater*, Webster's rhetoric was overwhelmingly placed in service of the white community:

Indian people and their sovereign governments are entirely missing in action in Webster's soaring orations and writings, surfacing only, as in the *Johnson* arguments, on occasions that advance the interests of white settlers.[6]

The 1823 case of *Johnson v. McIntosh* was the exception that proved the rule. Only here does Webster invoke Indian sovereignty in order to defend the rights of land speculators whose claims traced to early transactions with the tribes. When Dartmouth was founded, on ancestral Indian land, these rights, and their people, were invisible.

Back to Occom. Upon returning to New England he discovered that despite huge financial success, his mission had been undermined. Wheelock had reneged on two counts. First, Wheelock did not keep his promise to found a school for Native Americans. Wheelock's Dartmouth had become a school for English gentlemen rather than Native Americans (as Occom had been promising, and to whom the charter was primarily dedicated). Second, Wheelock broke his promise to support and care for Occom's family. Occom returned to find his wife and children living in abject poverty, largely abandoned by Wheelock despite the financial success of the mission to start the new school.

It is no hyperbole to suggest that from the perspective of enslaved blacks and Native Americans the founding of Dartmouth was a complete and utter failure. During the first two centuries of Dartmouth's existence only nineteen Native Americans graduated. Nor was the experience of racism at Dartmouth unique. As Wilder has shown, the history of the Ivy League is also the history of the power of those who profited from slavery and a culture of casual and endemic racism. It was also a culture of white supremacy in which it is easy to find ministers, representatives of the institutional church, advancing reasons for racism. Most of them had considerable financial interest in perpetuating the system of exploitation.

The Rev. John Witherspoon was one of the signatories of the Declaration of Independence. A Scottish Presbyterian minister, Witherspoon stabilized the finances of the College of New Jersey on the backs of human slavery. Witherspoon influenced countless denizens of the American state, including President James Madison and dozens of United States senators, college professors, ministers, and military commanders:

> He and his contemporaries had established their own intellectual freedom upon human bondage. They had also bound the nation's intellectual culture to the future of American slavery and the slave trade.[7]

Like the rest of the Ivy League, the origins of Dartmouth revealed an unholy alliance between higher education and the worst forms of prejudice. In Kipling's terms, the triumphal rise of eighteenth-century and early nineteenth-century higher education was a disaster for human dignity and the equal worth of all people.

After such inauspicious beginnings, with the arrival of President John Kemeny in 1970 Dartmouth reversed two centuries of ignoring its foundational promise in order to begin to serve Native Americans. Thanks to Kemeny's reforming zeal and awareness of Wheelock's failure to honor his founding promises, the institution began to make good. Dartmouth prioritized recruitment of Native Americans, offering scholarships that remain available to Native American students. Over 1,180 Native Americans from 200 different tribes have now graduated from Dartmouth. Wheelock's failure drove Kemeny's success. And yet, of course, the story is far from over. While Dartmouth is not alone in continuing to struggle to exorcise the specters of its institutional racism, its origin story makes it hard to ignore the depth of its complicity with white supremacy.

Samsom Occom is remembered as a saint in the Episcopal calendar. He continued to work hard for his people, despite being rejected by Wheelock. On one level his story is a story of failure. He did not succeed in creating a school for Native Americans. Yet, by other metrics his legacy is a story of astonishing success. Due to Occom's steadfast pursuit of donors and support in England, Dartmouth College received both its initial fortune and its name. While Wheelock betrayed him and used the funds for purposes contrary to the original intent of the donors, over time the institution remembered its charter commitment to serving Native Americans.

ORIGINAL SINS

As eighteenth-century ministers, both Wheelock and Occom would have known that their lives were lived under the shadow of original sin. And yet while they knew this theologically, it was not always easy for them to recognize the reality of sin and their own involvement with sinful structures. Wheelock thought nothing of coming to Hanover with a retinue of slaves. Just as he thought nothing of altering the mission of his new-found school.

The systemic failure of institutional racism is not found only in the past. It is also an ongoing social reality repeated across the generations and in every individual. Christianity has not always recognized racism as the sin it is, but it has always understood the inexorability and centrality of sin to human life. Life places monsters and obstacles in our course, most of which are best avoided. Unfortunately, not all the monsters can be avoided all of the time.

Sin is a frightening concept for seekers of the Goldilocks God. We wish we did not have any need for it. We prefer to imagine a life instead of porridge, comfortable chairs and cozy beds. Nevertheless, deep down every human being knows the visceral truth of sin. Sin, or what may better be translated as the absence of love, is everywhere. It is part of every human life, an inescapable part of shared human experience. The social operations of sin are seen more clearly in racism, sexism, homophobia, classism, and xenophobia. But there are many more ways that this originary absence of love infects and distorts relationships.

Goldilocks did not set out to break the little bear's chair. It simply turned out that way. Sin is an attempt to describe how despite not setting out to be hateful, divisive or unkind, we often find ourselves doing precisely that. Presumably, Eleazor Wheelock did not set out to betray his friend Occom. But lure of wealth or success combined with structural racism ensured that it played out that way. That is not to excuse or minimize his actions, but it does underline the omnipresent reality of failure.

Theologians have a particular name for the inevitability of such failure. It is called the doctrine of original sin. Today many good people are rightly suspicious about certain aspects of the church's theorizing around original sin. The teaching of original sin, as developed by luminaries like St. Augustine, risks rooting the start of all failure with one ancestor or, even worse, with the act of procreation. In identifying the entrance of sin into the world with Eve rather than sharing her culpability with Adam, there has also been a distinct sexism around traditional theorizing of original sin. Women and girls have tended to inherit the burden of original sin. Sexism is difficult to untangle from simplistic scriptural readings of original sin, making it the theological equivalent of bindweed or ground elder. It has deep theological roots, and for all the work that has been done to counter it, the church still has a long way to go in tearing up the tendrils of the sexist root systems we have inherited.

For travelers of the *via media*, original sin tends to be a deeply unpopular topic. Augustine's popularizing of the thesis that sin enters the world through human sexuality seems odd at best, and deeply disturbing at worst. Sexuality often seemed to the early church one of the great vices, looming greater than either Scylla or Charybdis. Instead of a story about human mutual curiosity, Eve becomes the fall girl for Adam's disobedience. Rather than treating it as an elegant story that mythologizes human failure, literalists framed Eve. In the more recent rush to repudiate sexism the church has been just as bad as the interpreters who put all the blame on Eve in the first place. Instead of challenging and dismantling sexism as an assault on the *imago dei*, and instead of rereading the egalitarianism of humanity within the story, we have written the story of Adam and Eve off as an embarrassing or inconvenient myth.

Before going further it is necessary to distinguish between some of the different significations to the word "myth." A myth in popular parlance is often a synonym for simple falsehood. There are other interpretations of myth, however, that affirm the capacity of myths to signify truth. It is in this latter sense that some of the ancient myths and legends of various cultures are better approached. Not as simple fabrications, but as poetic constructions that reveal truth. For the Greeks, theology was a form of poetry, and it is this mythopoetic dimension of theology that bears further reflection. Once again, the poetic imagination is better able to appreciate the complexity to how myths generate truth. In his analysis of *The Dream of the Rood*, the eighth-century Anglo-Saxon poem, Malcolm Guite delves into the stratigraphy beneath the words. Exposing the pagan roots of the words woven into this Christian poem, Guite encourages us to listen to the way words and myths are freighted beyond their mere surface appearances.

Guite suggests discussions of myth and metaphor would benefit from the account of Humphrey Carpenter, who recorded a debate that took place between C.S. Lewis, J.R.R. Tolkien, and Hugo Dyson in September 1931 as they strolled through the grounds of Magdalen College, Oxford:

> Lewis had never underestimated the power of myth. Far from it, for one of his earliest loves had been the Norse Myth of the dying god Balder. Now, Barfield had shown him the crucial role that mythology had played in the history of language and literature. But he still did not *believe* in the myths that delighted him. Beautiful and moving though such stories might be, they were (he said) ultimately untrue. As he expressed it to Tolkien, myths are "lies and therefore worthless, even though breathed through silver."
>
> *No*, said Tolkien. *They are not lies.*
>
> Just then (Lewis afterwards recalled) there was "a rush of wind which came so suddenly on the still, warm evening and sent so many leaves pattering down that we thought it was raining. We held our breath."
>
> When Tolkien resumed, he took his argument from the very thing that they were watching.
>
> You look at trees, he said, and call them "trees," and probably you do not think twice about the word. You call a "star," and think nothing more of it. But you must remember that these words "tree," "star," were in their original forms names given to these objects by people with very different views from yours. To you, a tree is simply a vegetable organism, and a star simply a ball of inanimate matter moving along a mathematical course. But the first men to talk of "trees" and "stars" saw things very differently. To them the world was alive with mythological beings. They saw the sky as a jewelled tent, and the earth as the womb whence all living things have come. To them the whole of creation was "myth-woven and elf-patterned."

This was not a new notion for Lewis, for Tolkien was, in his own manner, expressing what Barfield had said in *Poetic Diction*. Nor, said Lewis, did it effectively answer his point that myths are lies.

But, replied Tolkien, man is not ultimately a liar. He may pervert his thoughts to lies, but he comes from God, and it is from God that he draws his ultimate ideals. Therefore, Tolkien continued, not merely the abstract thoughts of man *but also his imaginative inventions* must originate in God, and must in consequence reflect something of eternal truth. In making a myth . . . a person is actually fulfilling God's purpose, and reflecting a splintered fragment of the true light. Pagan myths are therefore never just "lies": there is always something of the truth in them.

They talked on, until Lewis was convinced by the force of Tolkien's argument.[8]

At the risk of taking Tolkien's thought in a very different direction from that originally intended, it does not seem entirely inappropriate to transpose this argument about the truth of pagan myth onto the mythopoesis of scripture. Whether one reads Adam and Eve as revelation or myth (or both), Tolkien's suggestion seems to point to taking the truth of this story seriously, at least at the level of myth if nothing else. It also reiterates the connection between the human imagining, whatever the faith of that human and whenever their imagining occurred, and the human as a mirror of God, the *imago dei*.

Myth in the Tolkien sense makes it possible to listen to the story of the Garden of Eden once again. Goodness can always be abused. Reason, sex, and even compassion can always be (dis)oriented towards nefarious purposes. But there is nothing inherently necessary that these divine gifts must divert us from being kind to one another or seeking the divine. All are part of the spiritual thermodynamics of seeking God in the middle of everyday life. Once we stop approaching the story of Eden as the subordination of one gender to another we can hear its deeper music. Examined for its potential to carry deep truth, it becomes a tale about the inevitability of human failure. It is here that the linguistic code offered by original sin has much to commend it: as an ancient myth that nevertheless reveals much about who we have thought we are.

The scriptures cannot provide good answers about what the original sin was, who made it or how it is transmitted. The story of the Garden of Eden is not history. However, it does provide a poetic story about the inescapability of human failure. There is deep truth to the notion that brokenness is a non-negotiable part of who humans are. Contrary to the cultural coding that constantly promotes "Triumph" with sunny smiles, vapid inducements and superficial optimism, lovers of God know the unavoidability of sin. The faithful know that disaster is part of human life. Wherever we were born, we all come from Eden.

Unlike traditions that constantly emphasize fallen-ness or propensity to sin, those searching for God in the middle of everyday life are more sanguine. From the moment we fail trying to walk as infants, to the time we first fail to convince our parents that they owe us dessert, to when we crash the car, fail the test, or don't get the perfect job, the work of being human is characterized by failure. This is the alienation that we know from within. To speak about sin is simply an attempt to name how these negative experiences are nothing to be afraid of.

However hard seekers after the divine try to live good and faithful lives, they will make mistakes, hurt others, and fail to live up to the image of God within them. Unconscious failures, sins unknown, things done and left undone, are all a constant. Some of these human failures are so systemic and go so deep that the phrase original sin remains a powerful talisman to alert us to their horror. The original sin of racism is not something that can be avoided. It is to be named and resisted. And those of us who have benefited from the subjugation of others are the ones who have the most work to do.

In the HBO show *Watchmen*, we see a dramatic reimagining of a world after the Tulsa Race massacre. The original Tulsa Race massacre of 1921 saw a mob of white residents, including law enforcement, destroy what was at the time the wealthiest black community in America.[9] Large numbers of black citizens were killed, and about 10,000 were left homeless. *Watchmen* begins with the atrocity of the massacre, and then moves forward to present a society in which white supremacy is being challenged and systematically taken apart. The show imagines a society that has so transformed its structures as to drive white supremacy underground, while making reparations to descendants of the massacre. It is a fantasy, and aspects of it are not entirely utopian. But once again, fiction offers hope (though not without honesty about potential challenges) for how society may envisage new antiracist ways of living.

THE PSYCHOLOGY OF SIN?

Some sins are easily recognized as such. Others hide in plain sight. Doubters of the unavoidability of human failure would do well to explore the pioneering work of psychologists Amos Tversky and Daniel Kahneman.[10] Tversky initially led research into the way humans make decisions. Through practical experience, first in the Israeli army, Tversky shed light on the role played by human psychology in making poor decisions. Later, Tversky and Kahneman would expand this research into other fields. Whether analyzing the work of realtors and stockbrokers or performing creative field studies with students, their research uncovered a whole field of systematic human failure. What is most interesting about the findings of these psychologists is that in all cases the subjects responsible for making poor decisions were not poorly trained or ill-educated. Most of their research was conducted in fields of higher education or professional life where the barriers to access are very high. Yet, in experiment after experiment Tversky and Kahneman discovered how the brightest and the best consistently made poor decisions based on instinctual responses. One of the blind spots for the highly educated is that they may think they are immune from making poor decisions.

To reduce it to its simplest, Kahneman and Tversky realized that human beings are excellent at making assumptions. This is the "thinking fast" piece of their work. Even the most highly educated and mathematically sophisticated of their subjects repeatedly jumped to false conclusions rather than taking the time to discern the true nature of a problem at hand. What makes this even more extraordinary is how many of these intuitive or semiautomatic responses were not the product of human laziness or stupidity. Instead, Tversky and Kahneman identified a structural feature in the human mind dealing with the many different types of processing requests it receives.

To explain why this might be they posited the existence of two separate processing features within the human mind. "System one" way of thinking, Kahneman's "thinking fast" system, responds quickly, almost intuitively, to sensory and intellectual input. Then there is "system two" thinking, a "thinking slow" approach that takes more time to mull things over before reaching a conclusion. Most of human life is dealt with by the fast system. Right now, it is your fast system that is reading and translating the marks on this page into words. It requires little to no intellectual effort to read the words once one is familiar with the grammatical conventions of the English language. In the same way, it requires little to no intellectual effort to work out basic mathematical questions, like how much money is left in my wallet after I have bought lunch. But bigger questions are different. Questions like why is there life on planet Earth, or what does it take to make a good tank commander, stockbroker, or graduate student all require the "slow" part of our processing power. They require us to slow down and think deeply.

Tversky discovered that people, especially experts in their respective fields, were often drawn to responding with the "fast" part of their processing power when the "slow" part is what was required. Simply put, humans are not very good at hiding their bias or jumping to conclusions. What both psychologists found was that this insight applied equally to mathematical questions where there is only one correct answer as to more complex social questions. Even people who are meant to be particularly attentive to the nuances involved in mathematical problems involving probability or statistics, for instance, would frequently come up with the wrong answer. This was not because they were bad at math. Rather, it was because their "fast" thinking brain would take over before the "slow" part could kick in to properly situate the problem. Humans are naturally drawn to think fast. Even humans who should know better jump to conclusions when confronted with certain questions.

Tversky and Kahneman offer good psychological reasons for the structural inevitability of failure. Psychologically, humans are hard-wired to make impulsive and quick-thinking decisions that blind us to the complexity of many of the questions facing us. The pyschologists show how it could not be any other way. We rely on the speed of our brains to make sense of things around us without having to consciously reflect on what our mind is processing. There is no shame in this. If we did not, the most ordinary of human encounters would be extraordinarily mentally taxing. Even the smartest and most successful people are structurally incapable of keeping the "fast" part of their thought processes from taking over when the "slow" part needs to be engaged. Or to put it in the language of this chapter, the way we think is always failing us. We are always jumping to conclusions and making snap decisions based on faulty reasoning. Once we appreciate this we can try to make adjustments and attempt to anticipate and reason around our inbuilt biases and subjective leaps. Yet even then we remain human: heavily reliant on our ability to think "fast" when we should, instead, be slowing down.

For Tversky and Kahneman there are structural features of the human mind that means mistakes are more than accidental. Faults are part of the human psychological profile. Blundering about and not getting things right is not an aberrant or unusual experience. It is not something that can be avoided so much as mitigated. If we attempt to translate their work into theological language, it could be said that Kahneman and Tversky offer psychological confirmation for some aspects of the mechanisms of human sin and failure. Logically, there is no escaping the psychological flaws identified in the transitions between system one and system two thinking. The flaws are part of human nature. To be human, then, is not to pretend they are not there. Being human is instead about being attentive to where flaws in human psychology are most likely to derail individual thinking.

The trespasses of Goldilocks in the home of the three bears may reveal nothing more than her thinking too fast. In this sense, Kahneman and Tversky simply repeat Augustine's sense that humans will always make mistakes. This may even help us understand Augustine's own relative surprise at some of his own failings. In the famous episode from *The Confessions* when a young Augustine and his friends steal apples from an orchard, Augustine chastises himself for going along with an action that he later intellectually regrets. At the time he is confused at how he felt himself swept up in the power of the group to steal something he did not even really desire. We might add that he simply allowed himself to be led by the part of his brain that was thinking fast, rather than slow. Thinking fast he followed his instinctual desire for friendship and fruit. He didn't stop to think slowly about the ethics of stealing another's apples.

Tversky and Kahneman provide convincing arguments for the deep-seated presence of irrationality, or failure, in the way even the brightest humans think. Nevertheless, the theological view of failure is not simply about mental reasoning or psychological aptitude for jumping to conclusions. It goes even deeper. Spirituality speaks of brokenness as something that permeates the whole of life. It is part of who we are. As Brené Brown showed, failure reveals courage and wholeheartedness for what they are: powerful ways for reconstituting the self that enable us to shrug failure off as something that need not drag one down. There is clearly an intersection between Tversky and Kahneman's psychological theories of failed thinking, Brown's treatment of vulnerability, and the spiritual understanding of failure. However, there is a more significant reason for the emphasis on failure in theology that has not yet been discussed. Only failure can convince of the necessity for forgiveness.

THE DRAMA OF FORGIVENESS

Forgiveness is one of the core habits of spiritual practice and the most classic Christian virtue. It is also the hardest and least well practiced of all Christian habits. Experiences of personal failure and being let down provide two of the major routes into forgiveness. The genius of Christianity, or at least the genius of Jesus, was to see that failure in the eyes of the world does not preclude divine forgiveness. Time and again, Jesus forgave outsiders and those on the margins: tax collectors, the ritually unclean, lepers, the sick, and the possessed. While many of these situations may not strike us as ones that even require forgiveness, Jesus used forgiveness to liberate those whom society had deemed unacceptable or untouchable.

In the same way that God is mystery, so forgiveness is also incapable of being reduced to rational explanation. Rationally, there is no conclusive argument for the existence of God any more than there is an argument for forgiveness. It is natural to bear a grudge or plot revenge. Forgiveness is not natural. Nonetheless, the experience of failure frees us to receive the positive news of divine forgiveness. Human beings need ways of releasing themselves and others from the burden of failure, and forgiveness provides just this.

Jacques Derrida famously turned to increasingly explicit theological themes during the last phase of his career. Tellingly, he analyzed the subject of forgiveness, a somewhat shocking move for his predominantly secular and rarefied academic audience.[11] Always a student of paradox, Derrida articulated what he described as the impossibility of forgiveness. But this "impossibility" has a very technical meaning. Derrida's impossibility of forgiveness does not deny the possibility that forgiveness can occur. Forgiveness is impossible, in the same way that God is *the* impossible, or the impossibility *par excellence*.

Yet, as Derrida investigates, these seemingly "impossible" events of forgiveness do occur. Derrida never once denies the (impossible) possibility of forgiveness. Instead, this thinker who famously confessed, "I quite rightly pass for an atheist," directs us to the divine nature of forgiveness.[12] Derrida signals how forgiveness is quite foreign to human conventions of reciprocity. To borrow explicitly theological language, forgiveness is, a gift. Although Derrida does not actually say this, perhaps even the pre-eminent gift.

While forgiveness follows a divine logic of its own, the liturgy of the church scripts this essentially unscriptable experience. Through public or private confession the faithful are transformed through their experience of failure to encounter divine forgiveness. Failure is the prerequisite for forgiveness. Part of the way liturgy creates genuine potentiality is by drawing the faithful into a renewed experience of grace by delivering the pronouncement of absolution to them.

So is there any failure or sin that God does not forgive? Or, to put it more starkly, are certain kinds of people outside God's forgiveness? The idea that certain heinous acts are unforgivable makes intuitive sense. This is certainly my initial "thinking fast" response to many of the most awful crimes against the person or against humanity. And yet, if there are unforgivable crimes, then God's hope for humanity would seem to be unraveling whenever these awful events occur. This is critically important. If failure is how humans experience the need for forgiveness, and if forgiveness originates in God, then an unforgivable sin would seem to delimit the scope of God's power. Remembering the true character, the *dunamis* of God's power, it may be more helpful to understand forgiveness as the way God's possibilizing power breaks through.

Another way of asking this is to reflect on what is going on when murderers amend their ways and genuinely seek to repent and start over. Or what of a notorious persecutor who ends up being one of the great cheerleaders for divine forgiveness? The story of St. Paul is exactly that story. The tale of one who was intent on destroying Christianity, who ends up proclaiming it more ardently than any other person. Christianity simply makes no sense without the possibility that there may be forgiveness of genuine hurt. Indeed, it depends on the reality of forgiveness to reveal alternatives to the endless cycles of recrimination and hatred. The obligatory society of Mauss and Christakis would seem to benefit from a certain openness to forgiveness if humans are to continue to be defined by reciprocal giving.

Nor is the instinct for forgiveness unique to Christianity. The Dalai Lama recounts the story of Lopon-La, a Tibetan Buddhist who the Chinese kept captive for eighteen years, forced to do hard labor in appalling conditions, with barely enough food and little heat or creature comforts. For much of his captivity the prisoners were tortured. On one occasion the only thing available to eat was the flesh of a dead prisoner that was so frozen that it was too hard to bite. When Lopon-La met the Dalai Lama, he explained that during these eighteen years the worst thing to face him was not any of these physical torments: instead it was the spiritual temptation of losing his compassion for his Chinese guards.[13]

The capacity to have compassion for others is part of the drama of forgiveness. Lopon-La is a spiritual giant for his ability to see the spiritual danger of not having compassion for those who were torturing him. He also reveals something critical about the nature of forgiveness and compassion. These spiritual practices are just as important for our individual thriving as the basic necessities of food, warmth, and shelter. Even when we are the ones who are wronged, there remains hard spiritual work for us to do.

To go through life adamant that we have been more offended against than offending is to go through life spiritually cauterized, shorn of possible avenues for spiritual growth. As the familiar quote goes, "Resentment is like drinking poison and hoping it will kill your enemies."[14] To avoid resentment requires embracing failure, and enjoying being both recipient and giver of forgiveness. Only by embracing and acknowledging failure can individuals experience God's grace and forgiveness. Without having the experience of being forgiven, it is very hard to go out and forgive others.

Experiencing forgiveness and showing others they are forgiven are how we orient ourselves to the divine. Forgiveness heals would-be believers, unbelievers, and the faithful alike. It is how we learn to pick ourselves up.

THE JOY OF FAILURE

The city of Pamplona in northern Spain is a wonderful place to viscerally experience the Christian drama of failure and forgiveness. I discovered Pamplona almost by accident when walking the Camino Frances to Santiago de Compostela. We set out from Saint-Jean-Pied-de-Port in southern France, and walked along the winding trail that crosses the snow-topped Pyrenees before descending into the Basque region of Spain. After several days of beautiful walking through picturesque villages, forest, and undulating farmland we reached Pamplona. Famous for the tradition of the running of bulls through its streets and playing host to Ernest Hemingway, Pamplona also boasts a magnificent medieval cathedral.

Within the cathedral lies the Occidens Museum, an exhibition dedicated to telling the story of the West. Making full use of the ancient architecture of the cathedral, the exhibit weaves in and out of the different centuries of the cathedral's history. At one point visitors are taken down into a darkened subterranean level to explore its original foundations, including skeletons of early martyrs. Later visitors are taken through room after room with highly colored images and statuary of Jesus, Mary, and countless saints.

At the conclusion of the exhibit visitors are confronted with something that has all the appearance of a pink garden shed or playhouse. Every surface was coated in flat monochrome pink. It was unabashedly superficial and a striking contrast to the cathedral's enormous collection of artifacts, reliquaries, and paintings. It had none of their astonishing ingenuity and none of the complexities of color, texture, or material composition. The museum communicated a clear message, and it was impossible not to be struck by just how utterly inane this final structure was.

The exhibit pushed visitors to reflect on the contrast between the flatness, uniformity, and dullness of contemporary life compared to the strange and often disconcerting richness of the imaginative synthesis of scripture, art, and tradition within the medieval fabric of the cathedral. To encourage further thought, visitors are shown their reflection in a mirror. Before leaving we had to look at the reflection of our own image and ponder what we saw staring back at us.

The Occidens museum is an astonishing bit of visual preaching. What makes it incredibly powerful is that so many, if not most, of the statues on display are not particularly enticing or attractive images. There are, to be sure, some glorious and awe-inspiring liturgical items, gleaming gold chalices, monstrances, reliquaries, and all manner of precious ecclesiastical treasures. Nevertheless, so many of the statues and images were representations of failure, hurt, or suffering. The bones of the martyrs. Images of Jesus dying on the cross. Pictures of saints and the Virgin Mary, many of them looking particularly doleful. Weeping at the feet of Jesus. There were almost no shiny happy faces in the entire exhibit. In fact, much of what was on display was deeply heart-breaking. And yet, despite the sadness and tragedy these religious artefacts depicted, they pointed to deeper joys.

The superficially unthreatening and uplifting pink of the playhouse suggests an entirely different emotional trajectory. Stripped of anything that might cause hurt or even hint at resistance, the pink void of the shed was strictly utilitarian: a safe, barren, play space. It was not the empty throne of Agamben's reading of glory. It was simply empty. Signifying the challenge of relativism to the West, the museum asks whether our deepest desire is for anything more than a safe space where edges and roughness have been removed. Without texture or depth, even the merest hint of potential challenge or difficulty had been erased, making the playhouse devoid of complexity. On leaving the cathedral museum, the most disturbing image to linger was not any one of the many depictions of crucifixion streaming with blood, nor the uncovered bones of martyred saints. Instead, it was the image of the emotionally neutered playhouse.

Failure is necessary if we are to grow and find meaning in the whole of our lives, the dark parts as well as the brighter parts. Failure is also the way that humans, like the statues at Pamplona, radiate something of the forgiving love of God. Michael Ramsey concluded his exploration of Anglican identity by recognizing that the credibility of the church lay not in its virtues or successes but in its Lord: "And the Lord of the church is Jesus, crucified and risen, who through his church still converts sinners and creates saints."[15] Without the failure of the cross there is no grace or hope. Faith that is not forged through the cross will never be able to cope with failure: instead, it will remain hostage to idolatrous and false human ideals. Perfection is not the goal of the spiritual life. Rather, repeated encounters with failure and its spiritual twin, forgiveness, expose us to the perfecting possibilities provided by the divine. If to err is human, and to forgive is divine, failing is sanctity's catalyst.

NOTES

1. Michael Caine, *Blowing the Bloody Doors Off: And Other Lessons in Life* (London: Hodder and Stoughton, 2018), 202–4.

2. Søren Kierkegaard, *Practice in Christianity,* eds. Howard V. Hong and Edna H. Hong (Princeton: Princeton University Press, 1991), 223.

3. Bonhoeffer, *Life*, 27.

4. Craig Steven Wilder, *Ebony and Ivy: Race, Slavery, and the Troubled History of America's Universities* (New York: Bloomsbury, 2013), 95.

5. Wilder, *Ebony*, 113.

6. Bruce N. Duthu and Colin Calloway, *American Indians and the Law* (New York: Penguin, 2008), 175.

7. Wilder, *Ebony*, 111.

8. Humphrey Carpenter, *The Inklings; C.S. Lewis, J.R.R. Tolkien, Charles Williams and their Friends* (London: George Allen & Unwin, 1978), 42–44, quoted in Guite, *Faith,* 50–51.

9. I am grateful to Craig J. Sutton, professor of mathematics at Dartmouth, for educating me about the Tulsa Race Massacre and introducing me to *Watchmen*. At the time of writing, Sutton, together with colleagues and students, is engaging the Dartmouth campus in a shared antiracist experience around themes raised by *Watchmen.*

10. For an excellent overview of their work see *Thinking, Fast and Slow* by Daniel Kahneman (Farrar, Straus and Giroux, 2013).

11. Jacques Derrida, *On Cosmopolitanism and Forgiveness* (London: Routledge, 2001).

12. Jacques Derrida, "Circumfession." In *Jacques Derrida*, ed. Geoffrey Bennington (Chicago: University of Chicago Press, 1993).

13. The Dalai Lama, Desmond Tutu, and Douglas Abrams, *The Book of Joy: Lasting Happiness in a Changing World*, (Avery: New York, 2016), 155–56.

14. Nelson Mandela, Carrie Fisher, Anne Lammot and countless others have had the quotation attributed to them.

15. Michael Ramsey, *The Anglican Spirit* (New York: Seabury Classics, 2004), 134.

Chapter Eleven

Treasure Hidden in the Field

During the sixteenth century, debates between traditional Catholicism and rapidly proliferating reform movements became progressively more vitriolic. Like the contemporary hyper partisan coverage of many American news outlets, loaded, sharp, and angry rhetoric was all the rage. Character assassination was one way of communicating the seriousness of the stakes, and religious opponents were frequently tarred with the opprobrium of being if not the devil himself, then certainly his willing instruments. Both sides carved salacious or scatological images into wood to demean and caricature of their opponents. Printings from these woodcuts were the fastest way of sharing and disseminating visual propaganda. It was a brutal age, and hacks on both sides did not hesitate to deploy whatever weapons of coarseness and vulgarity they thought might make an impact: they would have loved cable news, twitter, Facebook, TikTok, and Instagram. And with immortal souls hanging in the balance, between eternal torment or heavenly bliss, the stakes could not have been higher.

Through the images of woodcuts or the screeds of pamphlets, it required no great imaginative leap to demonize the opposition. Reformer Martin Luther is explicit about why:

> I was born for this purpose: to fight with the rebels and the devils and to lead the charge. Therefore my books are very stormy and warlike. I have to uproot trunks and stumps, hack at thorns and hedges, and fill in the potholes.[1]

The one thing Luther and his enemies could agree upon was that those they disagreed with were not simply wrong. They were in rebellion from God, and, quite literally, under the influence of devils.

With the passing of the centuries, many of the topics that led to such heated disagreements seem quaint or even ridiculous. For a long time many reformers deemed it the most diabolical Popishness to have candles burning upon an altar. Even the very object "altar" reeked of such Popery that Protestants made sure to take altars out and replace them with simple wooden tables. Protectors of candles had their own quibbles, not the least of which was the vexed issue of translating the bible from the Latin vulgate into the vernacular language of the people. Stoutly proscribed across Catholic Europe, the church in England was far from unique in prosecuting vernacular translations as an automatic heresy, punishable by death.

Even after the break with Rome that occurred the year earlier, Henry VIII followed a very traditional path when in 1535 the great English translator William Tyndale was strangled to death and burned at the stake after being tried and found guilty of heresy. Tracked down by agents of the Holy Roman Emperor, his crime had been to translate the vulgate into an English his contemporaries could understand. Ironically for Tyndale, his desire to return to the original text made him both the enemy of King Henry VIII (who was at this point seeking an annulment from his marriage to Catherine of Aragon) as well as the staunch Catholic loyalist, Emperor Charles V. Within just four years the politics had changed, and Henry would use Tyndale's words for authorized English translations. Seventy years later the Tyndale text would go on to form the heart of the King James "Authorized Version" of the bible. I have yet to meet a Roman Catholic who today argues against the bible being translated into English, just as I have yet to encounter a Protestant who would think it amiss to light candles in church.[2] Questions of candlelight and language may seem inconsequential or trivial today, but four hundred years ago they were the types of thing one died for.

Theological disputes in each generation echo the concerns of the wider culture. Candles now seem innocuous, but in the middle of the Reformation candles were complex, and contested, signifiers. More than just a symbol for the Light of Christ, it was the fundamental building block of an entire mechanism of salvation, what theologians call soteriology. Candles were the obvious and ubiquitous signs of a larger devotion to relics, cults, and saints. And so it made eminent sense to reformers to extend their rejection of the cult of venerating saints and relics to include a repudiation of images, vestments, and candles. All were essential parts of a medieval religious life concentrated on Eucharistic celebration. Every saint had candles burning in front of their altar, and every shrine offered the possibility for the pilgrim to make a financial gift in exchange for the hope of spiritual benefits. The candles themselves were the physical manifestation of this spiritual-cum-financial exchange.

Saints' relics were thaumaturgical commodities, providing the hope of miracles and access to the holy for royalty and the great unwashed alike. The shrines that held these relics burned enormous quantities of wax, providing historians a way to track the literal waxing and waning of a saint's popularity through financial receipts.[3] Candles were the most visible sign of a wider spiritual and economic ecosystem. When reformers targeted that system of shrines, saints, relics, and superstition, they naturally targeted the candles that were its popular point of access.

From a spiritual or theological perspective there is nothing intrinsically right or wrong with lighting candles in church, just as there is nothing intrinsically right or wrong with Latin. In a time of great illiteracy it made eminent sense to keep the language of the holy scriptures in the language of Latin. Latin was a universal language that could be read and understood by people who spoke vastly different mother tongues. It was the language of education, regardless of where one lived. To know Latin was to be part of an international community that transcended the linguistically and administratively complex patchwork of European kingdoms, duchies, principalities, and city states. Latin was to medieval culture what computer operating codes are to modern culture. Keeping the bible in Latin was not primarily about restricting access to a trained elite. The international language of Latin ensured that those who had been trained how to read and study would bring intellectual sophistication and doctrinal coherence to church teachings. While today we do not think twice about restricting the practice of law or medicine to a professional class that has been taught, passed examinations, and accredited, so the medieval church placed a high value on transmitting accurate saving knowledge. Medieval scholars appreciated unaccredited charlatans messing around with doctrine about as much as today's medical boards thrill to the idea of uncredentialed quacks performing open heart surgery. What was at stake was both a question of authority and a matter of life and death. Resistance to change was not simply an assertion of power. It was also born out of a desire for the guardians of the faith to be properly equipped to protect the immortal souls of those entrusted to them.

FROM BETRAYAL TO RESISTANCE

If one person's resistance movement is another's terrorist organization, so spiritual reform can look the same as spiritual betrayal. Perspective is key. What makes the spiritual thermodynamics of the Goldilocks God different from sixteenth-century partisans obsessed with correct belief and defeating theological opponents is not so much *what* is believed, but *how*. Those searching for the *via media* are open to learning from both the traditional and the reformed dimensions of Christianity. Even when we strongly disagree with aspects of either, we are uncomfortable demonizing those who have sincere beliefs that are different. Religiously, seekers after the Goldilocks God are pluralists, able to see the benefit from having a wide variety of interpretations about religion.

While it is easy to reject the sixteenth-century obsession with labeling different beliefs as "devilish," there remain times when it is necessary to take a stand. While our age does not detect demons lurking under every bed and hiding around every corner, in ethics and morals there remain areas of human life requiring resistance rather than accommodation. Part of the search for God requires distinguishing the life-giving middle way from death-dealing extremism. Seekers after the holy cannot be focused only on their own spiritual flourishing. They are also called to champion and advocate for the marginalized and those at the receiving end of injustice. Or to put it in classic theological language: the commitment to resisting evil and injustice is part of every baptismal vow—and these vows are meant to be kept. The faithful no longer need to defend candles or texts. Rather, we are asked to use them to illuminate and articulate how to defend the dignity of others.

While defending the dignity of others sounds simple, what this means in practice is no less perilous than sixteenth-century debates about candles. Søren Kierkegaard argues against reducing religious faith to ethics. Faith is different, and sometimes faith will require us to commit acts that are unethical. For many, this remains deeply controversial. Certainly, Kierkegaard does not win many adherents by pointing to the story of Abraham, who has gone to Mount Moriah to sacrifice Isaac, after God tells him to do just this. And yet, even journeying to kill his son, Abraham is still said to have trusted in God's promise that his descendants will spread across the face of the earth. Saved only by the intervention of a ram at the last moment, it is a powerful vignette for a faith that is not reducible to reason or ethics. Abraham's story also presents a clear instance of searching for a middle way when the alternatives look terrible. This is not a story about the search for the middle way being easy. Rather, if the story is to be believed, it is a story that points to the need for trust. A trust that for Abraham extends to suspending the ethical, in order to continue to tread the path closer toward the divine.

Many struggle to relate to this story, with its reliance on Abraham's seemingly supernatural ability to understand God's intentions. What of situations where faithful or ethical choices are not clear? Who has not been presented with an ethical dilemma where the correct moral or ethical choice lies hidden? Maybe the story of Abraham and Isaac has something to say about moral decisions where the only choice is between the lesser of two evils? To choose between going against God or sacrificing one's son is not really a choice. No action here can be correct. Which is why it is helpful to treat this story as a paradigmatic revealing of the middle way. The middle way is not the correct way. It is the space that is inhabited where, like Abraham, we live in the ambiguity of knowing that we do not know what to do.

The beauty of the story of Abraham and Isaac is that it shows how morality does not equate to spiritual maturity. We already saw how Jacques Derrida investigated this story as part of his analysis of the gift. Derrida underlines the essential challenge here:

> The sacrifice of Isaac belongs to what one might just dare to call the common treasure, the terrifying secret of the *mysterium tremendum* that is a property of all three so-called religions of the Book, the religions of the races of Abraham. This rigor, and the exaggerated demands it entails, compel the knight of faith to say and do things that will appear (and must even be) atrocious. They will necessarily revolt those who profess allegiance to morality in general, to Judeo-Christian-Islamic morality, or to the religion of love in general.[4]

Ethically, Abraham's decision is wrong. He should not be killing his son, or even going along with what looks like the preparation to do that. But spiritually, the story raises the possibility of the impossible: that there may be ethical situations where the right spiritual action is the wrong ethical action.

This seems to me to be the heart of the moral confusion of living a Christian life in the Goldilocks zone. On the one hand, morality and ethics are fundamental. If anything, Christians should adhere to much higher standards of morality and ethics. And yet, if faith signifies anything, it means responding to God with creativity and imagination. Those who seek God are ethical-cum-spiritual agents who make decisions on the basis of possibilities that are gray and confusing, laden with uncertainty. Derrida's reading of Abraham's experience again gets to the heart of what it means to be faithful:

> Our faith is not assured, because faith can never be, it must never be a certainty. We share with Abraham what cannot be shared, a secret we know nothing about, neither him nor us.[5]

Neither faith nor ethics simply can provide certainty, however much we crave it. Even if we wanted to, we cannot choose how to act against some unchanging moral plumb line. To be able to resist evil and seek the good requires a moral and spiritual sensitivity to the ambiguity of many of the challenges facing us. If we are to resist evil we also need to risk a certain vision of ourselves, even ethical and moral values that we hold dear.

The German theologian Dietrich Bonhoeffer shows how Christianity always comes with a price. Bonhoeffer was a pacifist who worked to resist the National Socialist regime. At a time when many in the church accommodated the prevailing antisemitism of the era, Bonhoeffer broke away from the Nazified church, becoming a member of the Confessing Church. Confessing Christ as their head, they sought to undermine and counter the spread of antisemitism by holding on to theological principles that included respecting the dignity and faithfulness of the Jewish people in the sight of God.

In 1933, when Jews were being excluded from professional and civic life, including the removal of pastors from the church who had Jewish ancestry, the Confessing Church counterculturally insisted on recognizing the full dignity and humanity of the Jews. Bonhoeffer was not alone, joining with his entire family to oppose the racism and totalitarianism of National Socialism. Unlike Abraham, Bonhoeffer did not act entirely in isolation without support. While there was nothing inevitable to his resistance to evil, and while it was undoubtedly heroic, it was also shaped by his privileged intellectual and religious background. Without his upbringing in a community of faith and the intellectual climate of his family, resistance may not have been possible.

In 1937 Bonhoeffer published an important book about how following Christ always comes at a cost.[6] To be a disciple, to follow Jesus, is to give of oneself without counting the cost. If Christians are unwilling to pay a price for their faith, then that faith is essentially a kind of "cheap grace," something not worthy of the name. Bonhoeffer recognized instead the preciousness and expense of grace, describing this "costly grace" as "the treasure hidden in the field."[7] One cannot help but think that this is the very same field that R.S. Thomas writes about in his poem "The Bright Field." Thomas describes seeing the sun illuminate a small field within which lies "the pearl of great price, the one field that had treasure in it." For Thomas this field also evokes Moses's encounter with the burning bush, which, in turn, anticipates the scene of Transfiguration.[8]

In the poem, Thomas knows that he had to give all he possessed for this treasure. In his life, Bonhoeffer proves similarly ready to pay the price required for this costly hidden treasure. Even though he was a pacifist, in the face of the great evil of the Nazi regime, he teleologically suspended the ethical, and joined those plotting assassination to end the terror of antisemitism. A man of peace, he did all within his power to resist the evil of his day, even when that meant suspending his own deep commitment to nonviolence. Taking part in a plot to kill Hitler, Bonhoeffer suspended his deeply felt pacifism to resist evil with action. Captured and imprisoned, just days before the end of the Second World War the Nazis executed him. Bonhoeffer was thirty-nine years old.

It could so easily have been otherwise. Bonhoeffer had the opportunity to wait out the war in safety. In 1939 he fled to New York where he was profoundly moved by the spiritual songs and traditions of African-Americans in Harlem. He was horrified at the casual racism and segregation of contemporary New York. Yet, as war broke out Bonhoeffer returned home to work from within to undermine the regime. What is particularly revealing about Bonhoeffer is that only six years earlier he had written the following:

> The only way to overcome evil is to let it run itself to a standstill because it does not find the resistance it is looking for. Resistance merely creates further evil and adds fuel to the flames.⁹

In choosing to be part of an active resistance Bonhoeffer must have understood that he was doing precisely the opposite of this. Faced with a situation much like Abraham on Mount Moriah, Bonhoeffer heard the call to sacrifice his cherished moral beliefs, and move from pacifism to active resistance. In joining the resistance plot to kill Hitler, Bonhoeffer was not simply opposing the National Socialists. He was also revising his own understanding of the nature of resistance in the face of profound evil. The constant for Bonhoeffer was not ethical theory, but the call of faith.

Bonhoeffer imitates Abraham's faithfulness in the face of apparent moral madness: continuing to follow God while sacrificing ethics. Living faithfully, he chose the path of costly grace, paying the ultimate price for abiding in the hope and trust that evil would not triumph.

Working out how and when to resist evil is probably the hardest part of the spiritual life. Less well known than Bonhoeffer's experience is the story of Marion Pritchard. At the height of the Second World War in 1944 Pritchard was living in occupied Holland. A social work student, she decided to help Jews escape who were at that time being rounded up by the Nazis. One night three Nazis and a Dutch collaborator came searching her home. They did not find the place where Marion was hiding Fred Polak and his three children, an infant, a four-year-old and a two-year-old. After the Nazis left, thinking the coast was clear, the Polaks came out of hiding. The Dutch collaborator, however, suspecting that they might do just that, returned and confronted Marion. Faced with certain death for herself and the family she was hiding, Pritchard killed the collaborator, keeping Fred and his children alive. Like Bonhoeffer she chose the path of Abraham.

Pritchard continued to help Jews escape the Nazis for the remainder of the war, saving 150 from certain death. Unlike Bonhoeffer, she survived the war, moved to the United States, and eventually become a psychoanalyst. In 1981 she was recognized by Yad Vashem, the Holocaust memorial and research center in Jerusalem, as "Righteous Among the Nations." Following her death, Deborah Dwork wrote, "Not only did she save lives during the 1940s, but she continues to save lives today through her influence."¹⁰ Pritchard resisted evil, and through her continuing influence and life's work she inspired others to do the same.

Pritchard and Bonhoeffer both knew the love of God first-hand. The source of their resistance to evil came from believing that in order to love their neighbor, this required putting both one's self at risk as well as one's cherished beliefs.

> Greater love hath no man than this, that a man lay down his life for his friends. That is the love of the Crucified.[11]

For Bonhoeffer, God's love is not some cloying sentimental feeling. Resisting evil was not an abstract idea for either figure. Rather, it was a demand for practical action that conflicted with the ethical and religious proscription against killing. While it is easy with hindsight to valorize and celebrate heroes and heroines of the resistance, their actions, like Abraham's on Mount Moriah, were not without their own "fear and trembling."

Resistance to evil appears straightforwardly heroic only in retrospect. Kierkegaard understood that the "moment of decision" is never so easy. The actual moment is always shrouded in ethical uncertainty, moral confusion, and physical danger. Neither Bonhoeffer or Pritchard were soldiers, part of a unit following orders and governed by the rules of war. In each case they were civilians behind enemy lines. Against those who actively collaborated with the regime, Bonhoeffer and Pritchard chose a path that was as morally and ethically hazardous as it was physically dangerous. While they had moral hesitancy and an aversion to violence, they also had the spiritual backbone to revise and to suspend these principles when faced with evil.

In the life of Etty Hillesum we see a third approach to how faith might provide resistance in the face of evil. Jewish and Dutch, Hillesum was deported by the Nazis to Auschwitz where she died. Her remarkable diaries and writings reveal an extraordinary perspective. Interned, and living among those being brutally and systematically murdered, Hillesum resists the evil all around her by choosing faithfulness. In the midst of the horrors and uncertainties facing her own future and that of her family and community, Hillesum's resistance points us back to the powerless *dunamis* of God.

Hillesum's faith helps reveal the centrality of the promise and potentiality of faith within the human experience, even when God is gone. Hillesum's faith turns the tables on a God who seems entirely absent and powerless in the face of evil:

> If God does not help me to go on, then I shall have to help God . . . I shall merely try to help God as best I can, and if I succeed in doing that, then I shall be of use to others as well.[12]

Acknowledging that God cannot help her, Hillesum nevertheless commits to helping God: "You cannot help us, but we must help You and defend Your dwelling place inside us to the last."[13] Hillesum's resistance brings God back to where God is gone, pointing us back to the presence of God's image and likeness within every human being. By choosing to resist evil, Hillesum refuses to abandon the God who is powerless and vulnerable, the God who is within her and the faces and bodies of those around her. As Richard Kearney notes:

> Faced with the certainty of imminent dispatch to Westerbork concentration camp, and the collapse of European civilization all around her, Hillesum could still write: "I have been feeling strong . . . so free of fears and anxieties . . . Perhaps I shall walk right across Russia one day, who knows? . . . [W]e are lost permanently and for all time unless we provide an alternative, a dazzling and dynamic alternative with which to start afresh somewhere."[14]

This dazzling alternative is the *dunamis* of the transfiguring potentiality of the divine, found deep within every human being. It is the astonishing testimony of Etty Hillesum that she was able to conceive of this dynamic alternative while evil raged all around her. Hillesum does not simply point to the possibility of God. She shows how to forge that possibility even in the worst possible circumstances.

Those searching for the *via media* need to be willing to make similar connections between the world around them and the spiritual life. It is impossible to find the holy while ignoring the tragedies and injustices of everyday life. It is always easier to see the evils of a previous age than our own, and part of the challenge of spiritual maturity is to recognize how we may defend against evil and bear witness to the possibility of God's love in our own times. To search for God is to join a resistance movement. Like the French Resistance in the Second World War, spiritual resistance movements cannot operate under the same conventions and rules as wider society. Theologically, Bonhoeffer and Hillesum both point us back, once again, to the powerless *dunamis* of God, as typified by the cross of Christ: "Christ helps us, not by virtue of his omnipotence, but by virtue of his weakness and suffering . . . Only the suffering God can help . . . man is summoned to share in God's sufferings at the hands of a godless world."[15] This is what they both did, from different religious traditions that shared an understanding of God in the image and likeness of all people. Writing from prison or concentration camp, Bonhoeffer and Hillesum resisted not solely by fighting against evil but by modeling lives of faithful grace. Bonhoeffer nurtured the souls of those around him, his compassion and fidelity to God earned him the respect of both fellow prisoners and guards. Hillesum refused to allow the evil of the camps to sunder her from the divine.

Heroic stands against unacceptable evil are not the only forms of resistance. Resistance is also a practice of calling the world to experience rebirth. Through the practices described in previous chapters seekers of the holy draw God into the world rather than set God against the world. Resistance to evil does not mean resistance to all that is worldly. The ancient Manichean idea that the world is the creation of an evil One and that everything within it is evil is spiritually infertile. Equally unpromising is the frigid moral reasoning that claims nothing ultimately matters and that all actions and perspectives are equal.

INNER DEMONS

As we saw with the Dalai Lama's friend Lopon-La and his worry that he would lose compassion for the Chinese guards, the greatest threats to spiritual growth lie not outside, but inside. Martin Luther made the same discovery four hundred years earlier, although he expressed it much more dramatically. Demons were real for Luther, because for years he had lived with them and fought them—on the inside. Which may also explain why he was so ready to identify demons in others.

After years of failing to earn grace by his own deeds, Luther had a spiritual awakening which, like Brené Brown's, was also a breakdown. Luther realized that his attempts to be devout enough to qualify for God's grace were all ultimately futile. However hard he tried, he could not get to the point where he felt justified in the sight of God. His world-upending revelation was ultimately very simple: God alone was capable of freeing Luther from his burden of guilt. Or in his own words, God alone saved and justified him, imputing to him a righteousness that was not of Luther's creation.

Luther's enduring legacy was the realization that he, and every other Christian, is neither simply a saint or a sinner. Things are more complex: we are *simul iustus et peccator*: both just and a sinner. Or to translate it better, the person hoping to be Christian is always a saint and always a sinner. Luther knew that the greatest challenge of the spiritual life is the challenge found within the heart. Like Augustine before him, he recognized that the hardest things to resist in life were not external, but the temptations that come from within. Luther underlined how resistance to those temptations could never be achieved by virtue of one's own strength and faithfulness. He had tried that route, and it had been a dead end. Ironically, each of us continues to have to learn that it is a dead end for ourselves before we can embrace the liberation of God's gift of grace.

A little more than eleven hundred years before Luther had his startling insight into the nature of God's grace, a British monk by the name of Pelagius was involved in a dispute about the same topic. Once again, much theology in this early period is distinctively adversarial. Heavyweights competed through their writings, and occasionally one of them would be decisively knocked out when certain positions were declared heresy. Pelagius was an ascetic who had a more optimistic view of human nature than the teaching of original sin might suggest.

Just how optimistic is still being vehemently contested today. For many centuries it was thought that Pelagius believed humans achieve merit in God's eyes by virtue of their own free will. St. Augustine countered Pelagius by affirming the more pessimistic view of human nature. For Augustine the depth of sin meant that God's grace alone could redeem. Augustine's view of original sin meant that apart from divine grace, humans can never achieve righteousness. While Augustine won the literary fight with Pelagius, as Nicholas Adams notes, Pelagius deserves sympathy for pursuing an approach that was more consistent, neat, and tidy.[16] By contrast, Augustine's teaching on sin and grace was complex, messy, and paradoxical. As a result in 418 Pelagius's ideas were declared heresy, and shunned by most later Christians, including those on different sides of later Reformation splits.

Grace, for both fifth-century Christians and later sixteenth-century Roman Catholics and Protestants, was at the heart of this dispute. What is most fascinating is that while Pelagius is held as having lost, he probably did not even believe that humans could attain salvation by their own free will. Doctrinal history is mostly written by the winners, and what these theological debates often teach is the enduring complexity of the relationship of divine grace and human free will. While there is no doubt that Pelagius stoutly defended free will, this is not the same as denying the grace of God. If salvation is purely a work of God, does this make human freedom entirely illusory? How should the faithful reconcile belief in human freedom and trust in divine grace? While Pelagius was labeled a heretic and Augustine the defender of orthodoxy, scholars are only really starting to recognize the complexity of their debate and how the two are much closer than the tradition (passed down by the victors) has led us to believe.[17]

Augustine's negativity towards the human will also needs to be rethought. Many commentators have been blind to the complexity of Augustine's thought, lifting it out of context. Augustine did not see the human will as something that was entirely opposed to grace. Rather, Augustine believed that true human will cooperated *with* grace. As Jean-Luc Marion's study of Augustine shows, the self in Augustine is not an isolated phenomenon set apart from God. Rather, the human self becomes truly a self, and discovers its true will, as the human self reaches out beyond itself to be constituted by God's grace. For all that Augustine recognizes how sin estranges us from God, he also points to an understanding of the human self (including our memory and will) that emerges as a gracious gift of God. The complicated thing about Augustine is that he is trying to articulate how the self and God are not separate objects, so much as interdependent. And it is grace that always draws the self out of itself—to God.

In some ways, Luther's insight was a return to the original Augustinian rejection of Pelagius. But in the intervening centuries the church lost sight of the centrality of God's grace as opposed to human action. The historical arguments, and contemporary ones, over the teachings of Pelagius point to how Christians are continually re-evaluating (and arguing about) the central mystery of how God's grace extends to us. Can human action trigger grace? Do we cooperate with God's grace? If we do, does God make it more or less possible for that cooperation to take root? Was Pelagius correct in teaching that human nature does have freedom and is inclined towards goodness? Or were his opponents right, that human nature is ineradicably fallen and incapable of working without grace? In the light of Christakis's work, maybe Pelagius deserves some rehabilitation. Is Christianity the mystery of prevenient grace (preemptive grace that comes from God before we do anything to deserve it)? Are humans capable of making good decisions on their own? Or is Augustine correct, what we think of as our will, is only ever properly our own will when it is cooperating with the desire for God's grace?

These questions hopefully show that the answers to them are not straightforward. Grace is not simply a substance infused into human life, grace is rather a metaphor for the essential need for a relationship between God and the human soul. The French theologian Henri de Lubac is helpful here. In discussing the relationship of nature and grace in Thomas Aquinas, he notes how profoundly interconnected the two are. While they are distinct, they both originate in God, and it is in human nature to desire the supernatural grace that comes from God. That grace does not come out from nowhere. It is God's response to human "velleity," a desire for something that each human being cannot achieve.[18] Seekers after the Goldilocks God hold a unique position on these questions. We admit a certain agnosticism in the face of such big questions. We understand why many embrace the Augustinian-Lutheran insight. We also appreciate how others wish to lean in different directions. Half a century after Luther first started ruffling theological feathers, the English Puritan William Perkins complained:

> Our common people bolster themselves in their blind ways by a presumption that God is all of mercy, and that if they do their true intent, serve God, say their prayers, deal justly, and do as they would be done unto, they shall certainly be saved.

Perkins lambasted such behavior as "vulgar religion" and "country divinity." Such notions were heresy.[19] He saw it as undercutting the Protestant ideal of God's grace through faith with the notion that humans might be able to attain salvation through their own works. One suspects that more than a few pew-sitters today would think Perkins was describing not heresy but the very foundations of Christian habit.

The "Pelagian" heresy that one's actions matter seems important today, even if it was overstating it to name it heresy, and even if it was not exactly what he taught. If God's grace is really all we need, then why would anyone bother with anything? Why waste one's time on something as silly as being kind to someone or saying one's prayers? The problem of the classical Reformation insight of Perkins and Luther is that it chipped away at the notion of human actions bearing any significance. It got rid of any awareness of Aquinas's "velleity" and how that drives us to seek grace in the first place.

Followers of Goldilocks lean toward Luther and Augustine in their reminder that God's grace makes us "just right." But we reel from the thought that this frees us from good works. Like Pelagius we believe in free will and that human nature does tend towards the good. Like Augustine, we believe that it is almost impossible to be a human self without knowing and desiring the truth of who we shall be, a truth that draws us closer to God. We are not at all averse to pulling ourselves up by our own bootstraps. Goldilocks is not a story about embracing fate or passively waiting for someone to save her from herself. Like Pelagius, followers of Golidlocks rather like the idea that we have free will to plot our course. Unlike devoted Roman Catholics and devout Lutherans, we lack a strong sense of what the "correct" way to answer the paradox of grace might be. Faith alone? Works righteousness? A bit of both?

My suspicions are that I am far from the only doctrinally unsound member of the Anglican Communion who wants to have all three, even sometimes inhabiting all three positions simultaneously. This is why we need Goldilocks to help ground us somewhere in the middle, seeing the necessity of both faith in God's absolute grace *and* the faithful response of human works. Divine grace is essential, but so is recognizing how human nature is grounded in divine goodness and capable of responding to the divine. While some seek to oppose nature and grace, a more incarnational approach emerges if we celebrate the interdependence of nature and grace.

The Reformers as epitomized by Luther and Calvin placed God's grace back in the center of human life. Yet all too often this was at the expense of nature, including the natural affection of human love. They risked forgetting Augustine's hunger and desire for God, a hunger he knew originated with God's love for us to begin with. By contrast, seekers of the Goldilocks God are not content to trade one for the other. We like to think that the pairs faith/grace and love/nature can work together. This desire to inhabit the middle ground, leaving such questions essentially undecided, forms the theological core of those befriending Goldilocks in their search for the divine.

Theologians and the faithful are familiar with the language of paradox. My suggestion is that we also become more comfortable with the experience of what Jacques Derrida called "undecidability." For Derrida this undecidability is not a cop out. It is instead an attempt to think a more infinite kind of responsibility. The undecidability of infinite responsibility resonates with what we already saw in the experience of Abraham journeying to Mount Moriah. As Derrida explains, for him and for Emmanuel Levinas, it also emerges from the responsibility to every concrete other, holy or otherwise:

> I would say, for Levinas and for myself, that if you give up the infinitude of responsibility, there is no responsibility. It is because we act and we live in infinitude that the responsibility with regard to the other (*autrui*) is irreducible . . . I owe myself infinitely to each and every singularity. If responsibility were not infinite, you could not have moral and political problems.[20]

Infinite responsibility is not simply a theological paradox. It is also what emerges in the encounter with every other (whether that is a person or the Holy Other). Navigating life creates situations that are, strictly speaking, undecidable. One moment they point in one direction, another the opposite. With lives that hover around indeterminacy, faith does not allow us to avoid the experience of the undecidable, it simply crystalizes it.

While it is good to trust in God through faith, seekers of the Goldilocks God believe that trusting in God does not exempt us from shutting down our critical faculties or absolving ourselves of responsibility for our actions. While we cannot earn our way into God's affections, we cannot simply be passive in the face of God's amazing grace. A spirituality that does not seek to love one's neighbor, and resist oppression, would be a hollow spirituality. Where some believers prioritize faith over works of love or works of love over faith, those on the *via media* find themselves uncomfortably caught between two equally coherent imperatives. Faith without works of love is as spiritually barren as works of love without faith.

The deeper challenge for those searching for the *via media* is realizing that resisting evil requires us to be simultaneously Protestant and Catholic. We know we need God's grace. We also know that grace requires action. I may well be naturally Pelagian in my predisposition for works of love. I also know that the hardest spiritual challenge has nothing to do with the power of evil as some external force. Far harder are the temptations found within.

In the face of the awesome power of apathy and inertia, the faithful developed a whole panoply of structures, sacraments, and doctrines with which to resist. All it takes for evil to flourish is for good people to do nothing. My natural sensibility is not to look out on the world and view it as an evil hostile environment. Following Augustine's own rejection of the dualism of Manicheeism that saw the world as inherently evil, it seems better to treat the world as a created good. The problem with this can be that in believing creation to be good, we do not do enough to counter injustice and evil when it is present. Too much piety can lead to quietism, just as too much action leads to forgetting God.

Lovers of the Goldilocks God are united in recognizing that the biggest challenges to finding the holy are resolutely inside of us. If the church is a resistance network, even before that it is a community of people trying to resist parts of their own nature. This is perhaps why the example of Pelagius is so appealing. We want to be able to transform ourselves. Even though we know we need God's grace, we are drawn to the idea that our inertia, our failings, and our peccadilloes might all somehow be manageable. We prefer not to go it alone, even as we worry that we may have to. Abraham's journey, with all its undecidability and uncertainty, needs to be seen not as a disturbing exception but as a paradigm of the holy life. This is not a life that necessarily looks holy from the outside. What it is, is a life that attempts to do justice to the insight of Emmanuel Levinas that we encountered right at the start of this book: to remain faithful to our responsibility to the other. The paradox of Abraham's infinite responsibilities is in remaining true both to the face of Isaac the beloved son—as well as the Infinite One who has promised so much that may be. Kierkegaard and Derrida never claim to understand the full extent of Abraham's impossible situation, but they do reveal the true undecidability of faith.

APPROACHING MOUNT DOOM

One of the great twentieth-century stories about the power of evil and the ethics of resistance is J.R.R. Tolkien's *The Lord of the Rings*. Wearers of the rings of power are creatures who are corrupted from within, by virtue of their own desire for authority and control. Whether they are the nine Ring Wraiths, ancient Kings of men, or Gollum, formerly the hobbit Sméagol, those who wield the ring of power are stripped of goodness, and fade away. Corrupted by their own lust for power, they become shadows of their former selves, living in almost perpetual darkness. What is notable about Tolkien's story is how the resistance to this evil is primarily located not in the mighty armies of elves or men but in the humble hobbits. Although part of a wider Fellowship of the Ring, the two hobbits Sam and Frodo epitomize the goodness that alone can destroy the ring. Unlike more powerful characters, their power lies in their vulnerable weakness. Their *dunamis* to possibilize a new future comes not through magic, strength, or political authority, but from within.

The journey taken by the hobbits to Mount Doom to destroy the ring in its fires echoes the drama of Abraham to Mount Moriah. Frodo and Sam have their own "fear and trembling" as they draw closer to their objective, shadowed by the despicable Gollum. As they near their objective, they almost fail, when Frodo gives into the enormously tempting power of the ring. Despite Sam's best efforts, neither hobbit is able to save Frodo. Instead it falls to the universally maligned Gollum to intervene, rescuing Frodo from himself, and destroying himself and the ring.

Rowan Williams reads this culminating scene as a triumph of grace:

> Somehow, the tangled web of interaction between these three ends in "salvation." Some force overrules and rescues them—but only through the weaving together of a whole set of flawed agencies, mixed motives, compassion, prejudice, courage and craving. Tolkien is seeking to model the way in which the creator works not by intervening but by interweaving.[21]

This is not a story of a heroic triumph, but the triumph of a constellation of forces that come together to see that evil does not succeed. Williams reminds us that there is no pure point of moral perfection from which resistance occurs. Resistance to evil instead entails living with moral ambiguity and confusion as well as an ethics of uncertainty.

Williams's reading of the Mount Doom denouement reminds us that power corrupts even the most single-minded and devout. Even at the very end of his journey, Frodo is not immune to the power of the ring. And yet, this pessimism is counterpointed by the deeply Christian affirmation that even a character as morally diminished and spiritually eviscerated as Gollum retains something of the good within him. This scene proves the truth of the Augustinian-Lutheran insight that grace alone saves. Just when all seemed lost, out of nowhere, hearts and minds conspire to allow the ring to be destroyed. On the other hand, it is an affirmation of the intrinsic goodness of human nature (assuming hobbits share in some of that). Evil does not completely destroy. Either way, it encourages us to shy away from any hard and fast determinations between those who are on the side of the angels and those who are not.

One of the ways evil is resisted is by refusing to believe that it has any abiding power. Those in search of the *via media* have much in common with the hobbit Sam: they are inveterate optimists whilst being complete realists. Part of the promise of the Goldilocks story as an archetype is that it is remarkably conflicted. Like the bickering hobbits with their failings, her interactions with the bears are far from perfect. But it is this brokenness that makes the story worth paying attention to. Humans experience moral confusion and ethical uncertainty.

Resisting is both an inner and outer struggle. As Jesus put it, "Do not think that I have come to bring peace to the earth; I have not come to bring peace, but a sword" (Matthew 10:34). These are frightening words, and he goes on to talk about setting children against their parents, and finding foes in one's household. Jesus locates division in our most intimate of relationships. But the greater divisions surely lie within the human heart. We are divided against ourselves. The task of resisting evil is also the task of resisting not just sloth and laziness, but also the less charitable and meaner aspects of our nature.

The Danish have a wonderful word for a spoilsport: *Lyseslukker*. Literally, this translates as, "the one who puts out the lights." Faith is a practice of resisting those who put out the lights. Bringing light to those living in darkness is the classic Christian understanding of the ministry of Jesus. Those who seek Christ will also be bringers and sharers of dazzling light. Great quantities of candles may no longer burn in shrines or on altars, but the fires of love still need to be kindled. Ultimately, it is through the brightness and brilliance of light that the darkness is resisted. The most reliable way for doing this is the subject of the closing chapter.

NOTES

1. Quoted in Andrew Pettegree's excellent *Brand Luther: How an Unheralded Monk Turned His Small Town into a Center of Publishing, Made Himself the Most Famous Man in Europe—and Started the Protestant Reformation* (New York: Penguin Books, 2016), 174.
2. This reflects the poverty of my social network more than anything. It is not hard to imagine that in certain religious contexts a flickering flame on an altar might continue to constitute the very definition of heresy. There will also always be lovers of the Latin who prefer its cadences to the vernacular.
3. See for instance, Ben Nilson, *Cathedral Shrines of Medieval England* (University of Rochester Press, 1998).
4. Derrida, *Gift*, 34.
5. Derrida, *Gift*, 80.
6. Dietrich Bonhoeffer, *The Cost of Discipleship* (London: SCM Press, 1959).
7. Bonhoeffer, *Discipleship*, 45.
8. R.S. Thomas, *Collected Poems 1945–1990* (London: Phoenix, 1993), 302.
9. Bonhoeffer, *Discipleship*, 141.
10. *The New York Times,* December 24, 2016.
11. Bonhoeffer, *Discipleship*, 130.
12. Etty Hillesum, *An Interrupted Life* (New York: Owl Books, 1996), 174, quoted in Kearney, *God Who*, 108.
13. Hillesum, *Interrupted*, 176.
14. Kearney, *God Who*, 108. Quoting Hillesum, *Interrupted,* 192–93.
15. Dietrich Bonhoeffer, *Letters and Papers from Prison: The Enlarged Edition* (London: SCM Press, 1964), 360f.
16. Nicholas Adams, "Pelagianism: Can People be Saved by their Own Efforts?" in *Heresies: And How To Avoid Them*, eds. Ben Quash and Michael Ward (Grand Rapids, MI: Baker Academic, 2007), 98.

17. Ali Bonner, *The Myth of Pelagianism* (Oxford: Oxford University Press, 2018).

18. de Lubac, Henri. *The Mystery of the Supernatural*. Translated by Rosemary Sheed. (New York: Herder and Herder, 1998).

19. Quoted in Keith Thomas, *The Ends of Life: Roads to Fulfillment in Early Modern England* (New York: Oxford University Press, 2009), 233.

20. Jacques Derrida, *Deconstruction and Pragmatism*, ed. Chantal Mouffe (London: Routledge, 1996), 86.

21. Rowan Williams, "Master of his universe: the warnings in J.R.R. Tolkien's novels," *The New Statesman*, August 8, 2018.

Chapter Twelve

Love in the Goldilocks Zone

We need to love, and we need to be loved. James Smith has argued with commendable clarity that you are what you love, showing how Christians are formed by habits of love.[1] The first eight chapters of this work have attempted to explore something similar through a series of themes: church, alienation, wisdom, Eucharist, scripture, Baptism, saints, and (Trinitarian) giving are all manifestations of the way divine love shapes seekers of the *via media*. The last three chapters explored how grace is continually encountered in the middle of ordinary life through a further three spiritual practices: prayer, failure, and resisting evil. This final chapter examines love as the "red thread" that connects these habits, and illuminates the Christian life. Taken as a whole these constitute the "spiritual thermodynamics" we have been investigating.

The unquenchable driving force of human connection, love, is the spiritual principle of countless different religions. For Christianity, love both orients humans to God and reveals something of the divine life. Love is both a synonym for the divine, and the imperative that alerts us to the possibility of the divine. Across two millennia, Christianity is the always evolving, yet abidingly familiar, plotline of how humans participate in love to encounter God. The corollary is also true. In the absence of love, the divine withdraws. Although central to spirituality, love is one of the most difficult of theological concepts. Love perplexes, partly because love is simultaneously a human experience and the revealer of divine identity. For Augustine, love is the shared substance of the triune God, forming the very fabric of God's being. For Jean-Luc Marion, rejecting the idolatry of philosophical and theological identifications of Being with God, it is precisely the nature of God as love that requires this rupture with metaphysics: "God can give himself to be thought without idolatry only starting from himself alone: to give himself to be thought as love, hence as gift; to give himself to be thought as a thought of the gift."[2] This gift of God is what we have been exploring: God giving God's self to be loved, and to be encountered in that love. The question posed by seekers of the Goldilocks God is how this gift of love is given, and how it is reciprocated.

Love summons us to action in the world. As well as orienting us to God, love also provides a trajectory for the growth of our souls. Bonhoeffer understood the radically secular implications of this divine love: "He who says he loves God and hates his brother is a liar."[3] To experience love is not simply to feel an emotional experience. It is to dwell within God, and invite others to do the same.

As scripture suggests with elegant clarity, "God is love, and those who abide in love abide in God, and God abides in them" (1 John 4:16). Love is how humans connect with God, as well as how the divine searches us out. Metaphors of abiding, living, or dwelling all share this same sense that love is relational and domestic. Love is a home where we encounter God. In the priest poet George Herbert's poem "Love (III)" this encounter is mapped as something that is immensely simple and remarkably ordinary. Love seeks out the writer, "sweetly questioning / If I lacked anything." The writer, who we have earlier learned feels guilty ("of dust and sin"), yearns for connection. In Herbert's first-person narration, despite lacking Love, he nonetheless responds to Love's enquiries by inviting Love in.[4] Profoundly aware of the absence of love, Herbert nevertheless shows how this absence draws Love out. Once at home with Love, the poem's climax is deep in its simplicity: Love extends an invitation to the soul to sit down and "taste my meat." Such a love is not concerned with interior belief. Love is instead the questioning that leads to transformation and renewal through feasting on love's "meat." As the poem reveals, Love desires relationship, in this case of guest to host (yet another pointer of the sacramental host that is the true meat of the poem). A parish priest who spent his time visiting the needy and the poor, eschewing the renown and lure of court life, Herbert's whole life points to the truth of encountering Christ as a guest at God's table.

In the face of what Cixous termed the mystery of other beings, it is not always possible to experience this blissful domesticity of Herbert's encounter with Love. Supping Love's meat is not the only response to guilty feelings of dust and sin. Absence does not always lead directly to Dickinson's "condensed presence." There are all sorts of good reasons for this. One of the most common is to do with the problem of discerning the reality of God's love in the world.

Part of the confusion is theological. If divine love is not sentiment, then what is its character? Dante's *Divine Comedy* concludes with the immortal line *"L'amor che move il sole e l'altre stelle"* (love that moves the sun and other stars).[5] Love powers the heavens, and it was the movements of the spheres powered by this love that medieval astrologers and astronomers sought to understand and predict. As we saw in chapter 3, Dante's belief in

God moving the heavenly spheres echoed Aquinas's theological program: combining the philosophy of Aristotle with the cosmology of Ptolemy. *The Divine Comedy* is not a pilgrim's progress into a fictitious heavenly realm. Rather, it is an existential ascent that for all of its undoubted emotional and theological power is one framed by a scientific conception of the planets, stars, and their nine associated heavens. Dante is led both by his love of Beatrice and the divine source of that love. And it is this love which Dante maps onto the medieval conception of the fabric of the universe.

Much later, C.S. Lewis revivifies and reclaims Dante's medieval cosmology. In his exploration of Lewis's Narniad, Michael Ward reveals how Lewis transposed the planetary symbolism of medieval astronomical thought, "tingling with anthropomorphic life, dancing, ceremonial, a festival not a machine," into the seven Narnia stories.[6] Lewis's familiarity with the medieval helped him understand the science of the soul of Hildegard and Dante. This love is not solely one of interpersonal intimacy: it is cosmic love pointing back to God. The creation and moving of earth and all the heavens is God's work, and it is a work of love.

Different Christian traditions have interpreted love in a range of different ways, reflecting a diversity of loves within the Greek New Testament. The classic form of Christian love is frequently identified with the Greek word *agape*, signifying a love that is boundless, selfless, and directed freely away from us without any expectation of reward. This is the word Marion uses for the love that is the gift that cannot but give itself. In his monumental and influential work *Agape and Eros* the Swedish theologian Anders Nygren contrasted *agape* love with *eros*, a love that is closer to the English word desire. Eros seeks out the beloved, because *eros* needs to love the beloved. *Eros* is also at the root of erotic experience and sexuality, and it is a hugely important aspect of the reality of love.

Christianity in all its iterations has probably done more damage by contesting, ignoring, or making light of *eros* than anything else. While the institutional preferences of Christendom for sacred virgins and monastic celibates have largely disappeared, these have simply been replaced by equally powerful proscriptions of sexuality and desire. Sex may not be the enemy of the divine it once was, but the church continues to struggle to talk about *eros* without revealing deep divisions and confusion. We may think we have freed ourselves from the medieval and early modern hegemony of the diabolical, yet we are still struggling to come up with a healthy spirituality of love and sexuality. As we saw in the exploration of the Trinity it is impossible to enter the mystery of the gift of God's love without also examining the theological centrality of desire.

To frame God's love as something revealed within the Goldilocks zone is to reject the contemporary Puritanism and compulsory asceticism that flees *eros* at all costs. At the same time, it is to chart a course away from the other extreme, that of the Dionysian. Erotic encounter no more inevitably leads to the divine than reading the scriptures inevitably leads to loving one's neighbor. Both are more than capable of being distorted, and to imagine otherwise is to misunderstand human nature. And yet, if God is love, God is not simply *agape* love. God is also one who desires with an intense *erotic* love. God does not love in a disinterested and generic way. As Hildegard, Anselm, and Gregory of Nyssa understood, God loves with all the fervor and passion of erotic love.

Mystics, saints, and theologians have repeatedly reflected on the passionate nature of their experience of God's love. So while the tradition rightly speaks of *agape*, perhaps it is better to think of God's love as a work of weaving between the warp of *agape* with the woof of *eros*. Christian love is not reducible to sentimentality. But that does not mean that it cannot also be purposeful and passionate.

If *agape* and *eros* are the dominant threads with which God's love is woven, *philia* is a mediating position often described as friendship. Like *eros*, *philia* seeks out the other because of something inherent in the other. Yet, unlike *eros*, *philia* is a kind of love that can be shared more broadly, like *agape*. Like *eros* this kind of love also has its historic weaknesses and dangers. Feminists and others remind us that too often philial love is simply the love of those who are identical to us. When C.S. Lewis wrote about philial love he imagined friendship between similarly educated privileged white males. There was no room for friendship between the genders, and little reflection on how others of diverse socioeconomic backgrounds might also experience this friendship of the like-minded. Just like *eros*, *philial* love can be exclusive and limiting. It is remarkable that in Pope Francis's Papal Encyclical on fraternal love there is no detailed examination of the naming of this fraternal love. Even though the Pope explicitly includes women in this fraternal love, and is arguing for a renewed sense of fellowship between human beings of all races, socioeconomic statuses, religions, genders, and nationalities, the language of fraternal love cannot help but sound limiting in its maleness. While it may be suggested that fraternal love is no more intended to be gendered than "man" was historically thought to be an adequate representation for the human race (but no longer is) it remains a puzzling turn of phrase for times that are more aware of gender dynamics. The gender bias signified to English speakers in the word fraternal, and the legacy of Christian reflection on *philial* love, should still cause us caution.

Which brings us full circle back to *agape*, and the Christian hope that the love of God is abundant and unrestricted. Not a love directed at only one part of the human family. And yet, it is even more complex. Whenever *agape* is held up as the pure archetype of divine love against *eros* and *philia*, something significant is lost. Sarah Coakley rejects Nygren's Lutheran bipolar separation of agape and eros, arguing that God's love needs to include a better and more positive understanding of erotic desire.[7] Coakley grounds this understanding in the writings of Gregory of Nazianzus, calling for an entirely fresh approach to the way Christians understand desire. To separate physical and sexual erotic desire from divine desire entirely is an unhelpful detour within the tradition. The Early Church was more explicit in their understanding of *eros* than moderns might imagine. Against Nygren, Coakley argues for a recovery of passion within our understanding of divine erotic desire. In light of the current argument, we might add that this recovery will also lead back to thinkers like Anselm and Hildegard. What is needed is not a radical separation of human and divine desire, but a better understanding of how connected the two have always been.

Theologian Janet Martin Soskice also argues for seeing greater connections and similarities between divine love and human experiences of love.[8] Too often, theologians and philosophers cogitate about God's love as if it were the ultimate extraterrestrial otherworldly kind of love. *Agape* at its worst becomes so loftily unreachable, and so distant from ordinary experience, that we may as well be talking about a UFO. Soskice encourages a different perspective, in which she examines love through the metaphor of the kinship God shares with humankind. The kindness for Soskice that matters is not about being kind: rather it is the kindness of God sharing love in kind, as kin to us. Soskice focuses on how incarnation, the entering of God into the messiness of human existence, is about God becoming part of humankind.

The kindness of God emerges as how God becomes kith and kin with us. The purpose of God in Christ is that we can know something of real love within ordinary life. Soskice tells a poignant story of a devout woman. Exhausted from having her first child, she was overwhelmed at the state of her spiritual life:

> She took advice from three priests. The first told her that if the baby woke at 6.00 a.m., she should rise at 5.00 a.m. for a quiet hour of prayer. The second asked if her husband could not arrange to come home early from work three times a week so that she could get to a Mass. This advice proved threatening to life and marriage. The third told her, "Relax and just look after your baby. The rest of the Church is praying for you."[9]

So much ecclesiastical writing about love is written from perspectives, often single, that appear clueless about the embodied nature of human love. Soskice encourages the church to reconnect instead with the wisdom of the third priest and a more ancient spiritual understanding of love's materiality. In dialogue with the philosopher Martha Nussbaum, Soskice argues for keeping reason or *nous* connected to humanity's physical animal nature. In the experience of pregnancy and lactation, Soskice highlights the intersection between involuntary and rational action. The physicality of love needs to be returned to the heart of theology. As Soskice wryly observes:

> What we want is a monk who finds God while cooking a meal with one child clamouring for a drink, another who needs a bottom wiped, and a baby throwing up over his shoulder.[10]

With the rise of the new monasticism, ordinary people living in faithful communities without all the traditional vows, one suspects this hope is coming close to being realized.

Soskice underlines how disinterested love cannot be seen as the highest or more supreme form of love. Where we do, we risk ignoring, or even denigrating, some of the most powerful and enduring experiences of love. The love mothers or fathers have for their children is neither disinterested nor erotic. Nor is it best described as a fraternal friendship with someone who is the same. Indeed, it is surely one of the most passionate forms of love, and one of the most giving. Feminist theologians have been leading the way here for quite some time, recovering the full range of human experience in the scriptures and in understandings of divine love.[11] At the same time, as Coakley helpfully reminds us, to strip the Trinitarian God of the gendered language of desire is unhelpful. We do not need a gender-neutral or an exclusively gendered God. What we need, is a God in whom the whole human experience is caught up, through the entanglements of the Holy Spirit and the human yearning for God. A God whom Anselm prayed to as both mother and father.

JULIAN AND THE MOTHERING LOVE OF CHRIST

Mother Julian of Norwich, the first woman to be recorded writing in English, also shows how this may be done. Julian wrote movingly of God in astonishingly intimate and maternal language that appears centuries ahead of her time. At the end of the fourteenth-century Julian lauded maternal love: "The mother's service is the closest, the most helpful and the most sure, for it is the most faithful."[12] God as mother, caring actively for us, remains strikingly and enduringly innovative. Julian writes out of her profound personal experience of having received revelations or "showings" of the richness of God's love.

Julian is anticipating and channeling the spirit of Cixousian *jouissance*, reveling in the intimacy, joy, and passion of abiding in God's love. It is hard not to come away from reading Julian without being struck by her inventiveness. This medieval anchoress chose the very archetype of an uncomfortable life, living as an enclosed spiritual guide, confined within the walls of the church. Yet through her writings she has drawn generations into a deeper, more complex, and richer understanding of the kind yet passionately embodied love of God. As Coakley and Soskice both recognize, Julian takes the Trinity seriously, refusing to identify one particular gender in the dance that unfolds among the three persons of the Trinity.

In one passage, Julian develops the maternal analogy to describe Jesus's maternal love. In our age of gender fluidity, when gender identities are no longer clear cut (if they ever were), Julian creatively explores gender fluidity in this holiest of areas. Something of the magnitude of her approach to God's love in Jesus shines through in the following passage:

> The mother can lay the child tenderly to the breast, but our tender mother Jesus, he can familiarly lead us into his blessed breast through his sweet open side, and show within part of the Godhead and the joys of heaven, with spiritual certainty of endless bliss.[13]

Is this *agape*? *Eros*? *Philia*? Something else? The one thing that is abundantly clear is that this love is not a disinterested substance-free type of love that is purely spiritual or intellectual. Nor can this be described as strictly fraternal. As Soskice reminds us, these descriptions are not fixed: all three persons of the Trinity are rendered as both male and female by Julian.[14] Julian's creativity is diametrically opposed to Nygren's view that a disinterested and disembodied *agape* lies at the core of Christian love. Instead, through the rich use of intimate metaphors of suckling and feeding Julian makes it clear that God's love is physically real, and frequently very messy. It is not a love confined to cogitation. It is a love that carnally knows us and physically builds us up. It is the primary way we experience the kinship and kindness of God. It is also profoundly Eucharistic: the way that Jesus "can familiarly lead us into his blessed breast" is through the sacrament.

Mother Julian expands the spiritual to take into account the material ways God reaches out in love. In that sense, she was standing fully within the medieval tradition of Catholicism that saw God acting more like a God of *eros* than Nygrens' Protestant God of *agape*. Thanks to the efforts of many medieval scholars we know that Julian's material spirituality is by no means unique. Caroline Walker Bynum quotes a powerful excerpt from the mystic Catherine of Siena writing to three women in Naples:

> Do as the child does who, wanting to take milk, takes the mother's breast and places it in his mouth and draws to himself the milk by means of the flesh. So . . . we must attach ourselves to the breast of the crucified Christ, in whom we

find the mother of charity, and draw from there by means of his flesh (that is, the humanity) the milk that nourishes our soul.[15]

One of the great tragedies of religious history is how reformed churches so often excised the experience of religious women like Julian and Catherine. Endemic patriarchy and misogyny did not lead to the flourishing of women's voices. In the tenth century "reforms" of Anglo-Saxon England, the earlier traditions of women abbess's ruling over double houses of men and women disappear. The seventh-century figure of Hilda of Whitby, exercising authority over a monastic double house of both men and women, is unimaginable by the later medieval period. By the eve of the Reformation, Bynum notes how "virulent misogyny" had led to both witch accusations and witch-hunting theology. Within this context witches and female saints were similarly threatening to theologians, canon lawyers, inquisitors, and male hagiographers.[16] Before the Reformation access to the holy was aided by a communion of saints, of both genders, many of them local, many of them renowned for their friendship, accessibility, and patronage. In countries that exercised reform, not only are most of these saints rejected, but even the ultimate intercessor, Mary, Christ-bearer, Mother of God, and Queen of Heaven, has seen her place usurped. A diverse communion of saints that included men and women, young and old, strangers and locals, was replaced with a theory of sanctity that by including all the baptized seemed to include no one.

Nothing about this is intrinsic to the spiritual life. Even a reformer as internally conflicted as Martin Luther was happy to break free of the shackles of monastic celibacy, clearly adoring his dear Katarina and the liberation of raising his own family. Luther also set about improving the educational system for girls, dramatically increasing the literacy rates of girls and women. Founding new schools for them, he even dreamt up innovative ways to encourage school enrollment, encouraging choirs to go recruiting in the streets and generating a powerful tradition of singing that continues to flourish. Under Luther's giant shadow, within a few decades Germany saw a surge of up to 50 percent of its girls enrolled in school. By comparison, Catholic Venice in 1587 had about 0.2 percent of its girls in school. Yet, as a swallow does not make a summer, so Luther was no feminist. Even this great advocate of female empowerment provided his drinking companions with what one commentator sensitively describes, "rumbustious reflections on female frailties."[17]

QUEEN ELIZABETH AND THE
POLITICS OF UNCERTAINTY

Despite educational progress under Luther, cross-party patriarchy continued to repress women. So anxious was the Presbyterian John Knox to target the Roman Catholic Queen Mary that he penned one of the most vitriolic tracts denying the ability of any women to have authority. Arguing primarily from scripture, the title of Knox's screed did not leave anything to the imagination: *First Blast of the Trumpet Against the Monstrous Regiment of Women*. Published in 1558 he endeared himself neither to Mary, who died shortly afterwards, nor her reforming successor Elizabeth. Knox's vituperative misogyny ensured that Elizabeth's England would never rush to embrace his Scottish Calvinism. While England would not bow to King Philip and his vast armies, neither would it embrace the religion of an intemperate Scotsman who denied the possibility that women might possess either authority or wisdom. Misogyny remained one of few areas of ecumenical agreement following the Reformation.

Half a millennium later it is still remarkable how radical the gendered writings of saints like Anselm, Hildegard, Julian, and Catherine sound. God was never solely identified with one gender, and often the genders were all mixed up. For them Jesus and God were both mother and father, offering a far richer interplay between divinity, authority, and gender than Luther or Knox could imagine. To speak of the Goldilocks God is to recognize a form of spirituality that stands both on the shoulders of saints like Julian and political operators like Elizabeth. Both produced revolutions within their own days. Julian's spiritual revolution was to reveal in the vernacular the love of God as a maternal love that was sacramentally and physically nourishing. Elizabeth's religious revolution was to mother her kingdom by mandating sacramental nourishment while turning a blind eye to interior belief.

Both women show how to enflesh love in rites and language that were accessible. In rematerializing and repoliticizing love, they shed light on how one might reimagine Aristotle's practical wisdom in Christian form. Theology is not philosophy with a Christian twist. Theology is embodied love. As Soskice puts it, "We may acknowledge that we are loved by God, but it is more difficult to accept that we will be made lovely; yet this too is implied by the bridal imagery of Revelation."[18] This eschatological promise echoes the potentiality of Agamben and Kearney's God Who May Be. A similar sentiment of eschatological lovely-making lies behind the poem of Samuel Crossman, sometime vicar of Little Henny in Suffolk in the seventeenth century. His poem describes the heart of divine possibilizing love. Even when we falter at knowing and describing God's love, that love remains the aspiration of Christian fellowship: "My song is love unknown, / My Savior's love to me: / Love to the loveless shown, / That they might lovely be." The spiritual thermodynamics of the Goldilocks God is both an historical and present process. Those who fall in love with God, also fall in love with others who have done the same, across space and time. Christian love requires remembering the lost and forgotten as much as preparing to enter a new future. The loveless are for whom we love. They are, after all, those for whom Christ gives himself both on the cross and in Eucharist.

The Golden Age of Elizabeth was a time of remarkable literary and artistic creativity. But her greater and more strategic legacy was to allow others, whether in the theater of politics, the exploration of the New World, or religious practice, the space to develop their own futures. Capable of being capricious, haughty, and rigid in her final years, this should not distract us from recognizing her as the first woman to steer the royal ship of the English state successfully through severe perils. Her political steering was also a kind of love, in which she cleaved not to a fixed ideology or theology. She located her constancy in keeping as many options open as possible. By contrast, her rival King Philip held to a profound belief in his religious destiny, doing God's will. Channeling the divine is difficult, and Philip almost incapacitated the Spanish realm through his need to micromanage every decision.

Elizabeth was quite happy to allow others to take the lead, granting autonomy where possible, and taking a step back (even if only to allow others to fail gloriously and face the consequences). As Gaddis argues, it was Elizabeth's remarkably relaxed approach to the New World colonies that forged in them habits of independence that ensured they would thrive and eventually throw off their English overlords.[19] By contrast, the Spanish colonies would wither on the vine, so dependent were they on centralized instructions coming from Madrid. Just as Elizabeth's deliberate indecisiveness shaped the political emphasis on freedom, individuality, and self-rule in England and America, so she forged the pattern of movement, one might say the dance steps, of the spiritual thermodynamics of the Goldilocks God.

Content to avoid micromanaging what people ought to believe, she makes space for the possibility that belonging (to the wider community) is more important than what one believes. Against serious advice to the contrary, her perspective prevailed. Although Aristotle is unlikely to have approved of all her decisions, he would have understood her practical wisdom in choosing to regulate exterior action rather than interior belief. This distinction remains remarkably uncontested today, although it was radical for its time. Elizabeth marshaled the resources of religion to produce a politics of prevarication rather than a politics of certainty. The fulminating Calvinist John Knox and the dutiful son of the Holy Church King Philip are excellent examples of opposing poles in the quest for religious clarity. Elizabeth's practical wisdom lay in a far more innovative and flexible approach: one that preserved her island from the bloody ravages of Christian certainty.

AUGUSTINE'S RULE OF LOVE

St. Augustine's life reveals other dimensions to the challenge of manifesting God's love in a time of conflict and change. Caught between the secular world and the kingdom of God, Augustine was deeply committed to the intellectual work of making God comprehensible. A member of a university elite, Augustine, much like many Ivy-League or Oxbridge professors, saw Christianity as crude and intellectually unsophisticated. However, after failing to find intellectual meaning in other accounts of the world, he returned to Christianity. Adopting it with a fervor that points to his own need for love and his own desire to find meaning, Augustine's conversion story is often portrayed as an encounter between Augustine and the voice of God that reaches out to him telling him to "take, read" the scriptures. Yet, we have to wonder, who made it possible for Augustine to hear that voice? What other context did he have for this encounter with the love of God?

The hidden figure behind Augustine's conversion to Christianity was his mother, Monica. Reading between the lines, it was Augustine's experience of Christian love through Monica that kept the Christian religious possibility alive. Monica's love made Christianity viable for Augustine. One way of interpreting his subsequent writings is as an attempt to make intellectual sense out of the gift God had given him through his mother's love. (Priests still see a similar desire in the young couples who come seeking baptism for their children. Trying to honor the miraculous gift they have received, they find themselves trying to make sense of the gift of love they received from their own mother.)

In writing about Christian teaching, Augustine addresses the problems of reading scripture. He knows that scripture often appears to encourage conflicting interpretations. He is also deeply aware how scripture speaks in different voices. Scripture is neither consistent nor transparent. As a teacher of rhetoric, grammar, and logic, steeped in classical culture, Augustine knew that the meaning of words is not simply a matter of surface appearances. To tackle the problem of scriptural interpretation, Augustine developed a strategy for choosing between competing (and often very different) interpretations. What he called the rule of faith (*regula fidei*) was deceptively simple. All one had to do was ask of a particular reading whether a certain interpretation strengthened love or weakened it. All things being equal, Augustine's rule invited the reader struggling to make sense of scripture to follow the more loving interpretation. The more genuine readings always maximized love. If love were absent, one had to question the scripturality of one's interpretation.

Augustine was an experienced consumer of religion by the time he landed on Christianity. He had rejected both the default paganism of the ever-expanding Roman pantheon and the ascetic extremism of the dualist Manichees. For him Christianity's Trinitarian monotheism was a third way between ethically vague polytheism on the one hand and world-denying dualism on the other. After growing up in a Roman culture in which everything was divine and nothing was sacred, his experiment with the Manichees was a failure. Viewing everything as the product of an evil creator, Manicheeism was the opposite extreme: a rejection of the goodness of creation as nothing more than the wiles of an evil God trying to derail us from the straight and narrow by all means necessary. By the time he gave Christianity a second chance, he had grown in experience and wisdom to see how it offered an intellectually sustaining account of the way goodness and love originate in the divine.

To seek God is always to recognize the same dynamic at work. We do not understand or fully comprehend what it means for the love of God to exist in the world. However, it is possible to identify where it gets too hot or too cold so that the conditions for its emergence are not present. It is natural to be deeply agnostic and uncertain about God's love. No one can explain God's love. Like Augustine, even after years of searching, it is not clear how God's love might be encountered in the world. At the same time, as Cixous showed us, we know that encountering love is about embracing a mystery. As Marion knows, building on Socrates's own essential uncertainty, the only certainties are negative ones: what we do not know. And these uncertainties cover not simply our knowledge of the divine, or our knowledge of ourselves, but also entire fields of supposed human knowledge.[20] The thoughtful, believers or not, know that they are mysteries unto themselves. And part of what makes us a mystery is the mystery of what may lie beyond us.

Seekers infused with the spirit of Goldilocks will share Elizabeth's suspicions of religious fervor. (Remember her comment to the French ambassador, "there was only one Jesus Christ and one faith, and all the rest that they disputed about but trifles."[21]) Travelers on the *via media* do well to remember that they have no novel insight not found in other Christian traditions. And yet, being open to the presence of the Goldilocks God is to be part of an inherently skeptical part of the human family. Like Cixous, Marion, and Richard Hooker, searchers for the Goldilocks God are unsure about the nature and extent of God's presence in the world. We are not overly credulous and we are quick to react against superstitions or zealotry. We have all witnessed enough religious charlatanism, nonsense, and rigidity to last lifetimes. In society and politics there remain more than enough confidence tricksters who will say anything to get what they wish. Faced with the thunderings of a John Knox, the shenanigans of an Eleazor Wheelock, or the twitter rants of politicians we prefer to keep silent; or read some poetry.

The image on the cover is of Elizabeth's accession to the throne in 1559. It shows a twenty-five-year-old woman clothed in coronation robes covered with Tudor roses and trimmed with ermine. She is framed with traditional Christian symbols of regal authority, the scepter of righteousness and the orb, the rod and sphere that reveal her ability to wield power over her domains. Her dress is golden, as is her crown. Unlike many of her later portraits, we do not know who painted this. What we can observe is that this image is both traditional in its symbolism, and unusual in that instead of red hair, it depicts long golden locks flowing into her golden coronation robes. She also seems somewhat happier than the portrait of Richard II to which this picture is often compared. This image is one of promise, a young woman not yet ravaged by political, religious, or personal challenges. The lens of this portrait, with its almost sardonic smile, reveals an Elizabeth who is different from later portraiture. For all that this is an image of authority, it is also an image of vulnerability: a slender young woman ruling a dangerous kingdom. And, again, unlike the coronation portrait of Richard II, she is not shown as occupying her throne. There is power here but it is also restrained. It is through this image that we enter the *via media*, not as a route that has been well charted and well established, but as a possibility, a new road that has potential, but also risk. The image is a construct designed to awe those beholding it, and it is in this same light that the *via media* needs to be approached: both a construct of human artifice, with all the positive and negative connotations of artifice, and also a path that opens up to awe and wonder.

The *via media* was coined to describe the historic evolution of a community that kept faith with the original ecumenical councils (before the split with the Eastern Church), and continued to maintain elements that were both traditional and reformed. Today that *via media*, or what we are reimagining as the spiritual Goldilocks zone, is even more diverse. It is no longer primarily a way of defining confessional or denominational differences. Instead, it represents a spiritual habit of always finding a middle way that remains faithful to God the divine lover.

The *via media* of the Goldilocks zone, is a spiritual way of making decisions in the face of undecidability and apparently opposing truths. Truth is rarely a matter of black and white, right or wrong, red or blue, up or down. Spiritual truth is never bipolar. As we saw with Abraham, Kierkegaard, and Derrida, the undecidability of faith discloses the nature of responsibility that is both *to* the infinite and *from* the infinite.

Like the scurrilous Goldilocks who tore through the three bears' house, and like the elliptical and constantly rotating orbits of planets, there is continuous movement in the Goldilocks zone. Life requires movement. Sometimes these motions are stately and predictable. Frequently they are chaotic. And more often than we might like, the motion appears backwards. For the love of God to become real there will always be the possibility of regression as much as progression. Like Goldilocks, we may not always be welcomed into others' homes, and like her we will probably not always be perfect guests. Nevertheless, to seek God is to be willing to embark on a lifelong adventure requiring curiosity, desire, and hope.

DECENTERING GOLDILOCKS

Goldilocks finds herself in an adorably familiar predicament. Our young heroine is intent on pursuing her own desire. She is also not very considerate about the property of the three bears. Part of the enduring popularity of the story is surely to do with the question of who is at the true center of the story. Maybe it is not Goldilocks at all. Perhaps it is the little bear who has so much to lose. After all, it is the little bear who loses his porridge, has his chair broken, and then suffers the indignity and trauma of finding her sleeping in his bed. What child has not identified with the poor little bear and wondered at the temerity of Goldilocks?

The origins of the Goldilocks story are uncertain, and it clearly circulated in oral form (like the Christian gospels and many other religious traditions) for at least four decades, if not longer, before it was written down. The first person to tell the story in published form was the poet Robert Southey. In 1837 he told the story under the title *The Three Bears*. Fascinatingly, Goldilocks is not original to that version. In Southey's telling, her part was played instead by an old woman who runs away at the conclusion of the story. A few years earlier in 1831 Eleanor Mure had produced a homemade book for a nephew in which the old woman meets a terrible fate. Her reward for invading the domestic tranquility of the bears was to be impaled on the steeple of St. Paul's Cathedral. When Joseph Cundall retold the tale in 1849, he replaced the old woman intruder with a little girl who remains through subsequent retellings.

One of the best parts of the story is the final scene when Goldilocks is chased out of the bears' house. One wonders whether she returned to make amends? How did the encounter change her? What happened to her, if and when, she reached her own home? What did she go on to do with her life? If she wasn't impaled by St. Paul's Cathedral, what *did* happen? In some modern retellings she becomes friends with the bears. There are so many unanswerable things about the story. It has deep mysteries. For all of its simplicity, it overflows with Agamben-esque potentiality, presenting a range of possibilizing futures for both the protagonist and her hosts. One possibility I have not seen explored is whether the whole thing might have been a honey-trap set by the bears. What if the bears knew Goldilocks was coming? What if it was their original plan for Goldilocks to find the food and rest that was "just right" for her.

That is also the question animating the spiritual thermodynamics of this book.

So far, we have been looking at the spiritual question of seeking the holy through the lens of what it is like to be a human in search of God. An alternative, and more classically theological, way of asking this same question is to ponder how God has always been in search of us.

What we see of the love of God is fragmentary, episodic, and incomplete. We never experience the love of God from God's perspective. We cannot, after all, because we are human. The beauty of *Goldilocks and the Three Bears* is that we start to imagine the world from the perspective of the bears. It anthropomorphises. It brings the bears to life by giving them human characteristics. And so, while we know that bears don't really cook porridge and live in houses, the story works. As with any fairy story, myth, epic, hagiography, or tale, there is always the possibility that the bears are more than just bears.

Given that there are three of them, this invites the question that maybe there is more to these ursine characters than meets the eye. In his monumental analysis of the seven possible plot archetypes that lie behind every story Christopher Booker holds up the tale of Goldilocks as a prime example of a story based around the number three. The threefold division of the story offers the opportunity to steer from one extreme to the other and then on to a deeper synthesis. Three is a deeply fulfilling number. It allows for progression and maturation as well as obstacles that can be overcome. As Booker explains, there is a narrative completeness when heroes and heroines transition first through two failures before finally attaining success. The third time is always a charm.[22]

Seen in this light, the three bears symbolize completeness better than Goldilocks. By entering their home, Goldilocks comes into a natural conflict with the harmony of the threefold ursine community. She can eventually find some kind of wholeness of her own, but only after symbolic and literal breaks have occurred within her self-centered world view. Curiously, Booker remains silent about the possible connections between the number three and the divine. Given that Goldilocks emerges in a society with at least a working familiarity with the Trinity, it does not seem entirely inappropriate to ask the question of whether the three might represent more than simply completion. Maybe the three also signify the Trinitarian God? One does not need to read the story from the perspective of Dan Brown to at least ponder this as one of a range of potential readings that enhances, or at least does no violence, to the text. I am not suggesting this is the "correct" or "only" reading. Rather, I am suggesting that such a reading increases the interpretive potential of the text, enlarging its horizon of surplus meanings.

What if the divine bears, the providers of all Goldilocks requires, are the protagonists? Might this have potential as a story about the divine hospitality of love? There is, after all, the very real love that the bear family has for one another. A love that is increasingly distressed by the intrusions of their uninvited guest. Is this a retelling of Herbert's "Love made me welcome yet my soul drew back"? Despite the disruptions ("guilty of dust and sin") the bears do not exact reprisals on their visitor. They maintain a remarkable equanimity in the face of all that they have suffered. They do not seek revenge. They are, in fact, rather friendly. They are open to one who is other.

Nor is this friendliness necessarily the product of an overimaginative fictional mind. Nicholas Christakis reminds us of the unusual friendship made between the eminent primatologist Jane Goodall and David Greybeard. After weeks of living in the remote forest of the Gombe Stream National Park in Tanzania, Goodall had barely seen more than a glimpse of a primate. And then David Greybeard appeared, befriending her, seeking her out. Coming to her campsite Greybeard sat for almost an hour picking out termites from their nests with a blade of grass. As Goodall recalled years later:

> Well, first of all, he was the very first chimpanzee who let me come close, who lost his fear. And he helped introduce me to the magic world out in the forest. The other chimps would see David sitting there, not running away, and so gradually they'd think, "Well, she can't be so very scary after all." He had a wonderful gentle disposition. He was really loved by the other chimps . . . And there was just something about him. He had a very handsome face, his eyes wide apart, and this beautiful gray beard.[23]

Ben Kilham has had similarly positive relationships with wild black bears. In the town of Lyme, New Hampshire, Kilham has raised dozens of orphaned black bears, rehabilitating them and returning them to the wild. One of these, Squirty, raised her own family and remained profoundly connected to Kilham.[24] Part of what makes Kilham's story so meaningful is that his own dyslexia may have been part of what enabled him to make his astonishing discoveries about the intelligence and sophistication of black bears.

For several years, a black bear named Mink, after the tributary where she tended to raise her cubs, visited the town of Hanover, New Hampshire. Mink and her cubs would hang out on the porches and in the backyard of residences. Faced with potential danger to human life the state wildlife commission decided to intervene and euthanize. Following an outcry, the governor of the State intervened to save Mink, transporting her into the northern reaches of New Hampshire. Within a few months Mink returned to town, and continued to forage peacefully near her human neighbors. Mink's lengthy sojourn, as a resident alien, earned her the devotion of townsfolk who rose to the challenge of adjusting their habits to ensure Mink's safety. When Mink eventually died there was an outpouring of grief in the wider community.

Countless millions of us depend on the love that our pets provide, and know at first hand their adaptability. Goodall, Kilham, and Mink remind us that even the animals of the wild can be channels of love. They also suggest that it is our human vulnerability that may make us better disposed to be able to live in fellowship with those who are perceived as profoundly other.

All these examples point again to Herbert's personification of "Love." They suggest a way of reading the three bears in the Goldilocks story. Following the rabbinic and medieval delight in multiple readings, what if one such reading approaches the little bear, the one who bears the brunt of Goldilocks's invasions, not simply as a son, but the Son of a divine Father? In the light of medieval writings about the maternal love of God, it seems entirely possible to read these three bears as a living embodiment of a family joined in a shared love. If not the Holy and Undivided Trinity of Christian tradition, then the three bears are at least a secular analogue. Like Oscar Wilde's story *The Selfish Giant* or C.S. Lewis's *The Lion, The Witch and The Wardrobe*, maybe Goldilocks is a thinly veiled Christian allegory? What if Goldilocks is a story of how the human soul and the divine are destined to encounter one another? Neither completely harmonious nor a total disaster, to read the story alongside those of Goodall and Kilham indicates the possibility that everything could have worked out.

Another way of reading this story is as a story of hospitality that has been abused. Goldilocks takes advantage of the bears' hospitality. As with the Last Supper, this reading places the focus on betrayal. Hospitality is enjoyed by Goldilocks, and in return, there is the betrayal of the breakages. Literary scholar James Heffernan is particularly attentive to the profound interconnections of betrayal and hospitality across Western literature. In Christ's institution of the Last Supper (on the night that he was betrayed) these are tightly braided: "To welcome the other is to risk being betrayed by oneself, but that is precisely what Christ himself did at the Last Supper."[25] Seen in this light Goldilocks is to the bears as Judas is to Christ. Without the one the other cannot be approached. Their betrayal by Goldilocks is also not the only sign of Eucharistic hospitality. The bears are a community of three whose food is set out, food that Goldilocks consumes. Matthew of Rievaulx's poem from the twelfth century seems particularly apposite:

> This food, which no hunger can expel,
> This is the bread which the Spirit has cooked in a holy fire.
> This is a liquid which no thirst can destroy,

> This is the wine which the grape of a virgin's womb has brought forth.[26]

The porridge is not obviously Eucharistic. But, like Herbert's, Matthew's poem underlines the sheer physicality of being fed in Eucharist. Anticipating the Goldilocks story, Matthew reminds us of the importance of heat, and the heat of spiritual yearning and Trinitarian desire. Whatever else Eucharist may do, Eucharist truly feeds this desire.

All of these Eucharistic hints point again to Goldilocks as a story framed by love. The "wholesome" love of the communion of bears and their domestic bliss stands on one side. The "desire" of Goldilocks and her quest for comfort and nourishment stands on the other. Goldilocks is the story of how these different loves collide. The Christian church has been working with a very similar plot. Human love and divine love are never in perfect harmony. There is always something undecidable about love's work. As Bonhoeffer explains, "The genuine work of love is always a hidden work."[27] In the same way that God's loving work is hidden from most of us most of the time, so the deepest acts of love are often ones that remain hidden from their recipients.

The hidden-yet-revealed love at the center of the Christian story is always a divine setup. It is the story of how God assumes and inhabits human language, human form, and human concepts to draw us into the reality of God's love. God hides in front of us in human form, first in the person of Christ and also in humans formed in the image and likeness of God. The mystery of the Trinity is the experience of remembering how God's love continues to be manifested within both human society and the divine life. And as with Christ, so in Eucharist. As human flesh hides and reveals the presence of the divine in the person of Christ, so bread and wine hide and reveal the presence of God in the sacrament. The apparent absence of the divine in the sacrament is the ultimate condensation of the presence of God. Bonhoeffer's hidden work and Dickinson's presence condensed are both manifestations of the spiritual thermodynamics of love.

As Cixous suggests, whenever we love another being we also encounter something of its mystery. The mystery of this loving is also the mystery of encountering God. The tradition of apophasis and negative theology also wants to affirm this mystery. As the cardinal, scientist, and mystic Nicholas of Cusa notes:

> According to the theology of negation, nothing other than infinity is found in God. Consequently, negative theology holds that God is unknowable either in this world or in the world to come, for in this respect every creature is in darkness, which cannot comprehend infinite light, but God is known to God alone.[28]

We already saw how Cusa's thought influenced Kearney's vision of the God who may be. It is honesty about unknowability that contributes to understanding God as mystery. The spiritual agnosticism of Hooker and Elizabeth can be said to reinforce the mystery. All point to freeing God from the constraints of human understanding, including the chains so beloved of theology. In the face of mystery, the only honest response is to eschew certainty and embrace the undecidable. Living into the mystery of God's love requires being open to the hints and glimpses that others have also had into the truth of that freely given, ecstatic, and superabundant love. As Marion puts it, "Only love does not have to be."[29] Divine love is gratuitous and without limit, unconstrained by external forces, metaphysical determinations, or cognitive blinders. Seekers after the holy are those who for whatever reason find themselves drawn to decoding and drawing near to the love of God. As Mother Julian of Norwich knew, we see God's love in the love of a mother for her children. By extension we cannot but think of God's love when we encounter those depths of human love. Such love is both natural and supernatural. Both ordinary and extraordinary.

This is perhaps the biggest paradox of the spiritual Goldilocks zone. Communities of faith are social organisms that testify to God's love as something that is simultaneously "not-yet," far off in the future, and also "always-already," something that has occurred and can be pointed to. Like great medieval cathedrals, these communities are not complete. There is great potential. Yet, parts of them are falling down and in disrepair. Other parts have been relatively unexplored. Some parts are so well trodden that the floor is worn and even the great flagstones show the imprint of centuries of pilgrimage. There is stained glass that lets in the light and offers a visual retelling of parts of the Christian story. There are also parts that are dark and obscure, features no longer clear to us, vandalized monuments and missing statues.

Cathedrals do not reveal everything. They also hide. However well-explored they are, there are always crypts, side chapels, and transepts to escape to. Secret and forgotten places hidden from popular view. Places that may turn up a couple of hundred years later quite by accident. Cathedrals are always being repaired and rebuilt, and someone is always exploring them for the first time.

It is the same for us. The community of faith is where the alien love of God is encountered in strangely familiar ways. Translating the divine into human form, God reaches out to us in the midst of our ordinary lives. The mystery of the divine is one of translation. We can never translate the love of God into our lives, and yet we try. The kindness of God is that even though we can never truly make sense of God's love, we receive sacramental gifts of bread and wine to help nourish us through times of spiritual famine.

The mystery of living in the Goldilocks zone is articulated by the tale of how a seeker receives hospitality from three persons joined together by love. It is a story of how seekers learn from their failures. A story of how one's deepest desires drive us into unfamiliar territory. The Goldilocks zone is not simply an apt metaphor for the astrophysics of life's emergence. It is also an illustration of the adventurous, and at times cheeky, spirit of trial and error that is required of those who would share their meat with the divine.

If love is the ultimate reason for why there is a universe, faith is how humans align themselves with that ultimate reality. The religious methodology that leads to the Goldilocks zone is deeply aware that human beings will never attain doctrinal or theological knowledge of how things really are. We are deeply uncertain and radically unsure of all the details of the Christian faith. We are also honest enough to know that our lives are spent in a fantasy of our own devising. Nevertheless, we trust in love. We learn to develop alien habits of loving strangers, enemies, and those who eat our porridge, break our chairs, and sleep in our beds. These are the really, truly, madly deeply alien parts of spirituality. They are also what guarantee we might have a hope of encountering God.

To love is first not to have loved, and noticed the difference. Mostly it starts by being the recipient of love. The fundamental purpose of God is to expose people to the experience and knowledge of being the beloved. Only in being loved can we learn to reciprocate love. Only in knowing what it means to be beloved of God can we treat others as similarly blessed. Socrates knew that humans do not know who they are. Augustine and Kierkegaard simply agree. Faith does not resolve this ignorance. Along with them, Nicholas of Cusa argues quite the contrary, faith compounds this unknowing:

> [S]urely then it is our desire to know that we do not know. If we can attain this completely, we will attain learned ignorance [*docta ignorantia*]. For nothing more perfect comes to a person, even the most zealous in learning, than to be found most learned in the ignorance that is uniquely one's own.[30]

The learned ignorance of *docta ignorantia* is the fruit of Cusa's mystic faith. To be human is to not know who we are, *and* to not know who God is. It is in the nature of God to be beyond our understanding. And it is in our own nature to share in being beyond understanding. Formed in the image and likeness of God, it is this mutual incomprehensibility that shapes who we are. To become a self, an individual, in this understanding is to recognize along with Augustine that we become our true selves only when we receive our life as sheer gift. As Marion glosses St. Augustine: "There where I find God, all the more as I continue to seek him, I find myself all the more myself as I never cease to seek that of which I bear the image."[31] Our yearning for God in this reading only truly becomes *our* yearning for God, as we start to recognize how we become ourselves in responding to the gift of God's love.

The dialectic of seeking and being sought is the fundamental dialectic of Christian experience. Moderns are not unique in seeing themselves as seekers. What I hope to have shown is how this seeking emerges as a response to the One who has already sought us out, and already disclosed something of the nature of the "not yet" and the "potentiality" of human experience. To be human is always to be *in via*, on the way, never arriving, never stable, never complete. This journeying is not simply one of pilgrimage or chronology, it is also a journey of return to the One from whom all comes. As Augustine puts in *On the Trinity*, we seek even when we have already found it, because this is how we seek the incomprehensible. Augustine knows that seeking God, the incomprehensible, does not suddenly turn the incomprehensible into the comprehensible. Why he asks, does our search spur us to search further, when we know that the divine unknown will always remain unknown?

> If not because one must not stop [seeking] as long as one is advancing in the search for incomprehensible things and as long as *one is become even better* from the fact of seeking so great a good, that one is seeking to find it, but that one finds it also in order to seek it still. That is, one seeks it so as to find it with all the more sweetness just as one finds it so as to seek it more ardently.[32]

The sweetness that Augustine names is intimated in the story of Goldilocks. The quest for the divine, so great a good, is one that rewards us with sweetness, inspiring us to redouble our search. Inspired by Augustine, the medieval writer Hugh of St, Victor summarizes: "As long as we live, we necessarily must always seek."[33] In the redoubling of our searching we discover more layers to this divine sweetness, as well as the gift of our own selfhood.

The best-known part of Mother Julian's "showings" is the refrain that recurs throughout the text: "all shall be well and all manner of things shall be well." Time and again she repeats this phrase throughout her writings, almost like a mantra. It is often forgotten that according to her narrative, these words were not hers. She ascribes them to God. In one chapter she described in detail Jesus coming to answer her questions and doubts.[34] Jesus tells her several times, in a deeply Trinitarian passage, that God "may," "can," and "will" make all things well. She layers the language of potentiality alongside the language of inexorability. For Mother Julian it is not just some kind of wishful thinking that "all manner of things shall be well." It is the centerpiece of her visionary experience of God's love.

Communities of faith flourish when they embrace their calling to be schools for love. To gather in the name of the divine is to seek to love more deeply. The more we are continually schooled in love the more we will practice generosity, hospitality, and service to others. Learning to love is one of the most alien and extraordinary things one can ever do. The Augustinian dimension to the Goldilocks search reminds us that whenever we try, we have to fail, and yet we have to try again. Being human we cannot but fall. And being human we cannot but get up and seek the One from whom we have come.

To search for the holy is to be willing to risk living in the middle ground between uncomprehending hostility to those who are different and militant certainty that one is right. It is to seek a love that is neither sentimental nor judgmental, but instead radically generous. Ultimately, to seek God is never about belief. It is about longing to be in the presence of God, belonging to God. Spiritual joy occurs when we are willing to receive the gift from the One who is Three who always graciously sets the table for us. God continues to set the table for ragamuffins and miscreants, sinners and failures, the broken and the vulnerable, the lost and the searching. In our search for God, we shall always betray Christ's invitation to hospitality. We shall fall, and we shall fail. And yet, in learning to love without complaint, and in responding to the breakages of life with graciousness and trust, truly, all manner of things shall be well.

NOTES

1. James K.A. Smith, *You Are What You Love: The Spiritual Power of Habit* (Grand Rapids MI: Brazos Press, 2016).
2. Marion, *God Without*, 49.
3. Bonhoeffer, *Discipleship*, 129.
4. George Herbert, *Love (III)* in *A Choice of George Herbert's Verse* (London: Faber and Faber, 1967), 91.
5. Dante Aligheri, *The Divine Comedy,* trans. Robin Kirkpatrick (London: Penguin, 2012), Canto XXXIII, 145, 482.
6. Michael Ward, *Planet Narnia* (Oxford: Oxford University Press, 2010), 24.
7. Coakley, *Asceticism.*
8. Janet Martin Soskice, *The Kindness of God* (Oxford: Oxford University Press, 2007).
9. Soskice, *Kindness*, 13–14.
10. Soskice, *Kindness*, 23.
11. Elizabeth Schussler Fiorenza (ed.), *Searching the Scriptures: A Feminist Introduction*, 2 Vols. (New York: Crossroad, 1993, 1994).
12. Julian of Norwich, *Revelations of Divine Love*, trans. Elizabeth Spearing (London: Penguin, 1998), Chapter 60, 141.
13. Julian, *Revelations*, 141.
14. Soskice, *Kindness*, 116.

15. Quoted by Caroline Walker Bynum, *Holy Feast and Holy Fast: The Religious Significance of Food to Medieval Women* (London: University of California Press, 1987), 176.

16. Bynum, *Holy Feast*, 23.

17. Pettegree, *Brand Luther*, 266.

18. Soskice, *Kindness*, 187.

19. Gaddis, *Strategy*.

20. Marion, *Negative*, 10.

21. Quoted Rex, *Tudors*, 156.

22. Christopher Booker, *The Seven Basic Plots: Why We Tell Stories* (London: Continuum, 2004).

23. Jane Goodall, quoted in Christakis, *Blueprint*, 205.

24. Ben Kilham, *Out on a Limb: What Black Bears Have Taught Me About Intelligence and Intuition* (White River Junction, VT: Chelsea Green, 2013).

25. James A.W. Heffernan, *Hospitality and Treachery in Western Literature* (New Haven: Yale University Press, 2014), 78.

26. Quoted in Rubin, *Corpus Christi*, 26.

27. Bonhoeffer, *Discipleship*, 159.

28. Nicholas of Cusa, *On Learned Ignorance*, trans. H. Lawrence Bond, in *Selected Spiritual Writings* (Mahwah, NJ: Paulist Press, 1997), 126–27.

29. Marion, *God Without*, 138.

30. Cusa, *Learned Ignorance*, 89.

31. Marion, *Self's Place*, 312.

32. Augustine, *De Trinitate* XV, 2, 2, 16, 422, quoted in Marion, *Self's Place*, 312.

33. Hugh of St. Victor, *De Sacramentis*, quoted by Henry de Lubac, *The Mystery of the Supernatural*, trans. Rosemary Sheed (New York: Herder and Herder, 1998), 164.

34. Julian, *Revelations,* Chapter 31, 83.

Bibliography

Adams, Douglas. *The Hitchhikers Guide to the Galaxy.* London: Pan Books, 1979.
Adams, Gillian. "Secrets and Healing Magic in the 'Secret Garden,'" in Frances Hodgson Burnett, *The Secret Garden,* edited by Gretchen Holbrook Gerzina, 302–13. New York: W.W. Norton, 2006.
Adams, Nicholas. "Pelagianism: Can People be Saved by their Own Efforts?" in *Heresies: And How To Avoid Them*, edited by Ben Quash and Michael Ward, 91–101. Grand Rapids, MI: Baker Academic, 2007.
Agamben, Giorgio. *The Church and the Kingdom.* Translated by Leland De La Durantaye. Photographs by Alice Attie. London: Seagull Books, 2012.
Agamben, Giorgio. *The Coming Community.* Translated by Michael Hardt. Minneapolis: University of Minnesota Press, 1993.
Agamben, Giorgio. *The Kingdom and The Glory: For a Theological Genealogy of Economy and Government.* Translated by Lorenzo Chiesa with Matteo Mandarini. Stanford: Stanford University Press, 2011.
Agamben, Giorgio. *Potentialities: Collected Essays in Philosophy.* Translated and edited by Daniel Heller-Roazen. Stanford: Stanford University Press, 1999.
Alighieri, Dante. *The Divine Comedy.* Trans. Robin Kirkpatrick. London: Penguin, 2012.
Anselm. *S. Anselmi Opera Omnia.* Edited by F.S. Schmitt. Edinburgh: Thomas Nelson and Sons, 1946. Volume One.
Anselm. *St. Anselm Basic Writings.* Translated by S.N. Deane. La Salle, Illinois: Open Court, 1962.
Anselm. *The Letters of Saint Anselm of Canterbury.* Translated by Walter Fröhlich. Michigan: Cistercian Publications, 1990. Three volumes.
Anselm. *The Prayers and Meditations of Saint Anselm.* Edited by Richard Southern and Benedicta Ward. London: Penguin, 1973.
Aquinas, Thomas. *Summa Theologica.* Translated by the Fathers of the English Dominican Province. London: Burns, Oates, and Washbourne, 1911.
Aristotle. *Aristotle's Nicomachean Ethics: A New Translation.* Translated by Robert C. Bartlett and Susan D. Collins. Chicago: University of Chicago Press, 2011.
Aristotle. *The Eudemian Ethics.* Translated by Anthony Kenny. Oxford: Oxford University Press, 2011.

Aristotle. *The Metaphysics*. Translated by Hugh Lawson-Tancred. London: Penguin, 1998.

Ashley, Kathleen, and Pamela Sheingorn. *Writing Faith: Text, Sign and History in the Miracles of Sainte Foy*. Chicago: Chicago University Press, 1999.

Augustine. *Confessions*. Translated by R.S. Pine-Coffin. London: Penguin, 1961.

Augustine. *De Doctrina Christiana*. Translated by R.P.H. Green. Oxford: Oxford University Press, 1995.

Baird, Joseph L. *The Personal Correspondence of Hildegard of Bingen*. Oxford: Oxford University Press, 2006.

Balthasar, Hans Urs von. *Prayer*. San Francisco: Ignatius Press, 1986.

Bartlett, Robert. *Why Can the Dead Do Such Great Things?* Princeton: Princeton University Press, 2013.

Bass, Diana Butler. *The Practicing Congregation: Imagining a New Old Church*. Lanham: Rowman & Littlefield, 2004.

Bonhoeffer, Dietrich. *The Cost of Discipleship*. London: SCM Press, 1959.

Bonhoeffer, Dietrich. *Letters and Papers from Prison: The Enlarged Edition*. London: SCM Press, 1964.

Bonhoeffer, Dietrich. *Life Together*. New York: HarperOne, 1954.

Bonner, Ali. *The Myth of Pelagianism*. Oxford: Oxford University Press, 2018.

Booker, Christopher. *The Seven Basic Plots: Why We Tell Stories*. London: Continuum, 2004.

Bowman, Hannah. "Communion without Baptism and the Paradox of the Cross." *Anglican Theological Review* Vol. 102.3 (Summer 2020), 373–92.

Brown, Bréne. *Daring Greatly: How the Courage to Be Vulnerable Transforms the Way We Live, Love, Parent, and Lead*. New York: Avery, 2015.

Brown, Peter. *The Cult of the Saints: Its Rise and Function in Latin Christianity*. Chicago: University of Chicago Press, 1982.

Bynum, Caroline Walker. *Christian Materiality: An Essay on Religion in Late Medieval Europe*. New York: Zone Books, 2011.

Bynum, Caroline Walker. *Holy Feast and Holy Fast: The Religious Significance of Food to Medieval Women*. London: University of California Press, 1987.

Caine, Michael. *Blowing the Bloody Doors Off: And Other Lessons in Life*. London: Hodder and Stoughton, 2018.

Caputo, John. *On Religion*. London: Routledge, 2001.

Carpenter, Humphrey. *The Inklings; C.S. Lewis, J.R.R. Tolkien, Charles Williams and their Friends*. London: George Allen & Unwin: 1978.

Chapman, Dom John. *Spiritual Letters*. London: Burns and Oats, 1935.

Chapman, Mark, Sathianathan Clarke, and Martyn Percy, eds. *The Oxford Handbook of Anglican Studies*. Oxford: Oxford University Press, 2015.

Charities Aid Foundation. "CAF UK Giving 2019." Accessed February 19, 2021. https://www.cafonline.org/docs/default-source/about-us-publications/caf-uk-giving-2019-report-an-overview-of-charitable-giving-in-the-uk.pdf.

Christakis, Nicholas. *The Evolutionary Origins of a Good Society*. New York: Little Brown, 2019.

Cixous, Hélène. *Coming to Writing and Other Essays*, edited by Deborah Jenson. Cambridge, MA: Harvard University Press, 1991.

Cixous, Hélène. *The Hélène Cixous Reader*, edited by Susan Sellers. London: Routledge, 1994.

Clanchy, M.T. *From Memory to Written Record: England, 1066–1307*. Oxford: Blackwell, 1993.

Coakley, Sarah. *God, Sexuality, and the Self.* Cambridge: Cambridge University Press, 2013.

Coakley, Sarah. *The New Asceticism: Sexuality, Gender and the Quest for God*. London: Bloomsbury, 2015.

Colish, Marcia. *The Mirror of Language*. Lincoln, NE: University of Nebraska Press, 1983.

Collins, Guy. *Faithful Doubt: The Wisdom of Uncertainty.* Eugene, OR: Cascade, 2014.

Countryman, Louis William. *The Poetic Imagination: An Anglican Spiritual Tradition.* Maryknoll, NY: Orbis Books, 2000.

Crombie, A.C. *Robert Grosseteste and the Origins of Experimental Science*. Oxford: Oxford University Press, 1971.

Crossan, John Dominic. *Cliffs of Fall: Paradox and Polyvalence in the Parables of Jesus.* New York: Seabury, 1980.

Dartmouth College. "Dartmouth Digital Orozco." Accessed March 20, 2021. http://www.dartmouth.edu/digitalorozco/app/.

Davies, Paul. *The Goldilocks Enigma.* New York: Mariner Books, 2008.

Derrida, Jacques. "Circumfession," in *Jacques Derrida*, edited by Geoffrey Bennington, 3–315. Chicago: University of Chicago Press, 1993.

Derrida, Jacques. *Deconstruction and Pragmatism*, edited by Chantal Mouffe. London: Routledge, 1996.

Derrida, Jacques. *The Gift of Death*. Translated by David Wills. Chicago: University of Chicago Press, 1995.

Derrida, Jacques. *On Cosmopolitanism and Forgiveness*. London: Routledge, 2001.

Descartes, René. *The Passions of the Soul and Other Late Philosophical Writings*. Translated by Michael Moriarty. Oxford: Oxford University Press, 2016.

Dickens, Charles. "Frauds on the Fairies." *Household Words. A Weekly Journal. Conducted by Charles Dickens*. No. 184, Vol. VIII. 97–100. London: Bradbury and Evans, 1853. Accessed April 13, 2021. https//Victorianweb.org/authors/dickens/pva/pva239.html.

Dozier, Verna. *The Calling of the Laity.* New York: Rowman & Littlefield, 1988.

Duffy, Eamon. *The Stripping of the Altars: Traditional Religion in England 1400–1580*. New Haven: Yale University Press, 2005.

Duhigg, Charles. *The Power of Habit: Why we do what we do in life and business.* New York: Random House, 2014.

Duthu, Bruce N. and Colin Calloway. *American Indians and the Law*. New York: Penguin, 2008.

Eadmer. *The Life of St Anselm*. Translated by R.W. Southern. Oxford: Oxford University Press, 1972.

Erdozan, Dominic. *The Soul of Doubt: The Religious Roots of Unbelief from Luther to Marx.* Oxford: Oxford University Press, 2016.

Falk, Seb. *The Light Ages: The Surprising Story of Medieval Science.* New York: W.W. Norton, 2020.

Fiorenza, Elizabeth Schussler, ed. *Searching the Scriptures: A Feminist Introduction.* New York: Crossroad, 1993, 1994. 2 Vols.

Flew, Anthony, and Roy Abraham Varghese. *There is a God: How the World's Most Notorious Atheist Changed His Mind.* New York: HarperOne, 2008.

Foot, Sarah. *Veiled Women I: The Disappearance of Nuns from Anglo-Saxon England.* Burlington, VT: Ashgate, 2000.

Francis. *Fratelli Tutti: On Fraternity and Social Friendship.* Washington DC: United States Conference of Bishops, 2020.

Fredrickson, Barbara L. "The Value of Positive Emotions: The Emerging Science of Positive Psychology Is Coming to Understand Why It's Good to Feel Good." *American Scientist,* 91, no. 4 (2003): 330–35.

Fujimura, Makoto. *Art and Faith.* New Haven: Yale University Press, 2020.

Galico, Paul. *The Snow Goose.* New York: Alfred A. Knopf, 1946.

Gallese, Vittorio. "'The Shared Manifold Hypothesis': From Mirror Neurons to Empathy." *Journal of Consciousness Studies,* 8 (2001): 33–50.

Gallese, Vittorio, Luciano Fadiga, Leonardo Fogassi, and Giacomo Rizzolatti. "Action Recognition in the Premotor Cortex." *Brain,* Vol. 119, 2 (1996): 593–609.

Geary, Peter. *Furta Sacra: Thefts of Relics in the Central Middle Ages.* Princeton: Princeton University Press, 1991.

Green, Hannah. *Little Saint.* New York: Modern Library, 2000.

Guite, Malcolm. *Faith, Hope and Poetry: Theology and the Poetic Imagination.* London: Routledge, 2016.

Gunn, David. "What does the Bible Say: A Question of Text and Canon," in *Reading Bibles, Writing Bodies: Identity and the Book,* edited by Timothy K. Beal and David M. Gunn, 242–61. London: Routledge, 1997.

Guy, John. *Tudor England.* Oxford: Oxford University Press, 1990.

Hampson, Daphne. *Christian Contradictions: The Structures of Lutheran and Catholic Thought.* Cambridge: Cambridge University Press, 2001.

Hauerwas, Stanley, and William H. Willimon. *Resident Aliens: Life in the Christian Colony.* Nashville: Abingdon Press, 2014.

Heffernan, James A.W. *Hospitality and Treachery in Western Literature.* New Haven: Yale University Press, 2014.

Heidegger, Martin. *An Introduction to Metaphysics.* Translated by Gregory Fried and Richard Polt. New Haven: Yale University Press, 2014.

Helfling, Charles, and Cynthia Shattuck, eds. *The Oxford Guide to the Book of Common Prayer: A Worldwide Survey.* Oxford: Oxford University Press, 2008.

Herbert, George. *A Choice of George Herbert's Verse.* London: Faber and Faber, 1967.

Heyward, Carter. *The Redemption of God: A Theology of Mutual Relation.* Lanham, MD: University Press of America, 1982.

Hildegard von Bingen. *Scivias*. Translated by Mother Columba Hart and Jane Bishop. New York: Paulist Press, 1990.

Hillesum, Etty. *An Interrupted Life*. New York: Owl Books, 1996.

Holmes, Urban. *What is Anglicanism?* Harrisburg, PA: Morehouse, 1982.

Hooker, Richard. *Lawes of Ecclesiastical Politie*. Edited by John Keble. Oxford: Oxford University Press, 1841.

Hooker, Richard. *The Folger Library Edition of the Works of Richard Hooker*. Edited by W. Speed Hill. Cambridge, MA: Belknap Press, 1977.

Illich, Ivan. *In the Vineyard of the Text*. Chicago: Chicago University Press, 1993.

Irigaray, Lucy. "Questions to Emmanuel Levinas," in *The Irigaray Reader*, edited by Margaret Whitford, 178–89. Oxford: Blackwell, 1991.

Jocelyn of Brakelond. *Chronicle of the Abbey of Bury St Edmunds*. Edited by Diana Greenway and Jane Sayers. Oxford: Oxford University Press, 1989.

Joseph, Dan. *Kabbalah: A Very Short Introduction*. Oxford: Oxford University Press, 2007.

Julian of Norwich. *Revelations of Divine Love*. Translated by Elizabeth Spearing. London: Penguin, 1998.

Kahneman, Daniel. *Thinking, Fast and Slow*. Farrar, Straus and Giroux, 2013.

Kallifatides, Theodor. *Another Life: On Memory, Language, Love, and the Passage of Time*. New York: Other Press, 2017.

Kearney, Richard. *Anatheism: Returning to God After God*. New York: Columbia University Press, 2011.

Kearney, Richard. *The God Who May Be*. Bloomington: Indiana University Press, 2001.

Kearney, Richard, and Jens Zimmerman, eds. *Reimagining the Sacred: Richard Kearney Debates God with James Wood, Catherine Keller, Charles Taylor, Julia Kristeva, Gianni Vattimo, Simon Critchley, Jean-Luc Marion, John Caputo, David Tracy, Jens Zimmerman and Merold Westphal*. New York: Columbia University Press, 2015.

Kierkegaard, Søren. *Practice in Christianity*. Translated and edited by Howard V. Hong and Edna H. Hong. Princeton: Princeton University Press, 1991.

Kierkegaard, Søren. *The Sickness Unto Death*. Translated and edited by Howard V. Hong and Edna H. Hong. Princeton: Princeton University Press, 1980.

Kierkegaard, Søren. *Upbuilding Discourses in Various Spirits*. Translated and edited by Howard V. Hong and Edna H. Hong. Princeton, 1993.

Kierkegaard, Søren. *Works of Love*. Translated by Howard V. Hong and Edna H. Hong. Princeton: Princeton University Press, 1995.

Kilham, Ben. *Out on a Limb: What Black Bears Have Taught Me About Intelligence and Intuition*. White River Junction, VT: Chelsea Green, 2013.

Lama, The Dalai, Desmond Tutu, and Douglas Abrams. *The Book of Joy: Lasting Happiness in a Changing World*. Avery: New York, 2016.

Le Guin, Ursula K. *The Left Hand of Darkness*. New York: Ace, 1987.

Levinas, Emmanuel. *Totality and Infinity: An Essay on Exteriority*. Translated by Alphonso Lingis. Pittsburgh: Duquesne University Press, 1969.

Loades, Ann. "Anglican Spirituality," in *The Oxford Handbook of Anglican Studies*, edited by Mark Chapman, Sathianathan Clarke, and Martyn Percy, 149–64. Oxford: Oxford University Press, 2015.

de Lubac, Henri. *The Church: Paradox and Mystery*. New York: Alba House, 1969.

de Lubac, Henri. *The Mystery of the Supernatural*. Translated by Rosemary Sheed. New York: Herder and Herder, 1998.

MacCulloch, Diarmaid. *Thomas Cranmer: A Life*. New Haven: Yale University Press, 1996.

Manseau, Peter. *One Nation Under Gods: A New American History*. New York: Black Bay Books, 2015.

Marion, Jean-Luc. *Being Given: Toward a Phenomenology of Givenness*. Translated by Jeffrey L. Kosky. Stanford: Stanford University Press, 2002.

Marion, Jean-Luc. *God Without Being*. Translated by Thomas A. Carlson. Chicago: University of Chicago Press, 1991.

Marion, Jean-Luc. *In the Self's Place: The Approach of Saint Augustine*. Translated by Jeffrey L. Kosky. Stanford: Stanford University Press, 2012.

Marion, Jean-Luc. *Negative Certainties*. Translated by Stephen E. Lewis. Chicago: University of Chicago Press, 2015.

Mauss, Marcel. *The Gift: The Form and Reason for Exchange in Archaic Societies*. Translated by W.D. Halls. New York: W.W. Norton, 1990.

McAdoo, H.R. *The Spirit of Anglicanism: A Survey of Anglican Theological Method in the Seventeenth Century*. New York: Scribners, 1965.

McGuire, Brian Patrick. *Friendship and Community: the Monastic Experience, 350–1250*. Ithaca: Cornell University Press, 2010.

McLaughlin, Megan. *Consorting with the Saints: Prayer for the Dead in Early Medieval France*. Ithaca: Cornell University Press, 1994.

McLellan, David. *Simone Weil: Utopian Pessimist*. London: Macmillan, 1991.

Miner, John N. *The Grammar Schools of Medieval England: A.F. Leach in Historiographical Perspective*. Montreal: McGill-Queen's University Press, 1990.

Moltmann, Jürgen. *The Crucified God*. Translated by R.A. Wilson and John Bowden. London: SCM Press, 1974.

Murphy, James Bernard. *Your Whole Life: Beyond Childhood and Adulthood*. Philadelphia: University of Pennsylvania Press, 2020.

National Philanthropic Trust. "Charitable Giving Statistics." Accessed February 19, 2021. https://www.nptrust.org/philanthropic-resources/charitable-giving-statistics/.

Nicholas of Cusa. *On Learned Ignorance*. Translated by H. Lawrence Bond, in *Selected Spiritual Writings*, 85–206. Mahwah, NJ: Paulist Press, 1997.

Nilson, Ben. *Cathedral Shrines of Medieval England*. Woodbridge: Boydell, 1998.

Oberman, Heiko A. *Luther: Man between God and the Devil*. Translated by Eileen Walliser-Schwarzbart. New Haven: Yale University Press, 2006.

Office of the General Convention of the Episcopal Church, *A Great Cloud of Witnesses: A Calendar of Commemorations*. New York: Church Publishing, 2016.

Oliver, Mary. *Blue Iris: Poems and Essays*. Boston: Beacon Press, 2004.

Parkinson, Carolyn, Adam M. Kleinbaum, and Thalia Wheatley. "Similar neural responses predict friendship," *Nature*, January 30, 2018. Accessed September 24, 2021, https://nature.com/articles/s41467-017-02722-7

Pascal, Blaise. *Pensees*. Introduction by T.S. Eliot. New York: E.P. Dutton, 1958.

Pattison, George. *Anxious Angels: A Retrospective View of Religious Existentialism*. London: Macmillan Press, 1999.

Pease, Donald E. *Theodor SEUSS Geisel: The Man Who Became Dr Seuss*. Oxford University Press, 2010.

Pettegree, Andrew. *Brand Luther: How an Unheralded Monk Turned His Small Town into a Center of Publishing, Made Himself the Most Famous Man in Europe—and Started the Protestant Reformation*. New York: Penguin Books, 2016.

Phillips, D.Z. *Faith After Foundationalism*. London: Routledge, 1988.

Pullman, Philip. "Why we Believe in Magic." *The Guardian*, September 1, 2018. Accessed September 8, 2018. https://www.theguardian.com/books/2018/sep/01/the-limits-of-reason-philip-pullman-on-why-we-believe-in-magic.

Quash, Ben, and Michael Ward, eds. *Heresies: And How To Avoid Them*. Grand Rapids, MI: Baker Academic, 2007.

Quinn, Frederick. *To Be A Pilgrim: The Anglican Ethos in History*. New York: Crossroad, 2001.

Ramsey, Michael. *The Anglican Spirit*. New York: Seabury Classics, 2004.

Reno, R.R. *Genesis*. Grand Rapids, MI: Brazos Press, 2010.

Rex, Richard. *The Tudors*. Stroud: Amberley, 2011.

Ricoeur, Paul. *Living Up to Death*. Translated by David Pellauer. Chicago: University of Chicago Press, 2009.

Ridyard, Susan. *The Royal Saints of Anglo-Saxon England*. Cambridge: Cambridge University Press, 1988.

Rollins, Peter. *Insurrection: To Believe is Human, to Doubt Divine*. New York: Howard Books, 2011.

Rowell, Geoffrey, Kenneth Stevenson, and Rowan Williams, eds. *Love's Redeeming Work: The Anglican Quest for Holiness*. Oxford: Oxford University Press, 2001.

Rubin, Miri. *Corpus Christi: The Eucharist in Late Medieval Culture*. Cambridge: Cambridge University Press, 1991.

Rushdie, Salman. *Haroun and the Sea of Stories*. London: Penguin, 1991.

Sayers, Dorothy L. *The Mind of the Maker*. San Francisco: Harper, 1987.

Schleiermacher, Friedrich. *On Religion: Speeches to Cultured Despisers*, edited by Richard Crouter. Cambridge: Cambridge University Press, 1998.

Schmidt, Richard. *Glorious Companions: Five Centuries of Anglican Spirituality*. Grand Rapids: Eeerdmans, 2002.

Schulenburg, Jane Tibbetts. *Forgetful of their Sex: Female Sanctity and Society, CA, 500–1100*. Chicago: Chicago University Press, 1998.

SETI Institute. "FAQ SETI Institute." Accessed March 31, 2017. http://www.seti.org/faq#seti2.

Sheingorn, Pamela, trans. and ed. *The Book of Sainte Foy*. Philadelphia: University of Pennsylvania, 1995.

Smith, James K. A. *You Are What You Love: The Spiritual Power of Habit.* Grand Rapids MI: Brazos Press, 2016.

Soskice, Janet Martin. *The Kindness of God.* Oxford: Oxford University Press, 2007.

Southern, Richard. *St. Anselm: A Portrait in a Landscape.* Cambridge: Cambridge University Press, 1990.

Spufford, Francis. *Unapologetic: Why, Despite Everything, Christianity Can Still Make Surprising Emotional Sense.* New York: HarperOne, 2014.

Stafford, Pauline. *Queen Emma and Queen Edith: Queenship and Women's Power in Eleventh-Century England.* Oxford: Blackwell, 1997.

Steinmetz, David. "The Superiority of Pre-Critical Exegesis," in *The Theological Interpretation of Scripture*, edited by Stephen E. Fowl, 26–38. Oxford: Blackwell, 1997.

Stock, Brian. *The Implications of Literacy: Written Language and Models of Interpretation in the Eleventh and Twelfth Centuries.* Princeton: Princeton University Press, 1983.

Tennyson, Alfred. *Selected Poems*, edited by Christopher Ricks. London: Penguin, 2008.

The Church Pension Fund. *Holy Women and Holy Men: Celebrating the Saints.* New York: Church Publishing, 2010.

The Church Pension Fund. *Lesser Feasts and Fasts.* New York: Church Publishing, 1980.

Thomas, Keith. *The Ends of Life: Roads to Fulfillment in Early Modern England.* New York: Oxford University Press, 2009.

Thomas, R.S. *Collected Poems 1945–1990.* London: Phoenix, 1993.

Threlfall-Holmes, Miranda. *How to Eat Bread: 21 Nourishing Ways to Read the Bible* London: Hodder and Stoughton, 2021.

Tillich, Paul. *The Courage to Be.* New Haven: Yale University Press, 2000.

Travis, Peter W. *Disseminal Chaucer.* Notre Dame, IN: University of Notre Dame Press, 2009.

Tronick, Edward. "Still Face Experiment." Accessed March 28, 2021. https://thepowerofdiscord.com.

Waal, Edmund de. *The Hare with the Amber Eyes: A Family's Century of Art and Loss.* New York: Farrar, Straus and Giroux, 2010.

Ward, Michael. *Planet Narnia.* Oxford: Oxford University Press, 2010.

Weil, Simone. *Gravity and Grace.* Introductions by Gustave Thibon and Thomas R. Nevin. London: Routledge, 2002.

Weil, Simone. *Waiting on God.* London: Putnam, 1951.

Wells, Emma J. *Pilgrim Routes of the British Isles.* Marlborough, UK: Robert Hale, 2016.

White, Susan J. *Introduction to Christian Worship.* Louisville, KY: Westminster John Knox Press, 2006.

Wilder, Craig Steven. *Ebony and Ivy: Race, Slavery, and the Troubled History of America's Universities.* New York, Bloomsbury, 2013.

Williams, Rowan. *Anglican Identities.* Cambridge MA: Cowley Publications, 2003.

Williams, Rowan. *The Edge of Words God and the Habits of Language*. London: Bloomsbury, 2014.

Williams, Rowan. "Lossky, the *via negativa* and the foundations of theology," in *Wrestling with Angels*, edited by Mike Higton, 1–24. Grand Rapids: Eerdmans, 2007.

Williams, Rowan. "Master of his universe: the warnings in J.R.R. Tolkien's novels." *The New Statesman*, August 8, 2018.

Williams, Rowan. *On Augustine*. London: Bloomsbury Books, 2016.

Wilson, A.N. *The Elizabethans*. New York: Farrar, Straus and Giroux, 2011.

Wright, J. Robert. "Anglicanism: *Ecclesia Anglicana,* and Anglican: An Essay on Terminology," in *The Study of Anglicanism*, edited by Stephen Sykes, John Booty and Jonathan Knight, 477–83. London: SPCK, 1988.

Yannaras, Christos. *Elements of Faith: An Introduction to Orthodox Theology*, trans. Keith Schram. Edinburgh: T&T Clark, 1991.

Zizioulas, John. *Being as Communion: Studies in Personhood and the Church*. Crestwood, NY: St. Vladimir's Seminary Press, 1985.

Index

Abraham, 123, 139, 141, 198–202, 208–9, 225
Adam, 154, 182, 184
Adams, Douglas, 48
Adams, Nicholas, 205
Adelard of Bath, 141
Agamben, Giorgio, 31, 106–9, 112, 170, 175, 191, 221, 226; coming community, 164; empty throne, 163
agnosticism, 72, 79, 80, 94, 206, 224, 231
aletheia, 81, 85
alienation, 15, 29, 37–39, 41–43, 51–52, 57, 117, 168, 185, 213
allegory, 88, 90, 229
anamnesis, 64–65
angst, 40
Anselm of Canterbury, 54–55, 89, 105, 120, 130, 132, 140, 143–45, 148–49, 216–18, 221; conversation and friendship, 122–24, 128–29; *Monologion*, 105; *Proslogion*, 123–24; *Vita*, 121
antisemitism, 199–200
apophasis, 20–22, 100, 105, 147, 230
Aquinas, Thomas, 35, 51–52, 55–56, 102, 144, 206–7, 215; analogical language, 21

Aristotle, 1, 14–16, 23, 37, 47, 49, 51, 55–57, 102, 107, 215, 221–22
art, 50, 152, 166, 191, 222
Ashley, Kathleen, 126
Athanasius, 96
Athelberht of Kent, 25
Augustine of Canterbury, 25–26
Augustine of Hippo, 6, 7, 35, 38–39, 53, 62, 74, 88, 109, 115, 123, 138, 141, 143–44, 146–49, 164, 182, 204–8, 210, 213, 224, 232–34; *The Confessions*, 49, 65, 187; *On Christian Teaching*, 89; *On the Trinity*, 61, 233; *regula fidei*, 223
Austen, Jane, 169
Authorized Version, 196

Baldwin of Bury St Edmund, 45
Balthasar, Hans Urs von, 111
baptism, 72–73, 76–79, 100, 106–13, 120, 130, 157, 198, 213, 223; the unbaptized, 74, 76, 111
Bartlett, Robert, 121
Basil the Great, 143
Bass, Diana Butler, 171
Bede, 25
beguines, 75–76
Berkeley, George, 178

Bernard of Angers, 125–28, 130–31, 137
Bertha of Kent, 25–26
Big Bang, 47–51, 53
Blake, William, 142, 152, 154
Boleyn, Anne, 11, 25–26
Bonhoeffer, Dietrich, 159, 176, 199–203, 214, 230
Booker, Christopher, 227
The Book of Common Prayer, 17, 19, 68, 70, 72, 168
Bowman, Hannah, 74–75, 77
bread, 61, 64–68, 70–72, 78–80, 108, 125, 230, 232; *hlaf,* 67
Breslaw, Elaine, 91
Brontë, Charlotte, 137
Brown, Brené, 38–39, 42, 138, 162, 188, 204
Brown, Peter, 120
Bullinger, Heinrich, 71
Bultmann, Rudolf, 118
Burnett, Frances Hodgson, 112
Bynum, Caroline Walker, 132, 219–20

Caine, Michael, 175
Calvin, John, 207
Camino de Santiago, 169–70, 190
Cappadocian fathers, 143–44
Caputo, John, 53
Carpenter, Humphrey, 183
Carroll, Lewis, 120
Cassian, John, 88–89
cataphasis, 20–22, 100
Catherine of Aragon, 11, 196
Catherine of Siena, 219–21
Chalcedonian orthodoxy, 96–97, 118
Chapman, Dom, 161
Charles V, 196
Chaucer, Geoffrey, 68, 171
children, 26, 41, 50, 52, 72, 107–9, 116, 138, 157, 168, 210, 218, 223, 231
Christ, 17, 19, 22, 26, 31, 71, 76, 79–80, 94–95, 106, 109, 148, 154, 162, 166, 188, 196, 199, 210–11, 214, 221, 229, 234; body, 63–70, 72, 74, 100, 107, 110, 123, 163; cross, crucified, 29–30, 40, 74–75, 77–78, 101, 120, 142, 158, 177, 191–92, 202–3, 219, 222; icon of invisible God, 119; imitation of, 128, 133; incarnation, 40, 90, 96, 118–20, 145, 157, 207, 217, 230; *kenosis*, 40; resurrection, 30, 64–65, 73, 108, 111, 113, 120, 157, 158, 171, 177; Son, 144, 148, 150, 171, 229; Word, 89–90, 104, 142, 147. *See also* baptism; Eucharist; face; God; love
Christakis, Nicholas, 140–1, 189, 206, 228
Civil Rights movement, 13, 133
Cixous, Hélène, 147, 149, 151, 153, 214, 218, 224, 230
Clanchy, M.T., 89
Clement of Alexandria, 88
Coakley, Sarah, 7, 142–43, 146–48, 151–52, 160, 170, 217–19
Colish, Marcia, 89
Comestor, Peter, 74
Conques, 124–26, 128, 133, 137
Constantine, 25, 31, 63
Corey, James S.A., 162
Corpus Christi, 63, 113
cosmologies, 51, 53. *See also* science
Countryman, William, 92
courage, 14, 33–34, 38, 41, 43, 93, 151, 162, 188, 210; to fail, 39, 42
Cranmer, Thomas, 68–69, 71
cross. *See* Christ
Crossman, Samuel, 221–22
Cundall, Joseph, 226
Cupitt, Don, 118
Cuthbert, 167–68, 171

Dalai Lama, 189–90, 204
Daniels, Jonathan Myrick, 133, 168
Dante, 56, 150, 214–15
Dartmouth College, 3, 41, 173, 178–81
Davies, Paul, 3, 49, 53
David and Goliath, 84–85
Democritus, 49

Denys, 148
Derrida, Jacques, 90, 139, 188–89, 198–99, 207–9, 225
Descartes, René, 55
desire, 7, 73, 76, 78–79, 96, 102, 116, 123–24, 137, 142–45, 147–48, 151, 154, 157, 160, 165, 187, 191, 209, 215, 217, 223, 226, 230–31; velleity, 206–7
Dickens, Charles, 137
Dickinson, Emily, 20, 138, 214, 230
Dodgson, Charles Lutwidge, 120
Donatists, 88
Donne, John, 92, 117
Dostoevsky, Fyodor, 40
doubt, 6, 12, 13, 22, 55, 117, 122, 157–58, 233
doxology, 109, 113, 163
Dozier, Verna, 13–16, 18–19, 23–24, 26, 52

The Dream of the Rood, 93, 183

Duchamp, Marcel, 50
Duffy, Eamon, 77
Duhigg, Charles, 129–30
dunamis, 101–2, 112, 164, 189, 202–3, 209
Dungeons and Dragons, 109
Dungy, Tony, 130–31
Duthu, Bruce, 179
Dwork, Deborah, 201
Dyson, Hugo, 183

Eadmer, 121–24, 128–32
Eden, garden of, 184–85
Edward VI, King, 11–12, 14, 68–70
Elijah, 163
Eliot, T.S., 92
Elizabeth I, Queen, 11–15, 17, 24, 26, 36, 68, 71–72, 79, 99, 103, 221, 224–25, 231; Elizabethan settlement 11, 18–19, 36, 70–71, 79; Golden Age, 13, 70, 222; middle way, 12, 14, 16, 18–19, 72

Emin, Tracey, 51
Emmaus, 65
epektasis, 111
epiclesis, 66
Epiphany, 163
equality, 3, 15–17
Eriugena, John Scot, 119
eros. *See* love
Esau, 86
eschatology, 78, 111–12, 143, 164, 221
Esmay, Judith, 172, 172n20
esse, 101–2
eternal life, 164–65
Eucharist, 58, 61, 63–68, 70–80, 83, 84, 99, 100–102, 104–5, 110–11, 113, 146, 171, 196, 219, 222, 229, 230; sacramental agnosticism, 72, 79
Eve, 154, 182, 184
evil, 18, 74, 110, 154, 198–204, 208–11, 224; *privatio boni*, 109
existentialism, 40
The Expanse, 162

face, 4, 29, 86–87, 118, 129, 162, 203, 209; of God, 86–87; of Goldilocks, 8; guarantee of ethics, 5, 129; of icon, 118–19, 146, 163; Still Face Experiment, 116, 163
failure, 1, 5, 8, 39, 40, 42, 54, 80, 93, 107–8, 112, 139, 142, 164, 175–78, 180–82, 184–92
Falk, Seb, 45
Flew, Anthony, 37
Foot, Sarah, 25
forgiveness, 2, 20, 30, 76, 100, 106, 111–12, 130, 154, 188–90, 192
Foy, St., 124–30, 132–33, 137, 140, 168, 171–72
Francis, Pope, 4, 216
Francis, St., 121
Fujimura, Makoto, 152, 165–66
Fulbert of Chartres, 126–27

Gaddis, John, 70, 222
Galen, 45, 48

Gallese, Vittorio, 115–18, 130
Gallico, Paul, 56–57
Gardiner, Stephen, 69
Geary, Peter, 125
Geisel, Theodor, 41
gender, 3, 11, 16–17, 19, 148–49, 184, 216, 218–21
Genesis, book of, 49, 86
George III, 179
glory, 42, 109, 113, 128, 162, 164–15, 170–71, 191; *doxa*, 163
God, 17, 32, 39, 46, 50, 53–56, 58, 63, 66, 70, 73, 78, 79–81, 83, 86, 87, 89, 93, 95, 97, 100–104, 107–10, 112–13, 117–18, 122–24, 129, 132–33, 137, 141–49, 151–52, 154, 157, 159–64, 166–67, 171–72, 176–78, 184–85, 188–89, 192, 195, 198–99, 201–7, 213, 215, 216–18, 221, 223–27, 230–34; without Being, 7, 102; dream of, 13–14, 16, 18, 26; kingdom, 32, 78–79, 108–13, 164, 223; as mother, 149, 218–19, 221; quest for, 6–8, 16, 20, 22, 39, 48, 97, 165, 181, 185, 197, 206, 208, 214, 224, 233; unmoved mover, 51. *See also* Christ; *dunamis*; face; Goldilocks God; Holy Spirit; *imago dei*; love; mystery; Trinity; wisdom
Goldilocks, 1, 3, 5–8, 12–14, 20, 26, 71, 73, 113, 124, 142, 163, 164, 175, 187, 199, 207, 210, 226, 229, 233–34; archetype, 5, 12, 26, 43, 72, 91, 96, 123, 178, 210, 224; porridge, 3, 5, 14, 110, 175, 181, 226–27, 230, 232; spirituality, 56, 110; *and the Three Bears*, 1, 5, 6, 7, 61, 73, 97, 142, 187, 210, 225, 227–29; three chairs, 163–64, 182; zone, 3, 13, 16, 20, 153, 199, 215, 225–26, 231–32. *See also* Goldilocks God; spiritual thermodynamics
Goldilocks God, 8, 17, 22–23, 32, 35, 37, 43, 47, 54, 57, 72, 94, 111, 153, 158, 165, 172n20, 175, 181, 197, 206, 208–9, 214, 221–22, 224
Goliath. *See* David and Goliath
Goodall, Jane, 228–29
Goudge, Elizabeth, 138–39, 150
Green, Hannah, 124, 128–29, 131, 133
Gregory of Nazianzus, 143, 217
Gregory of Nyssa, 96, 111, 119, 143, 147, 216
Gregory I, Pope, 25, 94
The Grinch, 40–41
Grosseteste, Robert, 75
Guite, Malcolm, 92–93, 117, 183
Gundulf, 122, 123, 145
Gunn, David, 85

hagiography, 121, 125, 127–28, 130–32, 137, 138, 220, 227
Hamlet, 99
Hanover, New Hampshire, 172n20, 178–79; Mink the bear, 228–29
Haroun and the Sea of Stories, 83
Hauerwas, Stanley, 30–32
Heaney, Seamus, 93
heaven, 37, 45–46, 56, 89, 108, 111, 121, 128, 129, 158, 167, 214–15, 220. *See also* eschatology
Heffernan, James, 229
Heidegger, Martin, 1, 48, 144, 153
Helena, 25
Hemingway, Ernest, 190
Henry VIII, King, 11–12, 18, 71, 196
Herbert, George, 92, 214, 228–29
heresy, 95–96, 196, 204–7
Heyward, Carter, 102–4, 107, 112
Hick, John, 118
Hilda of Whitby, 220
Hildegard of Bingen, 45–47, 51, 52, 58, 61, 74, 121, 168, 215–17, 221
Hillesum, Etty, 202–3
Hirst, Damien, 51
hobbits, 209–10
Holmes, Urban, 35
Holy Island. *See* Lindisfarne

Holy Spirit, 4, 21, 61, 66, 79–80, 142–43, 148–50, 152, 160, 171, 218; *vinculum caritatis*, 144. *See also* desire; imagination; love; Trinity
Homer, 24, 113
Hooker, Richard, 34–36, 71–72, 74, 79, 99, 224, 231
Hosea, book of, 86
hospitality, 1, 7, 19, 25, 61, 65, 73, 77, 80, 102, 142, 228–29, 232, 234
Hugh of Cluny, 124
Hugh of St. Victor, 90, 233
Husserl, Edmund, 153

icons, 118–19, 129, 146, 163
Illich, Ivan, 90, 147
imagination, 2, 26, 46, 48, 83, 92–93, 96, 108–9, 112, 118, 121, 131, 138, 151–54, 183–84, 199
imago dei, 4, 6, 16, 19, 113, 119–20, 142, 146, 152, 182, 184–85, 202–3, 230, 232
incarnation. *See* Christ
incomprehensibility 6, 119, 143, 149, 232–33
infancy, 107–9
Inside Out, 53
Irenaeus, 78
Irigaray, Luce, 147
Isaac, 141, 198–99, 209
Islam, 51, 118, 199
Israel. *See* Jacob
Ivy League, 1, 178, 180, 223

Jacob, 86–87, 97
James, St. (apostle), 170–71
Jane Eyre, 137–38
Jesus. *See* Christ
John, Gospel of, 147, 158
jouissance. *See* love
Judaism, 88, 91, 118, 159, 163, 199, 200, 202
Judas, 76, 229
Juliana of Cornillon, 63, 75, 77, 168
Julian of Norwich, 218–21, 231, 233

Kahneman, Daniel, 185–88
Kallifatides, Theodor, 37
Kearney, Richard, 53, 65, 100–3, 107–8, 112, 203, 221, 231
Kemeny, John, 181
Kierkegaard, Søren, 30, 33–34, 37–40, 115, 139, 141, 153, 176, 198, 202, 209, 225, 232
Kilham, Ben, 228–29
King, Martin Luther, 13
kingdom. *See* God
Kintsugi, 154, 165–66
Kipling, Rudyard, 176, 179–80
Kleinbaum, Adam, 116
Knox, John, 221–22, 225

Last Supper. *See* Eucharist
Lee, Stan, 137
Legge, William, Earl of Dartmouth, 179
Le Guin, Ursula, 48
L'Engle, Madeleine 19
Lethe, 61, 80–81
Leunig, Michael, 22, 100–101, 103
Lewis, C.S., 19, 183–84, 215–16, 229
Levinas, Emmanuel, 4–5, 7, 118, 129, 208–9
Lindisfarne, 167–68
Little Henny, 221
The Little White Horse, 138, 153–54
Loades, Ann, 37
locutio, 89
Lopon-La. *See* Dalai Lama
The Lord's Prayer, 163
The Lord of the Rings, 209
Lossky, Vladimir, 21
love, 7, 30, 33, 42, 46, 57, 61, 73, 79–80, 100, 104, 106, 110–12, 122–23, 128, 130, 133, 140–41, 143–49, 157, 161, 177–78, 192, 201–3, 207–8, 211, 213, 215, 222, 224–29, 230–34; *agape*, 215–17, 219; without being, 7; burning, 46, 73, 145, 211; *eros*, 143, 148, 215–17, 219; forgiving, 94, 192; gift of, 7, 144–47, 152–53, 214, 223; *jouissance*, 146,

148, 152–53, 218; justice in action, 13; maternal, 218–19, 221, 229, 231; *oikonomia*, 153; *philia*, 216–17, 219; qualitative difference of, 42; universal, 17, 19, 78, 108. *See also* Holy Spirit; Trinity
de Lubac, Henri, 64, 66, 206
Lucy, St., 125
Luria, Isaac 22
Luther, Martin, 35, 43, 64, 93, 95, 195, 204–7, 210, 220–21; *anfechtungen*, 39–40, 42; *The Freedom of the Christian*, 94

Machiavelli, 70
Madison, James, 180
Magdalen College, Oxford, 183
Manicheeism, 203, 208, 224
Mankell, Henning, 62
Manseau, Peter, 91–92
Marcel, Gabriel, 40
Marion, Jean-Luc, 6, 7, 21, 49, 62, 65, 79, 86, 102, 104, 111, 113, 118–19, 123, 129, 141, 144, 146, 148, 151–54, 163, 205, 213, 215, 224, 231–32
Mary I, Queen, 11, 14, 68, 70, 158, 221
Mathilda, Countess of Tuscany, 122
Matthew, gospel of, 163, 210
Matthew of Rievaulx, 229–30
Mauss, Marcel, 139–40, 154, 189
McAdoo, H.R., 18
McCulloch, Diarmaid, 71
McGuire, Brian, 123
McLaughlin, Megan, 132
medicine, 45–46
megalopsucia, 57
memory, 61–65, 80–81, 92, 128, 130, 148, 168, 205
Merryweather, Maria, 138–39, 153–54
metaphysics, 7, 21, 46–47, 56, 68, 102, 118, 144, 153–54, 163, 213, 231
metaxu, 171–72
middle way. *See via media*
midrash, 88–89, 91
mirror neurons, 115

Moltmann, Jürgen, 29
monasticism, 45, 90, 122–23, 125–27, 131, 138, 159, 165, 167, 218, 220
Monica, 223
Moses, 123, 163
Mure, Eleanor, 226
Murphy, Jim, 108
mysterion, 79
mystery, 20, 22, 29, 53–56, 58, 66, 71–72, 75, 77, 79–80, 93, 105, 137, 142, 145, 149–51, 153–54, 162, 168, 188, 206, 214–15, 224, 230–31

Nakamura-San, 166
National Socialism, 199–202
Native Americans, 178–81
Nicholas of Cusa, 102, 106, 107, 112, 230–32
Nussbaum, Martha, 218
Nygren, Anders, 215, 217, 219

Occidens museum, 190–91
Occom, Samsom, 179–82
Odysseus, 24, 113
Oliver, Mary, 93
Origen, 78, 88
original sin, 181–82, 184–85, 204–5
Osbern of Clare, 131

Pamplona, 190, 192
Pandolfini, Pier Filippo, 113
parable, 1, 35, 48, 87
Paradise Hill, 138–39, 146
paradox, 20–22, 29, 35, 54, 62–63, 83, 87, 94, 118–19, 165, 170, 188, 205, 207–9, 231
Parkinson, Carolyn, 116
Pascal, Blaise, 130
Paul, St. (apostle), 17, 88, 101, 119, 163, 189
Pelagius, 204–9
Penelope, 24, 26, 113
Perkins, William, 206–7
Peter, St. (apostle), 56
phenomenology, 153

Philip II, King, 70, 103, 221–22
Phillips, D.Z., 21
phronesis, 16
pilgrims, 62, 120, 124–26, 128–29, 167, 169, 170–72, 215, 233
Plato, 14, 111, 143
pneumatology. See Holy Spirit
poetry, 20, 92–93, 100, 102, 117, 137, 147, 153, 183–84, 225
popes, 46, 63, 122. *See also* Francis, Pope; Gregory, Pope
posse, 101–2
possest, 102
possibilizing, 99, 100, 102, 104–6, 112, 150, 169, 221, 226
potentiality, 76, 100, 104, 106–12, 150–51, 154, 164, 175, 189, 202–3, 221, 226, 231, 233
Potter, Harry, 138, 154
power. *See dunamis*
prayer, 7, 17, 35, 45, 65–66, 68, 77–78, 90, 96, 104, 112, 125, 133, 143–46, 148, 159, 161, 164–65, 168, 170–71, 207
Pritchard, Marion, 201–2
Proust, Marcel, 111
Ptolemy, 56, 215
Pullman, Philip, 151

quadrivium. See trivium
quaestiones, 89
Quinn, Frederick, 169

racism, 13, 109, 178, 180–82, 185, 200
Ramsey, Michael, 192
Rebekah, 86
Reformation, 33, 35, 39, 68, 94, 196, 205, 207, 220
resurrection. *See* Christ
Revelation, book of, 163
Richard II, King, 225
Ricoeur, Paul, 79
Robinson, John, 118
Rollins, Peter, 119–20
Roosevelt, Theodore, 41

Rothko, Mark, 152
Rowling, J.K., 19, 138, 154
Rubin, Miri, 63–64, 67, 74–76
Rushdie, Salman, 83

sabbath, 164
sacring, 77
saints, 25, 39, 42, 62, 66, 73, 75, 78, 81, 110, 120–21, 124–33, 140, 144, 160, 166, 169–71, 191–92, 196–97, 204, 216, 220–21
Salem witch trials, 91
Sales, Ruby, 133
Santiago de Compostela, 169–70, 190
Savery, Thomas, 49
Sayers, Dorothy, 150–52, 154
Schleiermacher, Friedrich, 2, 47
Schulenburg, Jane Tibbets, 25–26
Schweitzer, Albert, 29
science, 2, 4–6, 45–50, 53–54, 58, 137, 140–41, 215; astrophysics, 3; atomic theory, 49; empirical method, 5; evolution 5, 49, 140–41; genetic blueprint, 140; laws of physics, 49–50; medieval astronomy, 45, 214–15; M-Theory, 53; neuroscience, 115, 130; SETI, 6. *See also* Big Bang; mirror neurons
science fiction, 48, 162–63
scripture, 29–30, 35–36, 54, 65, 80, 83–96, 99–101, 103–4, 107, 109, 123, 139, 143, 149, 163, 184, 191, 197, 214, 216, 218, 221, 223; *glossa ordinaria*, 89; *poesis*, 92–93; vulgate, 196. *See also* midrash
The Secret Garden, 112–13
sexism, 109, 182
Sheingorn, Pamela, 126
Sisyphus, 5
skepticism, 34, 43, 126–27, 224
slavery, 178, 180
Smith, James, 213
The Snow Goose, 56–57
social suite, 140
Socrates, 6, 37, 53, 119, 224, 232

Soskice, Janet Martin, 217–19, 221
soteriology, 196
Southern, Richard, 123
Southey, Robert, 226
Spanish Inquisition, 3
Spenser, Edmund, 13
spiritual thermodynamics, 8, 16, 32, 61, 103, 110, 142, 175, 184, 197, 213, 222, 227, 230
squints, 77–78
Steinmetz, David, 90
Stilites, Simon, 166
Stock, Brian, 89
Stonehenge, 168–69
Stranger Things, 109

Taylor, Jeremy, 161, 165
Tennyson, Alfred Lord, 22
Thomas, R.S., 92, 200
Thomas, St. (apostle), 157–58
Thomas, St., Hanover, 77
Threlfall-Holmes, Miranda, 91
Thurman, Howard, 13
Tillich, Paul, 38, 118
Tituba, 91, 94
Tolkien, J.R.R., 183–84, 209–10
Transfiguration, 162–63, 171, 200
Travis, Peter, 68
Trinity, 7, 21, 61, 66, 73, 96, 105, 110, 122–23, 142–52, 154, 160, 163, 165, 170–71, 177, 213, 215, 218–19, 224, 227, 229–30, 233; *filioque*, 143, 145, 148; *hypostases*, 143; *perichoresis*, 143, 146; *prosopon*, 146; *vestigia*, 148. *See also* doxology; Christ; God; Holy Spirit; love
trivium, 45
Tronick, Edward, 116
Tulsa Race massacre, 185
Tversky, Amos. *See* Kahneman, Daniel
Tyconius, 88
Tyndale, William, 196

de Unamuno, Miguel, 40
undecidability, 207–9, 225, 230

velleity. *See* desire
via media, 4, 6, 8, 12, 14, 16, 18–20, 22–23, 32–33, 35–36, 68, 71, 73, 78, 83–84, 91, 93–95, 97, 111, 117, 142, 169, 172, 175, 182, 197–98, 203, 207–8, 210, 213, 224–25
The Virgin Mary, 58, 90, 129, 144, 175, 191, 220
virtue, 14–16, 46–47, 51, 57, 161, 188, 192
Voltaire, 12

de Waal, Edmund, 166
Wallander, Kurt, 62–63
Walsingham, Francis, 70
Ward, Michael, 215
Watchmen, 185
Webster, Samuel, 179
we-centric, 116, 118, 127
Weil, Simone, 23, 171–72
Wesley, Charles, 165
Wesley, John, 54
Wheatley, Thalia, 116
Wheelock, Eleazor, 178–81, 182, 225
Whitgift, John, 18
Wilde, Oscar, 229
Wilder, Craig Stephen, 178, 180
Wiles, Maurice, 118
Wilfrid, St., 120
Williams, Rowan, 6, 22, 35, 55, 80, 92, 100, 105–6, 159, 210
Willimon, William, 30–32
Wilson, A.N., 99
wine. *See* bread
wisdom, 2–16, 67, 94, 161, 217, 221–22, 224; personified, 46, 51–52, 58
Witherspoon, John, 180
Witten, Ed, 53
Wittgenstein, Ludwig, 23, 103
wonder, 43, 46–48, 50–58, 67, 93, 103, 141, 157, 163, 168, 172, 225
Wordsworth, William, 47
Wright, Robert, 12

Yad Vashem, 201

Yale, 178
Yannaras, Christos, 20

zimzum, 22
Zizioulas, John, 143, 146, 151
Zwingli, 71

About the Author

Guy Collins studied at the universities of St. Andrews and Cambridge. The author of *Faithful Doubt: The Wisdom of Uncertainty*, he has served parishes on both sides of the Atlantic. He is Rector of St. Thomas Church, Hanover, and the Episcopal Chaplain to Dartmouth College.

www.ingramcontent.com/pod-product-compliance
Lightning Source LLC
Chambersburg PA
CBHW020114010526
44115CB00008B/821